THREE
WISE
VIRGINS

THREE

WISE

VIRGINS

by

Gladys *Brooks*

E. P. DUTTON & CO., INC.

New York, 1957

LIBRARY OF CONGRESS CATALOG CARD NUMBER: 57-12754

For Elizabeth Ames

at Yaddo

Contents

I wish gratefully to acknowledge the help I received from:

Louise Hall Tharp, author of *The Peabody Sisters of Salem,* and Little Brown & Co., her publishers;

The Berg collection at the New York Public Library;

Helen E. Marshall, author of *Dorothea Dix, Forgotten Samaritan,* and the University of North Carolina Press, her publishers.

Preface

"Christ attacked sin as Apollo attacked the Python." So said Elizabeth Peabody, who dwelt on such acts of heroism with the pleasure that a faithful apprentice feels for the highly finished product of his master.

"I must work the work that is given me to do, and how is my soul straightened until it is accomplished?" Here was the phrase—though uttered by another among the band of beneficent humanitarians—that became the base upon which Dorothea Dix rested her life.

"How dignified, how exemplary in all her sufferings!" These words were spoken in praise of her mother by Catharine Sedgwick's father to the receptive tenderhearted child, thereby giving her a lifelong lesson in feminine behavior.

Here is the essence of that moment in our history when faith attached itself to duty, when hope attached itself to zeal, and miracles were born of the embrace. The three women whose aspirations and behavior are sketched in the pages of this book, and who shared this moment of history, were remarkable for their fortitude, their foresight and for their final accomplishment. They held a common aim which each in her own and separate way carried aloft. It was the betterment of men and women and the amelioration of their daily lives; it included also "the vigilant moral education of the young."

For these high ends, there was needed, from those who held the banner, both staying power and sacrifice. Sacrifice came first, as an often unconscious course; the staying power followed and to an extent so overwhelming as to obliterate all sense of martyrdom. It was the life of celibacy sometimes chosen by the women of that pre-Freudian day that encouraged and sustained their long devotion. And the amends that ensued were as the green growth sprouting from dormant seed brought forth by a late sun.

Hawthorne has, in *The Marble Faun*, given to Miriam the task of explanation:

It is a mistaken idea, which men generally entertain, that nature has made women especially prone to throw their whole being into what is technically called love. We have, to say the least, no more necessity for it than yourselves; only we have nothing else to do with our hearts. When women have other objects in life, they are not apt to fall in love. I can think of many women distinguished in art, literature and science —and multitudes whose hearts and minds find good employment in unostentatious ways—who lead high, lonely lives and are conscious of no sacrifice as far as your sex is concerned.

In contrast to the society of our day, the order of beings surrounding Dorothea Dix, Elizabeth Peabody and Catharine Sedgwick believed that the lives of such as they were more, rather than less, noble than the lives of those others who trod commoner paths edged with the homely field flowers. Thus confirmed in the approval of the wise of their time, these three vestals were buoyed also by their religion, recipients of that fresh and live doctrine of good will movingly enunciated by the Unitarian proselytizer, William Ellery Channing, saint and poet, whose intellect, conscience and heart had happily joined to bathe New England in a spirit of grace.

Boston, in 1820, was small enough to respond almost as a whole to the influence of one person, and it is not surprising that three women among his contemporaries should, each in her way, have been persuaded to adopt the faith of the delicate, impassioned little man of whom Mrs. Jameson, a visitor from England, wrote that he was "a human being more good, more wise, more pure than any other being I had ever approached."

Channing's religion, "the Boston Religion," so-called, he had made his own, transmuting the solid substance of Unitarianism into a moving doctrine for those who earlier were crushed by Calvinism's stony weight. He himself, as a little boy, listening in terror to the Sabbath utterance of an old-time Calvinist dominie, had been later reprieved from fear of fire and brimstone when, on the drive home following the service, he had noted the casual, matter-of-fact cheerfulness with which his father greeted the devastating tone of the sermon, accepting it as little more than routine. The truth was not there in that pulpit, the boy instinctively felt, but where, then, did it lie?

The passionate struggle brought by the ensuing years, the struggle against the forces of darkness, broke the health of the young student whose lamp burned far more than the allotted quota of midnight oil as he labored and inquired, sleeping then upon boards, fasting and mortifying the flesh in the long tradition of the saints. A spirited wrestler, famed in his youth for his physical prowess, he wrestled also with doubt as he prepared for the ministry, wrestled with despair, with the whispering voices of evil.

But the aura of aridity that the pursuit of theology might well have pressed into Channing's soul had been tempered by the soft air of Newport, his birthplace. There, the smell of the sea wrapped him and there the waves breaking lengthily along the shore, the swaying masts of the ships that he climbed one after another in upright progression, the bright flash of gull's wings in the sunshine, the deep cry of the night heron at dusk, made of the impressionable boy a poet in his own right who with delight fed his awakening senses upon those other poets, Byron and Wordsworth.

The victory that was presently his brought to Channing a fine amalgam of heart's warmth and moral discernment, thus enabling Coleridge, whom he later met in England, to say that he was "a philosopher in both the possible renderings of the word, being the love of wisdom and the wisdom of love." The victory, that balanced his inner with his outer life, so blended an intellectual fervor and a glow of goodness that he charmed his listeners and held them fast standing in the pulpit of Boston's Federal Church where, of short, slim stature, eyes unnaturally large, he preached the gospel of love and hope and bright renewal.

For Channing cared about goodness with a passion that was contagious. He communicated the sense of it to those about him as the perfume of flowers is wafted through a summer meadow. And he cared for human beings whom he saw as parts of a mighty and beneficent whole, seeing them also at close range as individuals capable of an upward soaring, emancipated, prodigiously free. The doctrine which he presented to those who heard him rested on God's tenderness and man's inherent virtue, on the nature of perfectibility. It released the faithful from brooding guilt, from a haunting sense of original sin, from preoccupation with eternal punishment. To Channing, the doctrine of Calvin spread ignominy on mankind, tainted it at the source, mankind whom God desired, rather, to bless, treasuring each man, each woman and child as intended vessels of heavenly essence.

Thus it was that William Ellery Channing set the seal of his blessing upon three exceptional women, augmenting the spirit of each, causing it to flower. He upheld, he advised, exhorted and soothed, pre-empting the place on the level of the spiritual that the amorphous husband might have held on the terrestrial, remaining as background to their lives until death brought his frail body to lie in Mount Auburn Cemetery while church bells tolled as for the passing of a saint. A greater fulfillment, perhaps, than they could otherwise have found, a fulfillment fairly won. For, as Channing had once written: "A noble school is profitable only to noble spirits. The learner must have something great in order to receive great lessons."

Described in terms of modern psychological parlance, the heroines of this book were three virgins who succeeded so far in sublimating their sexual drives that they escaped severe neuroses. In more human words that spring from the heart, they were three "exemplary women," spinsters all, whose emotions beating within their lonely breasts were of such intensity as to warm and enhance the patterns of posterity.

Gladys Brooks

Bridgewater, Conn.

I

Dorothea Lynde Dix

Dorothea Lynde Dix

"Your devotion to duty in starting off in that pitiless Monday's storm touched all our hearts. The lesson it inculcated was more than a chapter of moral maxims, and I hope we may never forget it."

These words were written in 1873 to Dorothea Dix by the superintendent of the Hudson River State Hospital. She was then seventy-one years old and had gone to the hospital on one of her periodic rounds of inspection. She had finished her tour of the plant and the grounds, the wards and the private wing, had talked with the nurses and orderlies, studied the figures attendant upon running the big institution and, with these things behind her, was ready for her next self-imposed assignment.

The years before Dorothea were unrolling more and more rapidly as they neared their end, like a carpet along a downhill slope until the bare spool proclaimed finality. She would not be able to control finality as she had controlled the pattern of her life. But neither would she wait upon its approach or pay homage to its power. She would not tarry, not for a moment of time. And so, pitiless or no, she confronted the Monday storm as she had ever confronted all physical obstacles: the wind, the rain, snow, flood, fire, plague, and her own ill health. She ignored them.

"America's Forgotten Woman" Dorothea Lynde Dix has been called and one asks oneself why this should be. For it is strange that a woman who revolutionized the status of the insane the whole world over, a humanitarian of the importance and caliber of a Florence Nightingale, or an Elizabeth Fry, has faded from memory so entirely as to be almost unknown less than a century after her death. Is it because the rational human mind prefers to ignore the eerie presence of the damned souls of our universe, those creatures disturbed and distraught to whom Dorothea Dix devoted her life, gathering them to her as a child gathers meadow flowers? Or was there something in her own character, "that terrible reformer but gentle lady," to repel rather than to beckon, something that held mankind at bay? Her last years seem, as we read of them, desolate and solitary, a guest for lack of a home of her own in one of the great asylums she had founded at Trenton, New Jersey, her "first-born child," as she called it. A lonely time it must have been, in spite of the capable care she received. And, as we are told of her burial in 1887 at Mount Auburn Cemetery in Cambridge, Massachusetts, this appears sadly unimpressive and ill attended:

Occurring when, in the height of the summer heats, so many are away at the seashore or in the mountains, a few friends only . . . stood by her grave. . . . Her funeral was marked by the simplicity she loved. . . . The marble marker bears neither epitaph nor date, only Dorothea L. Dix.

Thus her biographers describe the last rites, an almost anonymous committal to earth. If she herself had been standing there, an on-looker at the unattended graveside alone at the foot of a little hill, would she not have been distressed at so meager a display of emotion, of sorrow, of gratitude for a woman who had given the dreadful labor of fifty years to the grim cause of those frail souls who had slipped across the boundaries of our functioning everyday world?

A friend calling on Dorothea Dix in the hospital not long before her death writes of that last visit:

As the interview wore on it became evident that she wished to say something confidential and at her suggestion I tried to manœuvre the faithful nurse out of hearing. Failing, I said: "Oh, never mind now; tell me when I come again." "Ah, yes, if I am here, if I am here." "Oh, I hope you will be here for many a year to come." She started up with agitated eagerness and said with wild excitement: "My dear friend, if you hope that, pray for it: pray that I may be here. I think even lying on my bed I can still do something!" She fell back upon her pillow exhausted. I then rose to go. She threw her arms around me saying with unwonted tenderness, "O, darling!" and I had parted with my old friend forever.

They tell us that "O, darling!" is the exclamation that occurs over and over in the broken fragments of letters she wrote during these months of final illness when she was no longer able to hold aloft the façade of adamantine control erected by an unhappy girl in years long before: when the solitude and pain buried beneath the discipline broke through at last, seeking to be quieted. How pleasant if one could have been there to tell her then quite simply, before she had drifted beyond understanding, that her life had been an epic, that she belonged on the heights of Valhalla with that dauntless band of the Valkyrie, riding her wild horse through the clouds on some glorious errand of mercy. The armor she wore, confronting a world of despair, was the armor of those warrior maidens. Would not words such as these have brought a measure of renewal, at the last, to one who had given herself forever away?

There is the story of Abram Simmons of Little Compton, Rhode Island, whom Dorothea went to visit as investigator of conditions surrounding the insane. This was in 1842 when, in our country, there was no marked line drawn between paupers, criminals and the indigent insane, when they were herded together as animals of the lowest order, the evil and the damned, deprived of sun and air and decent food, the violent chained to the wall, scourged, their arms or legs pinioned, left unwashed, with matted hair, steeped in the diseases of filth: in fact, Bedlam. Dorothea, then on a tour of Massachusetts hospitals, almshouses and jails, had crossed the border into Rhode Island and, hearing of the poorhouse at Little Compton, had stopped to view its inmates.

"Your other patient—where is he?" she asked the wife of the superintendent who was showing her about by the light of a flickering candle. "You shall see," the woman said. "But stay outside till I get a lantern." Dorothea's account goes on:

Weary and oppressed, I leaned against an iron door which closed the sole entrance to a singular stone structure, much resembling a tomb. . . . Soon low, smothered groans and moans reached me, as if from the buried alive. At this moment the mistress advanced, with keys and lantern. "He's here," she said, unlocking the strong, solid iron door. . . . A few steps down brought us to a second iron door equally solid—this was unlocked and opened; but so terribly noxious was the poisonous air . . . that a considerable time elapsed before I was able to remain long enough to investigate this horrible den. . . . The candle's flickering rays illuminated a spectacle never to be forgotten. The place when closed had no light or ventilation. It was about 7 ft. by 7, and 6½ high. All, even the roof, was of stone. An iron frame interlaced with rope was the sole furniture. . . . There he stood, near the door, motionless and silent; his tangled hair fell about his shoulders; his bare feet pressed the filthy, wet stone floor; he was emaciated to a shadow, etiolated, and more resembled a disinterred corpse than any living creature. Never have I looked upon an object so pitiable, so woe-struck, so imaging despair. I took his hands and endeavored to warm them by gentle friction. I spoke to him of release, of liberty, of care, of kindness. Notwithstanding the assertions of the mistress that he would kill me, I persevered. A tear stole over the hollow cheek, but no words answered to my importunities; no other movement indicated consciousness or perception or sensibility. In moving a little forward I struck against something which returned a sharp metallic sound; it was a length of ox-chain, connected to an iron ring which encircled a leg of the insane man. . . . It was joined to bars of iron two feet long, linked together and at one end connected by a staple to the rock overhead.

"My husband," said the mistress, "in winter rakes out sometimes of a morning, half a bushel of frost, and yet he never freezes. . . . Sometimes he screams dreadful and that is the reason we had the double walls and two doors instead of one; his cries disturb the house."

"How long has he been here?"

"Oh, above three years; but then he was kept a long while in a cage first; but once he broke his chains and the bars so we had this built where he can't get off."

The words, "and yet he never freezes," echoed in Dorothea's mind and would not let her be. Nor could she forget the medieval instruments of torture that held such frail souls fast: the muffs in which their hands were bound, the metal anklets and wristlets, the strait jackets and restraining sheets, the "Utica Crib," a barred bed narrower and shorter than the human body in which one woman had been confined for fourteen years. Friends, these bewitched ones truly became for Dorothea Dix as she went the rounds, finding her way into their cells, taking their hands in hers, speaking to them with her beautiful voice that all through her life served to charm and compel. Keepers and attendants strove at first to keep her back, trying to frighten her with warnings of danger, but one after another they fell under her spell, withdrawing their objections, capitulating to the tall, quiet, large-eyed lady in the white-kerchiefed dress who moved forward toward some clamoring maniac as if she were keeping an appointment with a fair and chosen spirit.

At the time of her visit to Little Compton, Dorothea Dix had been gathering material on the insane of Massachusetts, her native state, with the idea of presenting a memorial, if need be, to her local legislature, thus bringing her labors to an end. But as her journeys touched on neighboring states she saw that conditions were no better in one place than in another, that horror existed everywhere, that there could be no quick end to her work. She had come on these cruel things a year or so earlier by an accident of isolated philanthropy at the East Cambridge jail for women where she had volunteered to go as Sunday teacher of the Bible. There, one raw spring day, she had had her first meeting with criminals, innocents, insane, a random group of unfortunates treated indiscriminately as animals without souls, except that the insane, apart in a room of their own, were deprived of the small stove furnished the others because, as the jailer explained: "Mad people do not know hot from cold and besides they might set themselves afire."

Dorothea, then a novice with a warm heart and a belief in human mercy, had thought that an appeal to the jailer would bring the needed changes. But no change was apparent as her Sunday visits continued and she learned then the first lesson in procedure against ignorance and cruelty, those stubborn, clinging attributes of the unenlightened. Radical changes, she began to realize, are brought about only by force, by the efforts usually of a single human being prepared to plan, to labor, to conquer. If the East Cambridge jailer would not voluntarily improve the condition of the inmates, he must be made to do so by law. And to the law she went, helped by the powerful humanitarian arm of Samuel Gridley Howe and by his friend, Charles Sumner. Thus her first battle and the winning thereof, a victory due probably in large measure to her own individual appeal, to her moving story that must have roused the judge of the court to act against the prevailing and more popular skepticism among nonbelievers.

And now, shining bright as any newborn planet, lay the direction of the future. All Dorothea's life had been but a preparation for the task she saw ahead. She would seek and rescue, where rescue was needed, bring the means of grace to those souls who waited day after empty day for the Samaritan who did not appear. There were doubtless thousands of them scattered over the state of Massachusetts, regarded, like the inmates of the Cambridge jail, as outcasts from God. But had not Dr. Channing preached that the lowest creature is redeemable in God's sight? Who could doubt the lasting power of mercy and faith? Not she. Her mission was clear. This was destiny. Did not "Dorothea" mean Gift of God? She had been called by Providence to do this work.

As a little girl, Dorothea had needed more hardihood than meekness in facing the daily scene. Her mother, Mary Bigelow of Sudbury, Massachusetts, was "poor, ignorant, uncouth and entirely unfit to become a member of the Dix household"—so runs the story of this unfortunate woman about whom very little is known. Dorothea's father was twenty years younger than his wife and they were married while he was still an undergraduate at Harvard. The rules of the college did not then permit a married man to remain as a student and Joseph Dix, therefore, the third son of Dr. and Mrs. Elijah Dix, formerly of Worcester, Massachusetts, had had to stop his formal education at that moment. The Dix family was of solid substance, conventional, cultivated, and the shame and disappointment brought them by Joseph's behavior must have cast an ineffaceable shadow over the little girl's life as soon as she was old enough to grasp the world's values and patterns. Perhaps she had had an intimation of tragedy as soon as her sensibilities began to develop in the crude log cabin at Hampden, Maine, where Joseph and Mary had gone to live when that territory was yet a part of northern Massachusetts. The cabin logs were chinked with plaster, floors were of puncheon, the small windows were covered with oiled paper and shutters kept out the sun as well as the cold. Dorothea slept on the attic floor while her parents slept below and the cooking was done in the fireplace before the chimney in the dim light of an unaired room.

Mary Bigelow Dix was not a rugged frontier woman and she could have had small help from her groping, irresolute husband whose uncertainties were accentuated by a tendency toward alcoholism. He had begun, at his father's request, to farm the harsh land about him, land owned by the doctor who speculated in real estate and lumber. But Joseph's training and his high-strung, delicate body made a preordained failure of his efforts in the open. At Harvard he had studied theology and he turned back to religion now as a safeguard against disintegration. One of Dorothea's vivid memories as a small child was the stitching of tracts, seated in a rude handmade chair, day after day, on and on, pushing the difficult needle through heavy folded paper, her father almost insatiable in his demands for the finished product.

For Joseph had experienced conversion there in that lonely land, from the persuasiveness of a Methodist clergyman, and he had himself become an itinerant preacher. He was at home after that only long enough to compose his sermons, then off again on his horse's back, saddlebags stuffed with the tracts he sold or exchanged for staples of food to keep his family alive. He was gone sometimes for weeks while Dorothea and her mother sat and cut and folded and stitched the sermons printed earlier at the press. Mary Dix could hardly refuse her husband this labor and she must have kept the little girl hard at it, too, for their very lives depended on the sermons that drew great crowds as Joseph became better known, when, carried away himself by fanatical excitement, he was able to rouse people to religious fervor. Now and then, hoping to make more money, he moved the family to a new town there to open a grocery or book shop. But these attempts, too, inevitably ended in failure and he died in his young forties burned through, presumably, by life's too ardent flame.

Meanwhile, Dorothea's mother, incompetent, lonely, overlooked by her husband's proud family, was on her way toward the invalidism that became a settled state after her two sons were born. She must, more and more, have depended on her daughter, shut away as they were together, in dullness and despair. That dominating quality, an asset to Dorothea Dix in later life, may well have got its start during these first years. Children of the frontier were often precocious and this child in particular would early have learned the lessons of stress and sorrow. With no companions of her age, she had only herself to rely on, and the growth of her own power. Even love she must find for herself within herself, there being so little of it elsewhere. "I never knew childhood," she once told a friend. And this is all she was willing to say in later years about that far-off time with its aura of a prolonged, unhappy dream that somehow she could never drive out of her memory.

One person there was, however, who now and then brought to Dorothea a glimpse of the civilized existence she had so far done without. Her grandfather, Dr. Elijah Dix, made a journey to the north, occasionally, to visit his son Joseph, and he and the small granddaughter became much attached to each other. Sometimes he took her back, as she grew older, to Orange Court, his fine house in Boston, to hand her over to her grandmother, Madam Dix, a great lady in her circle, who lived in grandeur and comfort on a scale most strange to the little girl from the frontier.

Here it was Dr. Dix whom Dorothea liked chiefly to be with. He was a constant delight to the responsive, eager child. While her grandmother corrected her manners, scrubbed and combed her, making her feel the disgrace of poverty and shiftlessness as it lay about her life at home, her grandfather was kind to Dorothea and they laughed together at the stories he told her of his patients' vagaries and their curious behavior. There were so many things that he knew. He took her on walks, pointing out the plants that grew by the wayside, giving her their botanical names; he drove her to Faneuil Hall, the State House, the Old North Church, as he told her the history of the young republic; he allowed her to watch him in his dispensary while he compounded his pills. He seemed the wisest and kindest of men and it was hard for Dorothea to understand why he should have to be on guard so often against his "enemies," men who resented his violent temper, his dictatorial ways and his unbridled tongue: faults of his virtues, born of fatigue, sorrow and an innate sense, possibly, of his superiority to the average man. His small granddaughter, however, the slim, impressionable child with the large questioning eyes, loved him with all her heart and, at his death when she was barely seven—back again in the desolate house in Maine—all pleasure must have disappeared from her life as the sun disappears under an eclipse by the moon.

For five years longer Dorothea lived on with her parents and the two baby brothers recently born. Space in the narrow, stuffy cabin was more than ever cramped, daily chores more confining, and outside, in the primitive village, less and less was to be gained from her intermittent visits to the schoolhouse. Tract stitching continued to be the one long-drawn occupation. Finally, in the tradition of so many other heroes and heroines, with a vision of the great and glowing world to beckon, Dorothea ran away from home. She managed to reach Boston and appeared one evening at Orange Court begging to be taken in, not for a few days or weeks but for good and all.

The bare statement of this remove, the mere fact of her leaving one place to arrive at another, is all that we come on as we turn the pages of Dorothea's story—like the brief mention of a hurricane that cuts a swath through a forest floor. But cataclysms may permanently change the climate. Dorothea's emotions, not only on that runaway day but during the weeks that preceded it, her guilt at leaving home, the terror of the secret, solitary journey, the fear of rejection, the joy of being accepted, were indeed tempestuous enough to cut a swath through her life—did, in fact, alter its course forever.

Madam Dix welcomed the ragged child with the large eyes and long brown hair, allowing her to remain within that polite and polished household which became the home she presently exchanged for the faraway cabin in the Maine clearing. And now Dorothea determined to forget the past, the shame of her parents' prolonged plight, the clinging boredom of those early years, the mean restrictions. But the pattern of upbringing had pressed deep into the mind of the twelve-year-old girl, a map in high relief, its contours never entirely effaced.

Her education was at once begun, an arduous training in character and manners, in sewing, reading and the doing of sums, in order and docility. Much of it must have come hard to a girl who had grown in the wilderness, her habits more like the wandering roots of ground pine in the woods than the upright delicate larkspur of her grandmother's garden. Indeed, there were battles to the finish between Dorothea and the redoubtable Madam Dix. No one had realized how strong-willed this untutored child could be. And no one realized, then or later, how passionate was her desire for affectionate acceptance and approval. This, while he lived, her grandfather had given her but Madam Dix, left to manage her complicated affairs alone, was too busy, too harassed, perhaps too unhappy to bestow on an adopted granddaughter the spontaneous love she craved. All the while, too, with each new effort to eradicate characteristics unpleasing to the old lady, there must have been outspoken criticism of Dorothea's parents and their manner of life. Did this not rouse buried loyalties in the girl's heart, strengthen her allegiance to the past, create a conflict forever renewed? And hidden conflict invites neither serenity of being nor docility of action.

Presently, after a two-year trial, Dorothea's recalcitrance became too much to bear. Madam Dix gave up the attempt to make the girl over in her own image, and, after a family conference, it was decided to send her off to Worcester to live with her great-aunt Mrs. William Duncan. This was a far pleasanter household, mellow, informal, with plenty of young cousins about, while Mrs. Duncan and her married daughter, the two Aunt Sarahs, were more flexible human beings than any Dorothea had yet known. One of her cousins, Edward Bangs, fourteen years older than she, befriended her at once, helping to break down her shyness, helping her to become an entity in her new surroundings. Here was the second real friend in her life and, with thoroughgoing gratitude, she began at once to love Edward Bangs.

However, the driving force that continually propelled her seemed not to let her be and, unlike most girls of fourteen, she felt she must work, earn money, send presents to her small brothers at home, become entirely independent, perhaps. In spite of the serene atmosphere of the Duncan house, she begged to be allowed to leave it each day for a certain number of hours in order to teach school. This was the career she had chosen, she said, that of schoolmistress. Why should she not teach other children what she had herself learned in Boston? She was not too young, she assured her aunts. In two more years she would be sixteen, a young lady. She begged to be allowed to begin the work which she knew would suit her very well.

Education for young children in 1816 was generally given at home. Private schools were few, and Dorothea's elders thought the idea a good one not only for the sake of sons and daughters of relatives, but for the girl's own development. They gave their consent and everyone set to work to find a suitable building. A vacant store was discovered, the place scrubbed, benches installed and a desk brought in for the fourteen-year-old teacher, who by this time had lengthened her skirts and coiled her hair in the fashion of a grown woman. The curriculum consisted of reading, writing, manners and sewing. The young mistress was serious and strict, going along with Solomon in his abhorrence of the spoiled child, and her punishments were severe. "It was in her nature to use the whip and use it she did," one of her boy pupils said later. The little girls were punished in a different way. One of them was made to walk to and from school during courthouse week wearing a placard on her back which stated: "A Very Bad Girl Indeed." The school became popular, nonetheless, often with twenty pupils at a time. In order to keep up the moral tone, young Dorothea required each child to memorize a weekly chapter from the Bible, and on Mondays the pupils marched to the front of the room, stood on a ruled line, and with folded arms and upturned faces recited the chosen passage. Later, when Miss Dix became famous, samplers were brought out to be exhibited, and her pupils remembered many Bible verses from these early days of pedagogy in masquerade.

Something tragic there was in the story of this determined child, in the zeal she gave to her labors, scepter in hand, on tiptoe above her subjects, ruling them without mercy as though to drive the evil out and away to kingdom come. Was she, by inference, attempting to drive the evil from her own soul, expiating thus the sins of the father as they had been visited on her young and innocent person?

At the end of three years the school closed, and Dorothea returned to her grandmother in Boston. Orange Court had not changed, but its inhabitants found an impressive change for the better in the young girl. She had left Boston impetuous, willful and still a child; she returned with the old eagerness and ambition, but a young woman whose manners were quiet, with habits neat and decorous. There was a new modest charm about her, too, the seeds of her future celebrated magnetism. She still kept her faculty for obtaining her own ends but the means she used were less apparent. One wonders whether the presence of Edward Bangs in the background had not had something to do with the softening process.

Now it was Dorothea's turn to go to school. Madam Dix was proud of her intelligent and capable grandchild and she provided her with tutors to supplement the classes at the public school. But it was from her reading that most of Dorothea's pleasure and instruction came. She borrowed books from the Athenaeum, from the old Boston Library over the arch on Franklin Street; books on science from the American Academy of Arts and Sciences; and she read for long hours in her grandfather Dix's substantial library and in that of her uncle Thaddeus Mason Harris of Dorchester. Later, she confided to friends, that until she was nearly twenty, she had 'determined to live to herself and enjoy only literature and art."

Meanwhile Madam Dix had reached the age of seventy-one and she might presumably have enjoyed the companionship of a grand-daughter disposed to sit by the fire and sew a fine seam, walk with her under the summer sunshine, arm in arm beneath a fringed parasol. But the simple everyday relaxations seemed as far from the unyielding temperament of this girl, with the tall erect figure and the "very stern expression," as the upright spruce tree is from the drooping willow. Only Edward Bangs' visits, his trips to Boston and hers to the Judge Bangs' house in Worcester, brought her something of the pleasures of a spontaneous, live exchange. They saw each other frequently, she and Edward Bangs, during these student years; the girl's passionate nature, with little other means of outlet, turned to him persistently in love and loyalty.

Two years of study brought Dorothea sufficient impetus to plan a new school of her own teaching. A fine opportunity in spacious Orange Court, she decided, to set up an academy, a dame school that would provide a stimulus to young minds found nowhere else. But she must first gain her grandmother's difficult permission. Madam Dix may have respected the girl's desire to earn money but she was not in favor of the school. She did not look forward to hav-ing her house turned into an institution, filled with children coming and going, soiling her carpets with their muddy boots, scratching with penknives and pencils the surfaces of her gleaming mahogany tables. Dorothea, however, was adamant, and in a battle of the wills it was the tough-fibered girl who was apt to win. Her father had died in April of 1821, and her mother and young brothers were now entirely dependent on the bounty of relatives. This situation filled Dorothea with worry and shame and it was an added in-centive to getting the school started.

Pupils arrived, first a few, then more and more. Dorothea was happy. She enjoyed teaching: "I love to watch the progress of a young being just emerging from infancy when thoughts first spring into existence and infant fancy is excited by every passing occurrence." As pupils increased she enlarged the curriculum, going beyond the vulgar fractions and handicrafts into the fields of astronomy, mineralogy and the natural sciences, subjects in which her grandfather had first interested her, and her intensive reading had disciplined her. She was presently so carried away by her success in molding the youthful mind that she persuaded her grandmother to one more step, that of allowing her to open another school, this one for the children of the poor, a "charity school," out in the carriage house above the landau, the pony cart and the brougham. "You have read Hannah More's life, you approve of her labors for the most degraded of England's paupers; why not, when it can be done without exposure or expense, let *me* rescue some of America's miserable children from vice and guilt?" These were words set down in a letter to her grandmother by Dorothea who evidently thought writing a surer means of gaining her ends than a face-to-face interview. The school was soon founded and it went on so well that it became a model eventually for others of its kind.

The days flew by and the nights, with the smallest modicum of sleep. For Dorothea there were not enough hours to contain her ever-swelling ambition for the growth of these children of hers. She wanted to answer every question they put to her and she planned to write a book for this purpose, a kind of Book of Knowledge, full of details about plants, animals, and the manufactured articles in daily use. To keep ahead of her pupils' inquiring minds and gather her material, to manage her grandmother's household, as more and more she came to do, to teach and conduct two separate schools, was the daily task she assigned herself. In summer she was up at four, in winter at five in order to read her Bible for an hour and have time also for her studies before breakfast. From then on there was no respite until long after midnight when her last letters and her final accounts were finished.

There could not have been many hours left to give to Edward Bangs, to whom she had become engaged somewhere about this time. Perhaps half hidden in the back of her mind was the thought that they were not entirely suited, he and she; perhaps Dorothea was afraid of marriage, in love with the joy of loving but not with the idea of bestowing her physical self upon the stranger a man always is for the young virgin. Perhaps, too, her hyperactive and determined nature gave the older man pause. How control such a woman once she had become his wife? How assure the serenity, the integrity of his own life once they were united? And so, one is not surprised to hear presently of the broken engagement, or surprised at the pyramiding of labor up and up, on and on. How else justify life's purpose, Dorothea asked herself, how else but to work with all that one had for the good of mankind?

We do not know the details of this episode, the one love affair in Dorothea's life, because of her talent for reticence. Letters were burned, in the romantic manner of the time, and no word of explanation spoken. She became more reserved, with an air of retiring melancholy that gradually mellowed her personality and brought an added poignance to her resonant voice. And her work went on.

She now had the consolation of religion to rely on, religion in the form of Unitarianism in its vibrant heyday. The Sunday morning came when she left the family pew in the Hollis Street Church to attend Dr. Channing's service in Federal Street, and she remained his loyal adherent from then on. Worship and doctrine now took the place of her lover, with William Ellery Channing as preceptor and friend, guiding her gently away from the Methodist hell-fire doctrines that she had heard preached by her father, teaching her the essential goodness of mankind. Love, for Dorothea, now supplanted fear, and mysticism took the place of dogmatism. Most of all, as it was to influence her future, did Channing's great doctrine: "Man must be sacred in Man's sight," come to lie upon her heart.

Another consolation, one of the several sublimations that Dorothea, in the fashion of modern psychiatry, chose for herself, was a thoroughgoing friendship with a young woman friend named Ann Heath. Ann, with her mother and father and a large number of sisters and brothers, lived in a big house on a hilltop in Brookline, a household that welcomed Dorothea as one of them, a bustling busy, open-hearted place, warming to a solitary nature. And so a friendship began between the two girls that lasted a full fifty years. Daily letters, when they could not meet, were exchanged between them, sisterly confidences and outpourings, enough on Dorothea's side to fill several chests discovered in the attic after Ann Heath's death.

Madam Dix wanted her granddaughter to step out into society, go to parties. There were other young men in the world besides Edward Bangs. She herself, as a girl, had been the belle of Worcester. Why not Dorothea, with her good looks and all her fine knowledge? But Dorothea was shy and inept in the social exchanges: "I have little taste for fashionable dissipation, cards, dancing; the theater and tea parties are my aversion and I look with little envy on those who find enjoyment in such transitory delights, if delights they must be called." In her nature there lodged an intensity, a search for perfection, an awful seriousness, dwelling there side by side with an unyielding reserve, that made for a deportment considered old-fashioned, ultra-ladylike, even in those days of gentle manners. It is not hard to see that this young woman of unbending dignity and serious purpose might have been a damper on any assemblage not committed to improvement of the human lot. There is no record that she was ever invited even to such sober gatherings as those of the Concord Symposium where Margaret Fuller, Elizabeth Peabody and Sophia Ripley were usually present along with Emerson, Orestes Brownson, Bronson Alcott, Channing and Theodore Parker. She was respected as a capable teacher but was not somehow thought of as timber for the cultured, brilliant coterie that made famous the Boston of that day. The "life of the party" she could scarcely have been, with her great unwavering eyes and her determined mouth. Her dark hair she wore parted and carefully brushed from her forehead, looped low over her ears and caught at the back of her head in a great overburdened knot. Her manner of dressing accentuated her dislike of frivolity: a somber-colored, severely cut dress surmounted by a fichu of white, a small brooch at the base of her throat that marked the live pulse sprung from her beating heart, a heart whose desperate tenderness held her fast, urging her on to scale grim and hitherto unattainable heights. The seeds sprung of her disparate inheritance, her longing and solitude, blended in her now to form that uncommon flower, lacking a specific horticultural name, but known to all the world while still it bloomed, as Dorothea Lynde Dix.

Finally she became ill, ill enough to be put to bed. For some time her voice had been husky and a pain in her left side had come to press and to pester. There was even an occasional hemorrhage. "Rheumatism of the lungs," was the family doctor's diagnosis and he advised closing the school for a year or more. To bed Dorothea went but not to rest. She spent the time writing books for children: hymns, moral tales and the *Conversations on Common Things* long in her mind. Although she was often in pain, she was not unhappy. She wrote to Ann Heath: "I am never less disposed to sadness than when ill and alone. The hour of bodily suffering is to me the hour of spiritual joy."

This was the inception of a pattern that came to establish itself as more or less fixed in the later years of her life: intensity of work to a degree not imaginable to most mortals, bodily discomfort and mental stress enough to destroy the average man, then a period of collapse when the dormant tuberculosis became active again or when malaria, contracted on a Mississippi River trip, returned to shake her as the proverbial terrier shakes his prey. Presently a recovery, or what passed for it in Dorothea's mind, spiritual recovery, at any rate, then the rising from the dead to carry on again.

Dr. Channing, who as a youth had broken his own health through arduous work, wrote Dorothea about this time:

I look forward to your future life not altogether without solicitude, but with prevailing hope. Your infirm health seems to darken your prospects of usefulness. But I believe your constitution will be built up if you give it a fair chance. You must learn to give up your plans of usefulness, as much as those of gratification, to the will of God. We may make *these* the occasion of self-will, vanity and pride as much as anything else. May not one of your chief dangers lie there? . . . The infirmity which I warn you of, though one of good minds, is an infirmity. . . .

Infirmity and indulgence, too, perhaps. Easier to plunge headlong into life-saving labor, under the guise of well-doing, than to plan carefully, judiciously, a course of action calculated to use but a minimum of energy. Dorothea wanted to forget the pain of her loss. She wanted to love. And she believed in God. She could not readily "give up her plans of usefulness." They filled her life.

A new plan was made, however, a compromise between invalidism and overwork. When she was twenty-five, Dr. Channing invited Dorothea Dix to Oakland, his place in Portsmouth on Narragansett Bay, as governess to his children. During two summers she was there, supervised by the man she admired above all others, walking out with him, sitting at his table, teaching his daughters. When, later, Elizabeth Peabody became Channing's secretary, she said that "such an experience might be set down as the first year of one's intellectual life." Dorothea was not content merely to bask in the aura of the great man, however, but took on as an extra job, besides her work with the young Channings, "a class of troublesome men and boys who succumbed to her charm of manner and firm will." Thus was she described by one of Channing's daughters who went on to say:

She was strict and inflexible in her discipline which we, her pupils, disliked extremely at the time . . . but which I suppose was not unreasonable as I find my father expressing great satisfaction with her tuition of her pupils. . . . She was a very accomplished teacher—fond of natural history and botany—calling our attention to what was of interest in the word around us . . . fixed as fate we considered her.

There were also the books for children she continued to write and an ambitious literary botany, a kind of drawing room adornment of the epoch, published as *A Garland of Flora*. Here, the flowers that grow are illustrated by quotations from Virgil, Pliny, Plutarch, Spenser, Chaucer, Ben Jonson, Shelley, Washington Irving, etc., and the book astonishes one by its erudition and extent.

Dorothea's fondness for plants was more than ever stimulated by a trip to the Virgin Islands with the Channings, who took her along for a winter at St. Croix. The air here, warm, sweet-smelling, altogether delicious, in contrast to the unequivocal New England seasons, so soothed and enthralled her that at first she could do little more than abandon herself to it, collecting the tropical flowers, like flowers in a dream, listening to the rapturous singing of the Negroes whom she thought the happiest people in the world. But presently, her balance rather more restored, one has glimpses in her letters of the old spirit returning; and, in close proximity as she is to Channing, her sorrow at man's suffering, the haunting need to bolster his well-being, her determination to act. She is distressed at the aspect of slavery in the raw, the illicit power of one set of men over another; she looks ahead to the day when there shall be freedom for all mankind; she pulls herself up out of languor under the soft blue sky to face duty, "Stern Daughter of the Voice of God." And then, rested, strengthened, her hands filled with the plant specimens she had pressed for her friends Silliman and Audubon, she returned to Boston and the school at Orange Court.

This time the school was to be an altogether ideal place. She had read widely on education; she had talked long and earnestly with Channing, prophet of the future; she would use untried methods, induce the bright new day already tingeing the horizon. During five continuous years the big house was crammed to capacity, some of the pupils coming from the neighboring New England states and living there as boarders. They sat about Madam Dix's long dining-room table, cleared for the purpose between meals, doing their sums elbow to crowded elbow; they walked out two by two, pigtails neatly braided, Dorothea in the rear holding the youngest by the hand; they worked harder for Miss Dix than they had ever worked before; they wrestled with their souls to drive away clinging evil and they reported progress by written notes thrust into a giant shell on the parlor mantelpiece, a kind of Ear of God by way of their headmistress. They learned, too, the "Art of Introspection," consid-

ered by Dorothea to be one of life's chief needs. And, following the
text of a sermon by Ezra Stiles Gannett, "An iron will can accomplish everything," a little girl wrote: "I *will* have this iron will and
I *will do* and *be* all that you expect from your child." One of her
pupils later said: "I was in my sixteenth year . . . when my father
placed me at school. She fascinated me from the first. . . . Next to
my mother I thought her the most beautiful woman I had ever
seen. . . ."

Fascination tied to exalted striving and hour upon hour of unre-
mitting work brought tensions and fatigue, however, that some of
Miss Dix's pupils looked back upon later with aversion. The combination of high idealism and too little sleep gradually overwhelmed
many of the girls and presently broke once more the precarious
health of their headmistress whose daily motto was: "I have *no right*
to stay my efforts." Inevitably, the overweighted school had to close.
The girls were disbanded and Dorothea's doctor ordered her to bed.
Once more, too, while the servants carried trays to the invalid above
stairs and her aged grandmother sat upright at the bedside dismayed
at her child's persistent cough, Dorothea felt that sense of spiritual
elevation, that rapture known to the saints, bequeathed to her in
direct descent by her spellbinding father.

Under the sway of this mystical stimulus, not knowing whether
she was to live or die, Dorothea, propped high against the bed
pillows, set to work on the future of her flock. The labor of these
last years, so earnestly begun, with possibilities so significant, must
not sliver away into nothingness; youthful memory must not be
allowed to lose precepts so painfully learned; the past and the future
must somehow be united. She therefore drew up a plan, in the
nature of a last will and testament, bequeathing the school, her most
valued possession, to George Emerson and his wife, he a teacher
and both of them admired friends. Day upon febrile day, in spite of
remonstrance from those who nursed her, she schemed and wrote
while her cough grew worse and the fever held on. When at last it
was apparent that in this atmosphere, this setting of work without
play, she would not grow better, the doctor stepped in again, advis-

ing a trip to Europe. Plans were made, she was hurriedly wrapped
like a baby bunting, carried aboard ship, and, with friends to tend
her, she sailed away.

The ship docked at Liverpool after a stormy passage and Dorothea
was so ill that she had to be put to bed in a local hotel. This was in
April, 1836, when she was thirty-four years old, her life of labor
apparently at an end. Dr. Channing, however, in the continuing
role of guardian angel, writing to friends in Liverpool to tell of
her arrival, brought about an introduction that was presently to
give Dorothea "the jubilee year of her life."

Channing's friends were Mr. and Mrs. William Rathbone, he a
rich, cultivated philanthropist with a sharply whittled social conscience, both of them hosts at Greenbank, their place in the rural
outskirts of Liverpool, to Quakers, Unitarians and to men of good
will the whole world over. An English historian, in his *Portrait of
Victorian England,* has said: "No one can read for long in the literature of the thirties and forties without touching a finer and deeper
pride . . . glowing with the authentic sense of war and victory, man
against nature, and reason against the tradition of the elders." And
he includes the phrase from William Blake: "Great things are done
when men and mountains meet." He continues with a glimpse of
Liverpool in particular: "To travelers descending from the moor-
lands the smoke and roar of Lancashire seemed like the discipline
of a great army. It is hardly an accident that the first history of the
Renaissance came from Liverpool."

Here, then, was fate intervening again in Dorothea's behalf. At
twelve, the broad doorway of her grandmother's house had opened
to receive her, and now, at thirty-four, another door propitious to
her future closed with her on the inner side. And, collaborating
with fate—or dictating to it perhaps, because of its force—Dorothea's
character absorbed from these fresh surroundings the vision and the
nourishment she needed to overcome the mountains she was eventually to meet.

The Rathbones were charming to the stranger. With that talent
for easy hospitality possessed by the English and an innate kindness

combining pleasantly with wealth, they made her believe she was a
blessed apparition as well as an invalid to be cared for, petted and
loved. She writes to friends: "You know I am ill. You must imagine
me surrounded by every comfort, sustained by every tenderness....
I write from my bed, leaning on the pillows in a very Oriental
luxury of position . . . one which I think will soon fall into a fixed
habit."

The habit, indeed, was to continue for eighteen months. Dorothea
had never before received this kind of beneficent affection and, since
she was physically unable to work, her conscience was at rest. True,
her grandmother became disturbed at the protracted visit and wrote
to warn her against being in the graceless position of one who out-
stays her welcome. But from the earliest days Dorothea had been
accustomed to visit relatives far less agreeably tied to her than were
these delightful people who introduced her to their many friends
and continued to make her feel she was indispensable. How bring
it all to an end? Like weighing the anchor that held her floating in
a pool of varicolored, sweet-smelling lilies. There were the intellectual and philanthropic aspects of life here, too, the good and the
great who came and went, the enthralling talk. And it was probably
during these months that Dorothea met Dr. Samuel Tuke, that
generous benefactor of "York Retreat," an asylum sponsored by
Friends, where the Tukes, father and son, followed the pattern of
the eminent Frenchman, Dr. Philippe Pinel, in bringing enlightened
care to psychotics in an age of unenlightenment.

Presently the news came to Dorothea of her mother's death. The
letter announcing it absolved the daughter of responsibility for her
absence, Mary Bigelow Dix having died quite suddenly at the end
of a protracted illness. There was the consolation for Dorothea, too,
that she had long been helping to support her mother and brothers.
Now, the brothers were old enough to look out for themselves and
there was, in consequence, less reason than ever to sail away. It was
more difficult, however, to persuade her conscience in the matter of
her ninety-one-year-old grandmother who had now begun visibly to
fail and who longed to see her grandchild once again. "You know

all my habits through life have been singularly removed from reliance on others," she wrote to a friend at this time by way of justification, ". . . the feeling, right or wrong, that aloneness is my proper position has prevailed since my childhood." And it was not until the autumn of 1837, her grandmother having died in April, leaving Dorothea a legacy, that finally she pulled herself away and returned to New England.

Boston has been a place of promise, a haven of security, a center of learning. It has also been a sink of despair for the uncertain, the dimly connected, the outsiders to whom it seems raw, provincial, hard, ugly. Dorothea Dix on her return from England found herself an outsider. The familiar house at Orange Court was closed and there were no relatives to take her in as one of them. The cousins, in fact, received her coldly. Had she not behaved in callous fashion to the dying grandmother who had given her so much, who had been generous and forgiving enough to make her economically independent? There was no thought in Dorothea's mind of opening another school. Her educational projects had twice ended in catastrophe. What to do next, where to turn? Another Boston propensity, that of bracketing people, setting them rigidly into categories, told against her now. In England she had been accepted as a young woman of talent and intelligence, entertained by the high-minded and the gracious. At home again, known only as a schoolteacher, cut off now from this former world yet not included among the reigning intellectuals, there seemed to be no society that beckoned. She wrote Ann Heath:

> I was not conscious that so great a trial was to meet my return from England till the whole force of contrast was laid before me. Then, I confess, it made an impression which will be ineffaceable. Perhaps it is in myself that fault chiefly lies. . . . I may hunger and thirst too eagerly for that cordial, real regard which exists not in mere outward forms or uttered sounds. . . .

Who, indeed, does not thirst for this?

Several years followed, years of search, of wandering, of listlessness. Dorothea must often have been drawn again toward England. Instead, she spent months in Alexandria, Virginia, crossing the Potomac each day to read for hours in the Congressional Library, while plans for social service, in some form, she held in the back of her mind as a steadying counteragent in her present irresolute life, the aimless life that so often sends weaker beings into limbo. Then, temporarily in Boston in 1841, she received a visit from a young Harvard divinity student, John Nichols, who spoke of the East Cambridge jail and the twenty women prisoners held there. Someone was needed, he said, to begin the reform of these desperate creatures, to conduct a Bible class on Sundays. Whom could she suggest? What older woman might be available? Quietly, Dorothea answered: "I will go myself." Nichols remonstrated. She was too young; these women were too depraved. "I shall be there next Sunday," Dorothea said. After this, she was never to be irresolute or aimless again. The world became her oyster for good and all.

Following the episode of the jail and the first triumph in her struggles with the law, the vision came to Dorothea of other Black Holes of Calcutta where human beings were held in hopelessness. She must find these beings, go to their aid, go at once. One could point to a few fine hospitals for the insane already in operation: the McLean Hospital, the Boston Lunatic Asylum; but these were only tiny islands in a wild sea strewn with shipwrecks. There had also been the work of Horace Mann, thirteen years earlier, who, in making his survey of prisons, almshouses and houses of correction and finding that "persons furiously mad" were committed to the nearest jail, had called attention to this fact, saying: "Had the earth been searched, places more inauspicious to their recovery could scarcely have been found." In consequence of this beam of light the great hospital at Worcester had been built. But should there not be many more like it? Could she, Dorothea Dix, let the whole thing lie? Could she allow herself to slip back into retirement, play merely the role of cultivated lady, for the rest of her time on earth? She would go for advice to Channing. It was he, after all, who first had taught her the value of human life, who believed that human nature, even in the most degraded form, held within it the germ of endless spiritual development. Channing would sustain her, would understand her—command her, perhaps.

Channing was not well, was growing gradually weaker in an illness from which he was not to recover. But he listened attentively to Dorothea and her moving story of the sufferings of the insane, to her plans for work in their behalf, and, as always, he supported her now. He foresaw her success. She was learning to overcome her bodily frailty, keep it within bounds; she would undoubtedly come into her own with this task before her. She needed to confront mountains in order to be happy. Here was an Alpine range waiting to be scaled. Let her go forth. The sooner the better.

The Channing house at 85 Mount Vernon Street was thus Dorothea's point of departure. During the next two years, notebook in hand, she went all over Massachusetts. She visited every jail, almshouse, workhouse, from Berkshire to Cape Cod, sparing herself no horror as one of them after another confronted her, at Dedham, Medford, Pepperell, Plymouth, Concord.

At Danvers, before reaching the shabby almshouse, she heard wild shouts, oaths, obscenities, and found in a shed apart from the main building a young woman "beating upon the bars of her caged apartment . . . space only for increasing accumulations of filth . . . a foul spectacle . . . disheveled . . . unwashed. . . . The irritation of her body produced by filth and exposure incited her to the horrid process of tearing off her skin by inches. She held up a fragment just torn off. . . . To my exclamation of horror, the mistress replied, 'Oh, we can't help it. Half the skin is off sometimes.'"

At Granville a man was losing the use of his limbs from being so closely confined. At Medford was another who had been kept in his stall for seventeen years. At Newton, asleep in the woodshed of the almshouse, she found an old man lying on a box, the stumps which had once been feet protruding from one end. He had frozen his feet one winter when the jailer did not "reckon how cold he was." But he was nonetheless chained, for he could still crawl.

Everywhere, brutality, degradation, despair.

Through the long hot summer and on into autumn, Dorothea continued her work, taking notes on the spot, elaborating them at evening when she reached the tavern where she was to sleep. Winter came, when traveling by stagecoach and hired carriage was not easy. There were few railroads in Massachusetts in 1841, and the springless coaches bumped along, producing headaches in the passengers, at fifteen miles an hour. Now and then Dorothea became storm- or ice-bound at some inn. This brought the chance to rest, to organize her notes, to write friends of her progress. These friends became, more and more, the people who had an interest in her work: heads of the three big aslyums who taught her the most up-to-date methods for dealing with the insane, and men of the caliber of Dr. Howe and Horace Mann, besides intimates such as Ann Heath.

As the months passed, returning, occasionally, several times to the same prison, she made friends with the keepers whom she sometimes converted to the idea of more humane treatment for their charges. But these few enlightened ones complained of lack of funds while the majority remained indifferent. None of them barred her entry, however, or refused her the information she sought. They responded to her quiet courage and her tact. She had learned that reproof was less effective than persuasion and she dealt with these people in measured fashion that she might not be thwarted in her work.

Finally, in 1843, she returned to Mount Vernon Street, her journeys temporarily halted. Dr. Channing had died in October of 1842 but Dorothea was welcomed by Mrs. Channing and there, with the aura of this beloved mentor enfolding her, she wrote her *Memorial to the Legislature of Massachusetts* so that the people might know what were the conditions of the insane in their state. She wrote simply, directly, emulating the sober, telling style of Sumner and the spiritual quality of Theodore Parker:

I proceed, gentlemen, briefly to call your attention to the *present* state of insane persons confined within the Commonwealth, in *cages, closets, cellars, stalls, pens; chained, naked, beaten with rods* and *lashed* into obedience.

On and on she told the story.

Dr. Samuel Gridley Howe was a member of the legislature at the time and it was he who presented the *Memorial*. It created a sensation and was followed by the kind of behavior usual at moments of unpalatable discovery. Legislators were indignant and unbelieving; they considered preposterous the sums of money asked for. Local overseers of the poor denied inhuman treatment of their charges; keepers protested; women gossiping across house fences asked what kind of lady this could be who allowed herself to enter such horrible places as she described. In answer to statements made by Miss Dix to the press, hints of libel were printed and, at Danvers, the overseers wrote a counter-memorial denouncing Miss Dix's report.

But her *Memorial* stood, a monument of flint not to be destroyed.

Men of Massachusetts, I beg, I implore, I demand pity and protection for those of my suffering, outraged sex. Fathers, husbands, brothers, I would supplicate you for this boon. . . .

Thus Dorothea had written. For a time, however, it looked as though the men of Massachusetts would not be moved, would remain incredulous scoffers. Then, Charles Sumner again came to the rescue, writing articles for the newspapers in support of Miss Dix, guiding public opinion gradually in her direction, popular as he was with the man in the street. Dr. Howe, meanwhile, watched for an auspicious moment in the legislature and the day came when he was finally able to get action on the Memorial. It was referred to a legislative committee, which presently reported on it favorably. By this time public opinion had swerved in favor of reform and the body of lawmaking politicians no longer dared to stem the tide, even though Dr. Howe still heard a few of them muttering: "We must find some way to kill this devil of a hospital bill!"

On the Saturday in February that the vote on the bill was to be taken, Dorothea waited for news in the Channing library, and it

was here, most fittingly, that she heard from Dr. Howe that the bill
had passed by a large majority. Her second triumph, this was, and
on a scale of far greater magnitude than that at the East Cambridg
jail. The scale was to increase on and on, in length, in width, in
depth, during the forty years that lay ahead, as Dorothea Dix be
came more and more proficient at the art of scaling mountains. Her
was to be no roughshod attack; the pickax, the clouted boots, at an
rate, were to remain concealed. She was to go forward in her long
sweeping skirt held with one hand high above the slime of prison
floors, with aristocratic bearing, with dignity and repose of manner
even at the moments when she was most moved by the sight of
suffering. Also, the indomitable force of will that had shown itself
in the fourteen-year-old schoolmistress, cane in hand, was ever in
reserve. And now, combined with high intellectual qualities and
quick perception, she possessed the equipment for action of a states
man or a military commander. Jeanne d'Arc had had no more
powerful weapons than these, and who knows but that even the
power of seeing visions was not also present in this intensely reli
gious woman who believed in God and in the perfectibility of the
human soul.

"I am the hope of the poor crazed beings who pine in cells and
stalls and cages and waste rooms," she was later to tell the men of
the general assembly in North Carolina. "I am the revelation of hun
dreds of wailing, suffering creatures hidden in your private dwell
ings and in pens, and cabins—shut out, cut off from all healing
influence, from all mind-restoring cures."

She was helped, then, in the work that followed, not only by her
own qualities and appearance, her low voice with perfect enuncia
tion, her fine eyes and high color; she was helped, too, by the
temper of her age, an age dedicated to reform largely instigated
and guided by Channing. People were intent upon projects: Ripley
and Alcott were concerned with Brook Farm and Fourierism; Gar
rison was busy with the *Liberator;* Margaret Fuller and Elizabeth
Peabody drove forward to change the status of women; Orestes
Brownson and Henry Hedge proclaimed universal brotherhood

while the *North American Review,* prophet of a new age, printed articles on spiritualism, animal magnetism, clairvoyance, as well as on philosophy and political economy. Everywhere, among the enlightened, men and women cared and believed; all good things seemed possible, seemed necessary, and those who strove did not count the cost in effort. What mattered the day's expenditure in energy, the evening's exhausting interchange of ideas, what mattered illness or death if the world moved on toward the spheres of light?

And so with her bill in the Massachusetts Legislature on its way to becoming law, thus providing adequate space for the insane in Boston and in Worcester, Dorothea crossed the border into Rhode Island, resolved that she would continue her work state by state until those wretched, helpless friends of hers should everywhere be given proper treatment. Rhode Island, indeed, could not be put off longer. Was there not there the pitiful case of Simmons at Little Compton and the several others she had come on? A large, well-equipped hospital was needed at once.

At Providence, Dorothea set to work on the lists of names given her of affluent men who were charitably inclined. She selected one name finally, that of Cyrus Butler, because of his vast fortune and because he had so far kept his money intact for purposes of speculation. People shook their heads, telling her she would fail, that Butler was immovable. She persisted and found her way presently to his study, found her way also to his heart as she told him the story of Simmons and the rest.

"Madam," he asked at the end of her tale, "what do you wish me to do?"

"I would like you to give me fifty thousand dollars, for the enlargement of the insane asylum of this city," she answered. "It will ever stand as a monument to your generosity." Thus the Butler Hospital was established.

But Dorothea realized now that, moving on from state to state, she would not always be able to rely on the generosity of one man nor perform the incredible feat of conversion as in the case of

Cyrus Butler—a kind of virtuous wooing, an alliance made between man and woman with the angels as sponsors and guardians. No single individual could stretch to the far limits, morally or financially, that her plans required. Moreover, the people as a whole should know what went on, should have a part in the regeneration of humankind.

In New Jersey, therefore, her next choice for action, Dorothea returned to the method she had used in Massachusetts. But now she was far from home, from friends, from substantial help; now she must rely only on herself, begin at the beginning. And this, perhaps more than anything else, contributed to her final success. She was forever able to begin again at the beginning even when, as was presently to happen, she believed she had come to the end.

In New Jersey, now, her visits to prisons and poorhouses began once more, town by town, county by county, all over the state. Then the taking of notes, the tiresome jogging in creaky horse-drawn carriages, the business—a real business it became—of making allies as she went, people who would help her in the battles to come. Dorothea had a flair for discriminating friend from foe, for finding the staunch and influential within a community. In New Jersey and Pennsylvania it was the Quakers to whom she chiefly turned, who stood by her in faithfulness. And in return for help given her, she gave it back in good measure: she tended the sick whom she met on her travels, she read to the children, she listened to tales of woe, becoming an itinerant fairy godmother. Next, came the presentation of the memorial to the legislature, through some representative of influence, followed by the writing of articles for the newspapers to instruct and rouse public opinion and, once the bill was up for a vote, the long labor with the various members of the House, dissenters, demagogues often, wanting only to be certain of re-election by keeping taxes low for their constituents. She was up before sunrise preparing for the day to come, and in the evening she often entertained the members in her small hotel parlor by lamplight. She seemed never to rest. She wrote a friend from her New Jersey base:

I am exhausted by this perpetual effort. At Trenton thus far, all is prosperous, but you cannot imagine the labor of conversing and convincing. Some evenings I had at once twenty gentlemen for three hours' steady conversation. The last evening, a rough country member, who came to overwhelm me with his arguments, after listening an hour and a half with wonderful patience, suddenly moved into the middle of the parlor, and thus delivered himself: "Ma'am, I bid you good night! . . . *I am convinced;* you've conquered me out and out; I shall vote for the hospital. If you'll come to the House, and talk there as you've done here, no man that isn't a brute can withstand you. The Lord bless you!" Thereupon he departed.

Dorothea was too wise, however, to appear in the House herself, to make any kind of speech on her own behalf. Far better to work behind the scenes, remain in the role of gentlewoman according to the pattern of the day. She was in no sense a dedicated feminist. She did her work because it had to be done, oblivious of her sex. And much of her appeal, especially in the South where chivalry was still an active code, came from the aura that wrapped her, that of the aristocratic lady. She had also the wit to realize when she had worked long enough in one spot, when it was time to move elsewhere, to sponsor another one of her memorials, leaving behind some locally powerful person as nurse for the impending bill while the battle raged back and forth. In fact, part of her genius lay in her knowledge of men. For, one of her self-imposed duties had been to study, within each legislature, the names, faces, personalities of the members, that she might ferret out the capable and magnanimous from among others. The smooth-spoken men she avoided, the orators who announced that she was a "heaven-sent angel of mercy," and then voted against her bills. She fared better with the hard-bitten country members in homespun, downright as they were. But she once wrote a friend her opinion of politicians:

"They are the meanest and lowest party demagogues, shocking to say . . . the basest characters."

Pennsylvania followed after New Jersey, then Utica, New York; Indiana, Illinois, Kentucky, Missouri, Louisiana; and presently

Georgia, Alabama, South Carolina. She marked each of the states—
following a successful campaign for a new hospital, new wing or
new measures for treatment—with a cross on her map. But nothing
appeared there to show the hazards of her journeys as she endured
them more in sickness than in health.

In the months between June, 1843, and August, 1847, she traveled
thirty thousand miles, from Canada to the Gulf of Mexico and from
the Atlantic to the Mississippi River. In her long skirt and bonnet
and shawl and a rug to cover her knees, she sat in stagecoaches,
carts, lumber wagons, while horses struggled through mud and
swollen streams. Or, seated on a tree stump, she wrote letters to her
friends as the driver strove to repair damage to the harness. "I
crossed the Yadkin where it was three-quarters of a mile wide,"
she wrote, "rough bottom—the water always up to the bed of the
carriage and sometimes flowing in. The horses rested twice on sand
bars. . . . A few miles beyond the river . . . the axletrees of the
carriage broke, and away rolled one of the back wheels."

After a few such experiences, Dorothea provided herself with a
kit holding tools, rope, axle grease, nails, leather for patching, that
the colored boy who drove might conclude his repair job quickly.
"I encounter nothing which a determined will created by the necessities of the cause does not enable me to vanquish," she wrote her
friend, George Emerson, he who years before had taken over the
school at Orange Court.

What gave Dorothea Dix this terrible intensity, this determined
will? Inherited in part from her embattled grandfather, it was born,
perhaps, out of childhood imagination that proffered golden promises during the long, solitary hours of tract stitching beneath the log
cabin roof, and it was stimulated by a loss of self-esteem needing
to be recaptured, guilt that clung persistently, unremittingly since
the day she had run away from home, abandoning her mother and
the family. Her power of will had been strengthened again when
she had been obliged to summon her every force at the time of the
broken engagement to her cousin, when, to give herself recklessly to
human beings became quite simply a matter of saving her life. And

now, with these early things behind her, with the fine caliber of her intellect to guide her and Channing's counsels ever in her mind, she became a well-nigh unconquerable creature.

People remonstrated, friends begged her to rest. A letter from Dr. Francis Lieber written at Columbia, South Carolina, in 1864, says: "Miss Dix has been with us again and leaves us tomorrow. . . . She is greatly exhausted and I always fear to hear that she has succumbed somewhere in a lonely place. What a heroine she is! . . . I have the highest veneration for her heart and head."

At approximately the same moment, Dorothea was writing as she traveled down the Mississippi River: "We have on our boat both cholera and malignant scarlet fever."

These were but spectacular additions to the ordinary plagues of malaria and other infectious diseases carried by the mosquitoes, flies and rats that infested the old paddle-wheelers. Night after night during epidemics on board, Dorothea nursed the sick, helping to deal out the quinine and laudanum, the hard liquor and turpentine which were the standard remedies. She gave no thought to her own danger. Illness meant nothing more to her than an unhappy interruption of her work: "Up again from malarial fever; off to Jackson, Mississippi, tonight." Her system became saturated with malaria, the returning bouts of fever occurring at regular intervals that alternated with hemorrhages, springing from the lung condition contracted in her girlhood. But once these maladies had temporarily subsided, there was nothing that could stay her course. Minor ailments she seems not to have known and she once told a friend she had never in her life had a headache. Caught now and then by flood or washout, she took to her bed and stored up sleep, sometimes thirteen to sixteen hours at a stretch to tide her over the next two or three nights of jolting in wretched carts over corduroy roads when, arrived at her destination, she was to be met by surly jail keepers, cold floors slimy with human filth, pitiful scenes of suffering and active violence—all, that she might subsequently write one more memorial to turn apathy into action.

Dorothea traveled with sparse luggage which included her Bible and the latest work on mental diseases. These she studied avidly, reading oftentimes far into the night by the light of a candle or sperm-oil lamp, seated alone before a banked fire after the tavern keeper had gone to bed. She was ever eager to learn and to know, that she might ask and provide for the best. She made notes along the margins of pages and she was in constant communication with the doctors of the larger mental hospitals: Bloomingdale, Mc-Lean, the Lunatic Hospital of Boston and the hospital in Worcester. These men acted as her mentors, admiring and grateful as they were for the manner in which she was able to secure from the Philistines that which they had despaired of realizing. Horace Mann, too, continued to be her constant adviser, chiefly in the cause of prison reform. But more and more as the years turned from spring to winter, she eliminated all else for the sake of the insane. One principle, however, she held to, within every institution dealing with human derelicts, the principle that regarded men as individuals to be reformed rather than as targets for social revenge. There would soon be an end, she hoped, of sending to jail men and women, young and old, there to punish and torture them for no other reason than that their minds refused to serve them properly. She and her doctor allies must never fail to insist upon this aspect of progress until at last it should become practice. Here was the dream that drove her on.

Before the close of 1845, Dorothea wrote Mrs. Rathbone in Liverpool:

I have traveled more than ten thousand miles in the last three years. Have visited eighteen state penitentiaries, three hundred county jails and houses of correction, more than five hundred almshouses . . . besides hospitals and houses of refuge. I have been so happy as to promote and secure the establishment of six hospitals for the insane, several county poorhouses, and several jails on a reformed plan.

It had become her habit to canvass the South from autumn to the following spring and to go North during the summer. These northern trips included eventually Nova Scotia, St. John, New Brunswick, and Halifax where she worked especially hard to found a much needed asylum. There she acquired an ardent admirer in the Honorable Hugh Bell, who, along with the Bishop of Nova Scotia, gave her all the support that he could muster. "With you by my side (like Minerva, in the shape of the Mentor, by the side of Telemachus) even *I* would become courageous. We shall conquer yet," Hugh Bell wrote her.

Meanwhile, as she went, her fame spread far and she made many new friends. More and more she was invited to stay in the houses of the people she met on her travels, so that gradually her existence became pleasanter. She formed the habit of important people, quite naturally, because the great and the influential were those who could be of most help to the cause. Three Presidents of the United States she came to know intimately: Polk, Fillmore and Lincoln, and, besides being asked to the White House, she often stayed in the various executive mansions with the governors and their wives. She charmed the young as well as the old, talking to the children in the households she visited, asking them to part with their toys to give them to the inhabitants of asylums, fascinating them with accounts of that strange world where grown-up ladies played with dolls and gentlemen rolled marbles and hoops. She allowed no social engagements to interfere with concentration on her job, however, and she spent little time on clothes. It was usually Ann Heath who sent her from Boston the few dresses she needed in order to be neat: a plain gray dress for her journeys, with white collar and cuffs, and one simple black silk dress for special occasions. A trunk holding changes of linen, etc., was expressed on to a new destination one week ahead, and, because of her fast-spreading fame as a humanitarian, the express companies refused to charge for their services while railroads and steamship lines presented her with annual passes.

In spite of constant traveling, Dorothea's business habits were meticulous and she managed to keep her correspondence up to date, a remarkable feat, as her advice was constantly being asked not only on how to expedite passage of bills through the various legislatures but how best to run the hospitals once they had been established. "Do please return, we can do nothing without you," was the tenor of the appeals sent her at this period, and indeed as long as she lived. Besides this, the choice of the site for a new institution often devolved upon her and it was she who must go over the building plans with the architect. Were the grounds for the proposed site suitable for the patients' outings, were there enough shade trees, was the spot accessible for the delivery of supplies? The real estate transactions in which she must also take a hand were usually more than difficult because of the unpleasant qualities in human nature that these dealings brought forward, and because land owners fought off the setting up of "madhouses" as being dangerous and unsavory, frequently refusing to sell.

Dorothea moved on undaunted, her own passionately persuasive powers a last resort, when all else failed, for those who worked at her side. There was the well-known encounter with Thomas Blagden who owned a magnificent stretch of land at the junction of the Potomac and East Branch Rivers outside Washington, D.C., and who lived an enviable life there with his wife and children. When Congress in 1852 appropriated $25,000 for an Army and Navy insane hospital, the Blagden site was the one chosen by Dr. John Nichols who was to head it. Mr. Blagden, however, did not want to sell, did not choose to leave the broad meadows that fell quietly toward the water, nor the great ancient trees and his view of Washington in the distance. Wherever again could he and his family recapture the idyll they enjoyed here? Besides, the sum of $25,000 was entirely insufficient were he forced to quit the present site for another one.

Then came Dorothea Dix, asking if she might call on the owner of the best situation for a hospital "in all the world." She went and spoke as she had spoken to Butler of Providence, at the start of her career, telling Thomas Blagden the story of the broken lives that might perhaps be mended here in this beautiful place, were they given the opportunity. Mr. Blagden walked the floor in perplexity and pain. How refuse this lady of grace? How deny to the unfortunates for whom she pleaded a gamble in favor of betterment or cure? His letter was written that night:

Dear Madam:

Since seeing you today, I have no other opinion (and Mrs. B. also) than that I must not stand between you and the beloved farm, regarding you, as I do, as the instrument of God to secure this very spot for the unfortunate whose best earthly friend you are, and believing sincerely that the Almighty's blessing will not rest on, nor abide with, those who put obstacles in your way. . . . Your obedient servant, Thomas Blagden.

So the hospital presently known as St. Elizabeth's was born.

And now, in 1848, Dorothea Dix embarked on a task which was to be, for six years, more or less, a labor so vast that, aware of it in full, beforehand, she might well have shrunk from attempting it. Certainly the average man shrinks even from contemplating so great an expenditure of fortitude, energy, self-sacrifice, such singleness of purpose. The mere thought of it brings distaste to the person whose existence is scattered, who is bored by persistence, irritated by a stubborn will and the lack of humor usually an adjunct of these qualities. The pinnacles of valor, unaccompanied by the romantic, do not draw the multitude.

For some time past, as she made her rounds, Dorothea had been concerned with the future. She would not forever be available to plead for the mentally ill, while their plight would not lessen in the years to come. The stresses of civilization would bring more and more of the unhappy and ill-fit to the fore. Something must be done —a major plan on a national scale must be conceived and acted upon. The federal government itself should take over the task of caring for the insane, near and far, across the continent. This was surely the answer.

Dorothea knew that large tracts of land, a part of the public domain, were being gradually ceded by the government to the various states as they entered the Union, for the establishment of schools and other civic improvements within their borders. Already over 100,000,000 acres had been given away but there was a similar amount left to be disposed of. Why not reserve a part of this huge remaining domain for the indigent insane who were, after all, as

Dorothea said, "wards of the nation"? And why not, as it concerned herself and her life work, concentrate her labors in Washington at the source of the national stream, there to encourage the flow until its branches should cover the land?

True to her established technique, with the new plan thoroughly in mind, Miss Dix set to work to compose one more memorial, the most stirring she had yet presented. It was written in bed as she lay during three weeks recovering from a severe influenza. She could not go forth when her temperature zigzagged up and down the chart. How better employ the time than to try if she might not one day move the gigantic composite heart of Congress? She asked now for an appropriation of five million acres of land to become a fund for the use of this "too much neglected and most hopeless class."

The memorial finished, there was the usual meticulous preparation for the campaign to come: the choice of the right senator to sponsor the bill, the rounding up of influential supporters within Congress. Many of these members had known Dorothea during her labors for their individual states and they were already her allies. The bill therefore was at once referred to a "select committee" of her own choosing and reported back favorably. This was in June, 1848, with the heat of a Washington summer beginning to sear the pavements, grip the rooms where men gathered and make for breathless nights. By courtesy of Congress an alcove in the Capitol Library was set aside for Dorothea's use and here, day after day, she came to interview members, to prepare them for the coming vote, to plead, to quote, to exhort, combining emotion with a dignity hard to resist, managing somehow to reiterate her arguments over and over again, for the benefit of newcomers or recalcitrants difficult to win. She had studied the use of the English language, the art of clear statement, making notes over the years, as she read, to increase her vocabulary. Language for Dorothea took the place of his sword for the soldier. It was hers to maintain, keen-edged and polished.

Her life was now even more that of the ascetic than in the days of her school teaching. She woke at four, before dawn, to spend an hour at her devotions and arise from her knees an ever-renewed spirit. Such is the power of concentration tied to faith. Then, before the eight o'clock breakfast bell each morning, she tended her immense correspondence, bringing to it the order that set her mind free for the greater task of the day. If there were moments available before ten o'clock when she was due in her alcove at the Capitol, she read hymns or composed one of her own on the pattern of early Latin church hymns or those of Bernard de Cluny or the German mystics. This pastime and her continued love of biology and botany seem to have been her only entertainments. Now and then she put on the black silk dress contrived under the Heath aegis in Brookline, Massachusetts, hanging usually idle in her wardrobe, to attend a reception at the White House or some formal diplomatic dinner. But chiefly she spent her evenings writing to friends or preparing for the next day's work.

These friends were more sanguine than was Dorothea as to the passage of the bill. From her own experience in these matters, as she worked with legislators—"in general a good deal more occupied with party politics than devoted to the duties of statesmanship"—she had found that, although alone with her they might behave as charitable, fair-minded men, when the aura of expediency wrapped them again in the House and Senate corridors, they reverted to another brand of being. Powerful lobbies were opposed to her plan: railroads, large commercial enterprises, land-holding companies, every possible money-making scheme, it seemed, was bidding for portions of the public domain. She herself held no powers of bribery, possessed no bait to dangle aloft; she had nothing but a cause and a cause repulsive to the average man who needed a very strong stomach to digest it. Also there had sprung up a "new democratic movement in the Northern States," as Dorothea wrote a friend, to check the powers of Congress in the bestowal of land. These things, during the long months of summer, hung over her as factors that might well undermine her purpose.

And so, when in March of 1849 the five-million-acre bill failed of passage, she was not surprised. "My bill has been deferred," she wrote Ann Heath. Deferred but not dead. Impossible that a glorious idea such as this could die. There was always the future. An election would be held in November, new members would be entering Congress, there would be fresh material to be molded, other souls to be converted. With the new Congress she would try for even larger goals. This time she would include the indigent deaf and dumb as well as the insane, and for their combined benefit, she would ask for more of the public land, she would demand twelve million, five hundred thousand acres.

In December she was back once again in her special alcove at the Capitol, meeting there with the initial success she had had at the inception of her first memorial: an important man as sponsor, a friendly committee of reference. Also, this time, there were pressures on Congress in favor of the bill coming from churches and other strong sections of the public, while a resolution of "unqualified sanction" was sent from the medical superintendents of the American institutions for the insane.

Through another spring and another summer of endless dragging heat, Dorothea sat at her walnut desk in the library window and labored at the job of explaining, cajoling, repeating the sordid stories of suffering her soul so longed to forget. She filled with a "divine magnetism" those whom she called to her side, Horace Mann wrote his wife in September, 1850.

But for the second time Congress adjourned without acting. Instead, during the final days of the session it chose to act upon a bill to increase the pay of soldiers serving in the Mexican war. In February of 1851, however, the tide seemed at last to have turned and the land bill was passed by the Senate in a ratio of two to one. Dorothea was elated, only to be thrown back into despair when an adjournment for the summer prevented its being put to a vote in the House. "Pray that my patience may not fail utterly," she wrote her friend Ann.

There followed an interlude, as Dorothea waited for Congress to

change its mood—an interlude which might almost have been la-
beled a pleasure trip in that she set out on one of her journeys of
philanthropic exploration with a companion, rather than breast
the hazards and weariness of travel alone—her usual pattern. Frederika Bremer, the Swedish novelist, had met Dorothea in Washington, and, as a professional creator of character, had been drawn to
the great humanitarian. How invent a heroine in fiction to match
this extraordinary woman? Miss Bremer wrote her niece in Sweden:

She is one of the most beautiful proofs of that which a woman, without any other aid than her own free will and character, without any
other power than that of her purpose and its uprightness and her ability
to bring these forward, can effect in society. I admire her—her courage
and perseverance. In other respects we hardly sympathize but I love the
place she occupies in humanity, love her figure sitting in the recess of
the window in the Capitol, where amid the fiery feuds, she silently spins
her web for the unfortunate. . . .

They went into the South together, these two women, through
Georgia, North and South Carolina, Florida, and Frederika Bremer
watched Dorothea with amazement as in one prison, one hospital
after another, she bestowed her vitality on those who suffered there,
comforting as she went, soothing, cheering: "She scatters about her
like morning dew as she goes along her way little miniature books
called *Dewdrops*—seeds of spiritual culture." And while Miss
Bremer rebelled at the quality of accommodation offered travelers
in the South, Dorothea took all in her stride, wasting no bit of energy in resisting the inevitable. Going down the Savannah River,
there was no fresh water to be had and they were obliged to drink
the muddy river water; presently in their cabin, mice scurried
across their faces as they tried to sleep and cockroaches attacked
their baggage. Miss Bremer was in despair but Dorothea got out of
bed, lighted a candle, moved their bags elsewhere and gradually
managed the situation as she had done on many another night.
Whenever the boat tied up temporarily at a wharf to unload salt
pork, barrels and staves, to ship tobacco, molasses and rum, Doro-

thea was first to cross the gangplank, going off into the outskirts on foot or in a two-wheeler to visit the local poorhouse, prison or hospital.

All this so impressed Frederika Bremer that she later stated there was no one in Europe, not even Mrs. Fry, the English reformer, who could compare with Dorothea Dix in self-denial and fearlessness. That trip down the Savannah! And yet to Dorothea it was but one of countless others. "Should I not kiss her hand?" Miss Bremer asks. "I did and do it again in spirit, with thanks for that which she is and that which she does."

Another diversion, this one far afield, broke in on Dorothea's vigil over recalcitrant Congressmen. During a summer recess of Congress in 1853, she went, in June, to St. John, Newfoundland, on the exacting business of a new asylum and, while she labored, there occurred a frightful shipwreck off Sable Island. In terror of the sea though she was, she decided to set forth in person for the dangerous isle to determine what conditions held there.

Sable Island, the instructed Dorothea knew, had made its mark on history in the epoch of Queen Elizabeth, for it was during that age of far-flung enterprise that one of the Queen's gallant courtiers, Sir Humphrey Gilbert, had lost his life there when his ship foundered in attempting an approach. Here was a sea-front of almost thirty miles, unprotected by any harbor and maintaining before it long strips of treacherous bars and shoals, while island beaches were strewn with the wrecks of ships full-rigged, of brigs, schooners and a flotilla of smaller boats. This island of ill omen had served as a penal colony for French Acadia, and tales of desperate men roaming its surface had given many a sailor the wish to drown in the waters about it rather than risk a landing. Finally, after the wreck of the *Princess Amelia,* a ship carrying the officers and servants of Prince Edward, all of whom perished, the provincial legislature had established at Sable Island a relief station with superintendent and crew of four men. By 1836, several buildings had been erected and two thousand pounds in money settled upon it annually. But still the wrecks continued, it being impossible to construct a lighthouse on the adjacent shifting sands.

Fortunately, for Dorothea, the sea was calm on the day she sailed across although a heavy mist made the landing seem like a confused dream of early morning. Fortunately also, perhaps, for her and her plans, a wreck took place soon after her arrival so that she was able, from the back of the small wild pony which she rode—one of the herd that roamed the island—to watch on the long south beach the island lifesaving methods and to help the survivors. The surf boats went back and forth between ship and beach and, because the wind fell steadily, all hands were rescued, all save the captain who, temporarily demented, refused to leave his ship. Dorothea, used to handling men in times of mental crisis, urged a few among the crew to return to the rapidly sinking ship, bind the captain hand and foot, if necessary, and bring him to shore. This done, she rode swiftly to his side, persuaded the poor man to thank his rescuers, soothed him with gentle words and sent him off for food and bed in the hope that rest and nourishment might restore him to his senses.

During several days following, Dorothea studied the island's potentials and its many lacks. Its lifeboats and equipment were far below standard, wanting a mortar for casting out line. Without a cart or a breeches buoy, the boats themselves were clumsy and unsafe. Then she took the train to Boston. Arrived, she wrote at once to request an interview with Robert B. Forbes, chairman of Boston's Humane Society, one of the organizers of the local Sailors' Snug Harbor and a passionate adherent of all things maritime. He called on her at once and Dorothea told him the Sable Island story while together they planned the start of a new era there. Robert Forbes was fascinated with the problem. His journal of September 16, 1853, says:

Trying experiments with life preservers and boat. I went into the river with a neighbor to show Miss Dix how to capsize and how to right a boat. We invited her to throw herself over, and permit us to save her, but as she had no change of clothes she declined.

A pleasant holiday Dorothea seems to have contrived for herself, all unplanned, that many might have envied her.

In Boston, seven merchants of distinguished name and fortune subscribed to a fund for building a lifeboat with proper equipment, and in New York, three more boats were promised, as well as one in Philadelphia, by rich bankers benevolently and nautically inclined. Meanwhile, touring the country in November on hospital business once again, Dorothea received a letter from Robert Forbes:

The boat is in Boston, and being fitted with her floats, some of which being smaller than I ordered, I am putting in copper airtight cases. All will, I trust, be ready for shipment in four or five days. . . . I made a long journey to Williamsburgh where your New York boats are lying in the shop of Francis. They are good boats, though rather heavy, and I predict that the *Victoria* will be queen of the fleet.

At the end of November the boats were ready and the three from New York, on exhibition in Wall Street, attracted great crowds because of their strength and beauty. Dorothea wished to have them all shipped by sailing vessel to Halifax, but Robert Forbes warned her against having "too many eggs in one basket," and the *Victoria* was sent to Halifax alone by Cunard steamer. She was destined to remain alone for almost a year, for the brig *Eleonora* in whose hold the others lay, foundered near Yarmouth off Cape Cod. One boat floated out to sea while the rest were more or less damaged. The saddened Dorothea gave orders for immediate repair work and the drifting boat was recovered. Also, as a kind of stopgap to disappointment, she collected a library of several hundred volumes, presented by friends and generous Boston booksellers, to be sent to the Sable Island inhabitants.

A year or so went by before the original shipment finally arrived at its destination. There seemed, however, to be the hand of destiny arranging matters here, for on the day after the new boats were received, a large American ship from Antwerp, the *Arcadia* with 160 passengers, men, women and children, went aground on a sand bar at the northeast end of the island. A spectacular rescue was made by the *Reliance,* largest of the Francis metallic lifeboats, that rode the waves "like a duck." The distance from the island station to the wreck was more than twenty miles and six trips were made during the afternoon before all passengers were landed in seas far too heavy for the use of the older island boats.

In a letter to Dorothea's friend, the Honorable Hugh Bell at Halifax, the superintendent of the Sable Island Station, Captain McKenna, wrote: "I am sure that our benevolent friend, Miss Dix, will feel herself more than compensated for her great exertions in favor of Sable Island Establishment when she becomes acquainted with what we have already done through the means she furnished. For my own part I shall think of her with feelings of gratitude while memory lasts."

This good news reached Dorothea later at the Rathbones in England where she recovered from her labors in connection with the land bill, and congratulations inundated her as so many waves on Sable Island's shores. One letter in particular interested her, coming as it did from Miss Anna Gurney, a Quaker woman who possessed much of Dorothea's fire and imagination. Crippled in her youth by paralysis, Miss Gurney spent her days in a wheel chair, living on the seacoast of England. She was a scholar in Greek, Hebrew and the Teutonic languages, engaged in translating the Anglo-Saxon Chronicle and, for relaxation, she wheeled herself up and down the beach hoping for rescues to be made with apparatus for which she had provided the funds.

My dear Miss Dix,

I congratulate you intensely! I never heard of such success, and to have it exactly the day after your boats arrived! I can only tell you, I have been on the look-out these thirty years, and tolerably sharp too, I hope, and never got so much as a pussy-cat to my share of a wreck, though I have had plenty to do with crews and dogs and cats too. But I never had really the joy of being the instrument of deliverance, as you may truly feel yourself. . . . Once, indeed, my servant threw a rocket line over a stranded vessel, and my gang of fishermen were very indignant that the men would not give me the honor and glory of letting them-

selves be dragged through the breakers upon the sand, but would wait
to come ashore comfortably, in a lifeboat which just then came in sight.
So, in fact, I have had no luck at all, though, as I say, I have been gap-
ing for it like an oyster these five and thirty years.

During the rest of her life Miss Dix remained interested in the
art of lifesaving. Her journal, written a few days after the rescue
at Sable Island, says: "I have been trying lifeboats and visiting
shipyards, listening to lectures on the variation of compasses, also
much interested in a project for supporting lighthouses in loose
soils by anchors that work deep down in the sands."

In 1854, when Congress assembled for its first session, the atmosphere appeared more propitious for the land bill than ever in the
past. Letters backing Miss Dix poured in, petitions were signed,
newspapers published enthusiastic accounts of her work and the
temper of the members themselves was co-operative. It seemed as
though this was to be the moment of final victory. On March 9
the bill passed the Senate by a wide margin and soon after the
House followed suit: the end of six years' storming of the citadel.
What heaven for Dorothea! The opening of the Pearly Gates—"bliss
beyond compare." And now all that was needed was the President's
signature. From then on the future of America's insane would be
secure while her journeyings to and fro into darkness and horror
would have an end and she could walk in peace.

The President of the United States in 1854 was Franklin Pierce,
a friend of Dorothea, who had several times told her of his interest
in the measure. She would not have long to wait before the bill became law—a month or so, perhaps. A serene prospect stretched
ahead. And then the incredible happened. Word came that Pierce
was considering vetoing the bill on the ground of its transcending
States' Rights. The rumor gained ground, Dorothea's friends were
outraged, hospital heads were in despair. What was to be done?
Dorothea went to work again, more intensely than ever before.
Granted the veto: since the bill had had such large majorities in
both Houses, might it not be passed again? But every single member of Congress must be got at, his favor asked, his promise gained

For Dorothea there was barely time to sleep, no time to eat.

The veto followed: "If Congress have power to make provision for the indigent insane *without the limits of this district,* it has the same power to provide for the indigent who are not insane and thus to transfer to the federal government the charge of *all the poor* in all the states." The President declared he had been "compelled to resist the deep sympathies of his own heart." Many senators were indignant with Pierce. William H. Seward of New York called the message "desultory," "illogical," "confused." But there the measure stood poised, ready to take on new stamina or to collapse. Could the necessary two-thirds majority be found to pass it again? Could Dorothea count on all of her former allies?

The debate began in May, continuing on through June and into July. On July 6 the vote was taken: 21 yeas to 26 nays. Many previous supporters had deserted the ship. It was all over. No further help from the federal government. No more hope for the land bill, that once living entity now became a phantom.

What was Dorothea to do now? Her friends feared a general collapse, of her body, her soul, along with that of the measure. Suggestions tied to sympathy engulfed her. One of the hospital superintendents begged her to write the story of her life, a valiant tale that needed telling. This Dorothea refused categorically to do. The story of her life would have to include a picture of that dimly lighted cabin of her childhood, the escape, the battles with her grandmother, the episode of Edward Bangs—all buried deep and never to be exhumed. The true and proper story of her life was that of the insane, their progress, their well-being. The little things that happened to her personally as she faced the years were unimportant by comparison. What is an individual life, wherein its significance except as a minor part of the mighty whole? God grant that she might have the fortitude to continue reaching out toward the future as she had been able to do in the past, begin once again at the beginning when, only yesterday, it had seemed that she was well on toward the end.

There was still plenty to accomplish, of course, in the individual

states, the Government Hospital on Thomas Blagden's land to supervise, the hospitals in Canada. But even Dorothea's courage
drooped in facing at once the smaller tasks when so lately she had
been confronted with immensities. Besides, she had begun to realize now that there were such positive factors as fatigue, languor,
the wilting of the spirit. A new scene, a fresh outlook might be the
means of restoring her to eagerness. Various people had suggested
a tour on the continent. This in no way tempted her but the hospitals of Prussia and Austria, the far-famed cottage asylums at
Gheel in Belgium, for instance, of which she had read—these places
she would be interested to see. Moreover, there were her friends the
Rathbones at Greenbank, ever ready to receive her, serious of mind,
warm of heart, hosts in their generosity to the great among humanitarians. She would go to them. There she would find peace.

In September, therefore, Dorothea took passage on the S.S. *Arctic*
bound for Liverpool. When she went to the steamship office to pay
her passage, her money was refused. The owner of the line, the
clerk told her, wished to make her a present. The owner himself
came to the ship's sailing and led Miss Dix to a cabin which she
was to occupy alone. This, in order to try to repay the nation's debt
to her in tangible form, he said. The scene, onlookers tell us, was
very moving as Dorothea greeted the news with an outburst of
tears. Her emotions were not yet stabilized after the ordeal she had
been through.

The passage being unusually stormy, Dorothea was unable to
work at her writing, but one bit of charitable accomplishment came
her way. On a Sunday morning she watched several men who were
forming a pool to bet on the ship's run. Waiting until the winner
had gathered in the money, she introduced herself and begged him
to turn it over to the "Home for the Children of Indigent Sailors."
She also went the rounds asking each passenger for a donation to
the fund, hoping to raise $150 by means of this rather dubious
frontal attack. The crusading spirit, nourished by her daily work
and her many successes, plus the lack of self-consciousness in per-
forming acts such as this, increased Dorothea Dix's reputation for

being self-willed and arbitrary. The balance necessary to maintain a sense of proportion seems not always easy to achieve within a dedicated life.

The Rathbones met the ship at Liverpool and Dorothea rejoiced at being with them again, as well as being safe on land. An ocean voyage was the one prospect, throughout her life, that frightened her, obsessed as she was with the idea of shipwreck. Indeed, the *Arctic* on the return passage foundered and went to the bottom of the sea with many lives lost. Dorothea's fears seemed to have been justified here.

At present, rest and pampering were offered her at Greenbank, as when twenty years earlier she had visited there, but now she fretted at the bit, longing to be off, a war horse restive in pasture. To quiet her and at the same time fill her need for specific occupation, the Rathbones suggested a visit to Ireland and its hospitals. She acquiesced and spent four weeks under the healing soft green beauty of the Emerald Isle. She delighted in her happy awareness of "cloud canopied skies" and it rested her to jog slowly in a jaunting car along country lanes where the smell of peat came from the chimneys of whitewashed cottages and the small unruly black cattle blocked her way. Also, she permitted herself one diversion here, capitulating to a long-time eagerness for exploring scientific fields and, being in the neighborhood of the famous observatory at Parsontown, sent word to Lord Rosse at the Castle to ask if she might visit him and his telescope. She received a note within half an hour at the Parsontown Arms inviting her to dine at seven that evening, and, soon after, Lord Rosse's assistant arrived to conduct her to the Castle ahead of time in order that the instrument and the machinery might be seen by daylight.

"I reserve all details until we meet," she wrote Mrs. Rathbone, "simply saying that I was swinging in mid-air 60 feet from the ground at two in the morning . . . on a massive gallery . . . looking through the most magnificent telescope in the world."

But Dorothea's conscience would not for long let her rest in peace, and to Ann Heath she later writes from Ireland: "Romanism and Church of Englandism are waging as hot a spiritual war as is maintained in the Crimea by physical force, and the heart of pity is petrified under the assaults of bigotry. . . ."

Back in Liverpool, Miss Dix was taken on a tour of English hospitals for the insane by Dr. Hack Tuke, the third of that name to be in charge of the York Retreat for the Society of Friends, and it was soon evident to her trained eye that there had been a great improvement in all these institutions during the twenty years that had elapsed between her visits. She was glad to find how many forward steps were due to the "Society for Improving the Conditions of the Insane," promoted largely by the efforts of the Earl of Shaftesbury and the physicians he had summoned to the fight. The Society's object was to spread information among doctors and the general public as to the causes and the nature of mental disease. There were monthly public meetings and prizes given for the best essays on the subject, an idea that Dorothea considered excellent. But from the North, from Scotland, rumors were rife as to the appalling conditions that existed there. To step across the Scottish border, it appeared, was to go from the glowing light of the Renaissance back into medieval night.

Dorothea resolved to penetrate this night. She must help the day to dawn. Her friends remonstrated. Scotland was a place entrenched. The Scotch were stubborn, cautious, slow-moving, could not be swiftly aroused, resented interference. This was not America and Dorothea was an American. The Rathbones, the Tukes and the others spoke frankly, as Frederika Bremer had also spoken frankly when, at an earlier date, Dorothea had mentioned going to inspect the hospitals of Sweden. It would never do. Enough was enough. Let Dorothea's crusading spirit limit itself to her own land, splendid and necessary as it was there.

To Scotland Dorothea went, however, to Edinburgh, and at first confined herself to dining out with the charming and cultivated people who invited her to their houses. But superstition and neglect were rampant in the few institutions she had a chance to see at close hand and she realized that here she was back at the beginning of things as when first she had felt the obligation to survey the jails and poorhouses of her own home state. Within a fortnight she wrote her English friends that she intended to stay, to find a way of bringing abuses into the open. Mrs. Rathbone replied begging her to return, pleading Dorothea's health, her general debility. To this Dorothea answered:

I am not so very ill, only variable. . . . I am not *naturally* very active, and never do anything there is a fair chance *other* people will take up. So, when you know I am busy, you may be sure it is leading the forlorn hope—which I conduct to a successful termination through a certain sort of obstinacy that some people make the blunder of calling zeal. . . . I have no particular love for my species at large, but own to an exhaustless fund of compassion. . . . I do not see the *end* of this beginning but everybody says . . . that if I go away the whole work will fall off. So I pursue what I so strangely commenced.

Conditions, even in Edinburgh, were appalling. In his book, *History of the Insane in the British Isles,* Dr. Hack Tuke wrote:

Scotland, south of Edinburgh and Glasgow had not, until 1839, any retreat or place of confinement for the insane, except six squalid stone cells attached to the public hospital at Dumfries. Violent or vagrant lunatics were physically restrained in their own houses, allowed to roam at large, or incarcerated in prisons or police stations. . . . No country ever exceeded Scotland in the grossness of its superstition and the unhappy consequences that flowed from it. . . . The horrible treatment of the insane from the prevalent and, for long, inveterate belief in witchcraft, we cannot find language to characterize.

Private institutions existed for the care of the mentally ill but, being permitted to operate without supervision from the state, they had no fixed policy of procedure, no guarantee of humane treatment, and many of these places, in the hands of the grasping, were quite simply money-making schemes.

Writing some years later to Dorothea's official biographer, Dr. Tuke said: "Her intrepid raid upon the dwellings where lunatics and idiots were stowed away, confirmed her worst misgivings, and her revelations took many of the Scotch by surprise."

Dr. Tuke also touched on familiar patterns in Miss Dix's behavior: "She was very much out of health and indeed was confined to bed for some days, but the indomitable energy with which she pursued her mission was extraordinary . . . and I remember that on our driving in a hired vehicle . . . she showed her sympathies were not restricted to the insane by remonstrating with the driver for his treatment of the horse."

As she went the rounds of horror, Dorothea found that Scotch doctors generally resented her intrusion and sheriffs blocked the way of the "American Invader." At Musselburgh, outside Edinburgh, where a minor Bedlam existed in a private sanitorium, owing to the irresponsibility of its proprietors, she appealed to the Lord Provost and the various Justices in order that they should overrule the local authorities who denied her admittance. But her course remained more than difficult.

"The sheriff is a bad man, wholly despotic, and ridicules the idea of reform," she wrote Mrs. Rathbone, ". . . I have an odd sort of work on my hands. But ultimately good will result from this. I certainly hold myself much better occupied . . . than in strolling about Rome or Florence."

Determined as she was to get action out of existing apathy, she now asked advice of a Justice and three doctors who assured her that only by an appeal to the Home Secretary, Sir George Gray, in London, could the proper tools be assembled with which to scale this most difficult mountain. Who was to go? The doctors could not leave their patients, the Justice was loath to intervene. Could not Miss Dix herself manage the trip? Dorothea acquiesced.

Meanwhile the Lord Provost, opposed to the idea that an English commission should regulate Scottish affairs, himself decided upon a trip to London. Word of this reached Dorothea a few hours after her own decision had been made. There was not a moment to lose. Hers must be the first interview with the Home Secretary. He should have the story stripped of all padding, stark and grim as it was in reality. She set to work. Bradshaw was consulted. The evening train left at 9:15. Time only to gather up cloak, shawl, a fresh fichu, to send a wire to Lord Shaftesbury in London—that other long-time friend of the insane—and presently, while the Lord Provost's valet packed his bag for the trip on the following day, Dorothea established herself in the night carriage, traveling rug over her knees, prepared to face the long journey alone. London was on ahead, a town in which she knew not one being, except by name, had no idea of hotels or lodgings, of streets and distances. "I did not sleep but was comfortable," she later wrote a friend.

At King's Cross Station, as she stepped from the Royal Mail carriage, a man who waited on the platform came forward to inquire if she were Miss Dix. He was a messenger from the Earl of Shaftesbury who asked her to be at his office in Whitehall at three o'clock, Shaftesbury, friend to the poor and the criminal and the demented, Shaftesbury, whose parliamentary life was spent in conceiving and bringing to passage bills such as the Factory Act, the Lodging House Act, the Lunacy Act: legislation of the most far-seeing kind. A fit companion in labor to Miss Dix was this peer of the British realm who responded now to her appeal, urgently believing that the Bible was an open sesame to all wisdom and goodness.

The hour was then eleven, too late, Dorothea decided, to go to a hotel to freshen herself. But it would be possible to call on the Duke of Argyll, great Scottish nobleman, known for his courageous espousal of causes and his dramatic eloquence. She hailed a cab and appealed to the driver to help her work out the day's timetable. Then, seated inside the cab with curtains drawn, she changed her traveling cloak for a velvet one carried on her arm, draped a cashmere shawl about her and "did not look so much amiss as one traveling so far might look."

There follows in the unfolding story of this London episode, a roster of great names, worldly and political, Dorothea's genius drawing her instinctively toward those who were favorably placed for action and command. By twelve o'clock she had reached Argyll Lodge and a few minutes later had been shown into the Duke's library where the Duke and Duchess received her "most courteously." Telling them the fearful tale of Scotland's demented, she

asked for a personal introduction to the Home Secretary, that she
might beg him to appoint a Royal Commission. "An hour and a
half settled matters. His Grace would call for me at Whitehall
Place at three and a half, to go to Downing Street." Dorothea later
wrote a friend, Mrs. Torrey, in Boston.

At two-thirty, she appeared at Whitehall to keep her engagement
with Lord Shaftesbury who previously, at a meeting of his board,
had already got through a motion to demand from the "usually
tardy" secretary a Commission for Scotland. This good news was
temporarily qualified, however, by the present arrival of the Duke
of Argyll who told them that Sir George Gray could not see Miss
Dix that day, being summoned to a council at Buckingham Palace.
Furthermore, Gray doubted his authority to appoint a Commission;
the Lord Advocate of Scotland must first be consulted and his ruling made. Dorothea's letter to Mrs. Torrey continues:

> It was 4 P.M. I could do no more till the following day, so sent for a
> cab and drove to 38 Gloucester Square to my banker's [Mr. Morgan],
> asked for a basin of water to wash my neglected face and hands, a cup
> of tea and bed, all of which Mr. Morgan's prompt orders secured.

One more instance of her native faculty for heading, in times
of stress, straight for the fonts of wealth and power where, although
a stranger, her feminine dignity, her modesty, allied to the strength
of her cause, ever earned her a welcome.

Days of waiting followed. The Duke of Argyll reported that Sir
George had sent for the Lord Advocate of Scotland who would be
in London within a few days. The days went by: Monday, Tuesday, Wednesday. The Lord Advocate did not appear. Meanwhile,
fortuitously perhaps, because of ensuing events, Dorothea caught
a cold after permitting herself a tour of the chill spaces of Westminster Abbey and St. Paul's Cathedral. She called in to attend
her no less a person than the Queen's own physician whom, in the
course of treatment, influential man that he was, she quite naturally
converted to the cause.

And now, tired of waiting for the Scotch advocate, Dorothea

summoned one more willing cab and had herself driven straight to Downing Street where she sent her card in to the Home Secretary himself. She "was ushered up in some state and received courteously by his Lordship." This, in Dorothea's account, was an understatement of some magnitude, for it appears that as a result of her interview with Sir George Gray she was able to add his name to the list of her other conquests: Cyrus Butler, Thomas Blagden, as presently, in Rome, she was to include Cardinal Antonelli and Pope Pius IX. So that when at last the Lord Advocate came to London it was immediately found that the Home Secretary did indeed have the power to appoint the Royal Commission for Scotland. Here was the culmination of her labors, comparatively brief though they were. In her own words, as she finishes her unusually long letter to Boston:

This assures, first, reports into the condition of all the insane in Scotland. Next, the *entire* modification of the Lunacy Laws, the *abrogation* of all *Private* establishments. . . . My odd time I have spent chiefly in securing the interest and votes of members of Parliament for the Bill soon to be introduced, and now I go back to Edinburgh tomorrow to report this to parties interested and to rest if I need it, which is more than probable.

Several years later, in December of 1861, Sir James Clarke, the Queen's physician, who had remained her friend, wrote her: "The treatment of the pauper insane in Scotland is now more carefully attended to than in any other part of Great Britain." While Dr. Tuke, in 1865, wrote Miss Dix: "I think you might say to the Scotch, 'You are my joy and crown' for they have gone on wonderfully since 'The American Invader' aroused them from their lethargy."

In May of the year 1855, as Dorothea sat in the waiting room of a doctor's office in Edinburgh, a lady recognized her, her fame being now widespread, and asked whether she had considered a visit to the Channel Islands. Conditions there were very bad indeed for the insane. Would not Miss Dix go as soon as possible to set things right? Dorothea replied that she could not go to the Islands at once, but she "laid these things up" in her mind for future reference. This was a period at the close of one of her campaigns when, characteristically, she allowed herself to become aware of her disabilities, "the irritation of the mucous membrane of the stomach . . . the inaction of the heart." She writes a doctor in America: "Counting time since I left the steamer, I find that rather more than half the period I have been either really too ill, or too languid to do anything."

And now, in order to have the rest that was to set her on her feet again, she accepted an invitation from the Tukes and went to them at York for one of those protracted visits with sympathetic friends that she counted on to restore the soul. That these friends were always well placed materially, socially, intellectually, was understandable; they provided Dorothea with a padding of pleasure and security, to insulate body and soul against so much misery and despair at the other end of the human scale. At York, "very feeble but not helpless and never cheerless," she was wheeled, on each fair day, into the garden in a Bath chair that had, before his death, belonged to Lindley Murray, author of the famous grammar which brought back "child-time tearful memories," she tells Ann Heath, asking this old friend if she, too, does not share these. Many hours she spent here reading pamphlets and letters that described the condition of the insane on the Island of Jersey where flourished a veritable "Insanity Trade," as one doctor put it. This trade owed its success to the absence of laws that prohibited the setting up of private mad houses run for purely mercenary ends. In England the laws were growing continually more strict and Jersey, therefore, had now become a repository for the demented who were brought over in a kind of "chain-gang" from the larger island. One Dickensian villain in particular, a Mr. Pothecary, carried on a lucrative business with the help of his own private physician employed to "inspect" the institutions under his control, while reputable doctors felt powerless to change matters.

The fusion of pity and anger that served always to rouse Dorothea from inaction roused her now. "This must help me to get well

soon!" she exclaims. By July she had determined to set sail for
Jersey in order to release from their "dismal dark dungeons" those
who were helpless. "I shall see their chains off," she writes Ann
Heath. "I shall take them into the green fields, and show them the
lovely little flowers and the blue sky, and they shall play with the
lambs and listen to the song of birds, 'and a little child shall lead
them.' This is no romance; this will all be, if I get to the Channel
Islands, Jersey and Guernsey, with God's blessing."

Get to the Channel Islands she did, in July, and presumably with
God's blessing, for there, too, she left the stamp of her dauntless
spirit in the form of baring the evils that grew in place of flowers.
She planned a new asylum and she chose the site for its future erec-
tion. She also had the vivid satisfaction of turning Mr. Pothecary's
unfortunate patients over to the proper authorities and seeing their
slave-driving owner into the custody of the High Constable of Jersey. "There will be nothing more needed," a Jersey doctor told her
on her departure, "but keeping up a brisk fire." And this was accomplished above the embattled opposition of "three dozen members of the States, viz: 12 *rectors,* 12 yeomen, 12 chief constables,"
who were brought to heel only by means of force tied to persuasion.

Every reason there was at this epoch in Dorothea's life for her
to believe herself vested with divine right, a power above the law,
because of the triumphant course of her progress. Indeed, a letter
from her old and admiring friend, William Rathbone, as she set
sail for Jersey, warned her of the "pride that goeth before a fall."
It also added to the general praise accruing to her, praise in the form
of countless personal encomiums, testimonials from associations of
doctors and welfare workers as well as votes of appreciation from
twenty state legislatures, the United States Congress and the British
Parliament. Mr. Rathbone's letter from Greenbank on July 8, 1855,
says in part:

Not being inclined to sleep, I have thought that a quiet hour before
breakfast could not be better employed than in saying, God bless my
valued and loved friend, and speed her successfully in her progress.
. . . He has *tried* you in the success of what you have undertaken beyond

what I have ever known or . . . have read of any other person, male or
female . . . far beyond that of Howard, Father Mathew, Mrs. Chisolm,
or Mrs. Fry. I speak now of the entirety of the success as much as of the
extent, and it has not turned your head or, as I believe, led you to forget the source from which your strength has been derived. . . . May He
fit the burden to the strength and not try you too far by allowing you to
carry the *World* before you.

That Miss Dix's head had not been turned by those who wrote
they wished to "kiss the hem of her garment and bless God that our
country has produced such a noble heart," seems due to the fact that
her sense of power and self-reliance and the knowledge that she
"differed from others" was balanced by an awareness of human suffering that seemed never to leave her in peace. This, and her faith
in an all-seeing God whose servant she believed herself to be, were
strong deterrents to a desire for personal aggrandizement. So much
so, that she treated with scorn and anger any person who strove to
lionize her. As she sailed on, a galleon full-rigged, set on her proper
course, the plaudits of the crowds on shore were lost in the sound of
the driving winds.

The Rathbones, who had long since become Dorothea's guardian
angels, taking over the role from Channing in the days of her
youth, now presented her with a new plan: she was first of all to engage a lady's maid to tend her, to help make her difficult and complex life more endurable, and, next, she was to join them in a tour
of Switzerland. Although grateful, Dorothea forcefully turned down
the first proposal. She could not tolerate the close proximity, she
said, of a woman who would serve only to block her way, something
to stumble over, when her path should remain uncluttered as a
springboard ever ready to catapult her into a fresh arena. She wrote
in reply: "You desire that I should have someone with me, a maid,
to save me from fatigue and prevent my *feeling desolate* when
alone. A maid would only be in the way, with nothing to do; and,
for feeling desolate, I never felt desolate in my life, and I have been
much alone in both populous and thinly settled countries."

But the invitation to visit Switzerland she accepted with a delight that was to grow as the trip proceeded. Indeed, she remembered and spoke of it often during the rest of her life: Chamonix, the Bernese Oberland, "those grand snow peaks piercing the skies." And her steadfast interest in natural phenomena, in geology, the formation of glaciers and arctic flora, so stirred her that she was able momentarily to forget the "sound of the many afflicted ones" and let herself drift into pure pleasure. Later, in her reading, she turned back with avidity to Agassiz, Lyell and Tyndall, finding that the Swiss trip had increased her enjoyment here, too.

And now, with recovered vitality and energy stored, as was her habit, against the future, she planned an expedition of reconnaissance into the asylums of Europe, Turkey and possibly Palestine. William Rathbone's pleas that she draw in her horns before they locked with the world, seemed on their way to being entirely unheeded. At the end of August she left her friends as they returned to England and went across to France, stopping off at Rouen, going next to Orléans, Blois, Tours, Mettray, before beginning her organized work in the hospitals of Paris. Here she "became possessor of a full Police and Magisterial Sanction under seal—for which nine official parties were to be reached—for entering all the prisons and hospitals of Paris, without exception." This, in spite of the fact that she spoke only the most rudimentary French and had arrived in France with no sort of advance preparation or introductory letters. She was pleased to find that charitable institutions, liberally supported by the government, were generally good but with two radical defects: the lack of ventilation which explained the "amazing mortality" and the unenlightened viewpoint of nuns and priests, although a few of the Sisters of Charity "are very self-denying."

During early January, 1856, finishing her inspection of France, Dorothea was ready to go south into Italy. "It is just as easy traveling alone here as it is in England or America," she wrote in her letters home. And she therefore planned to continue on through Greece, Turkey, Slavonia, Russia, Germany, Norway and Holland, with a possible side trip into Austria. For conversing with people in these countries she had no equipment whatsoever, but converse with them she managed to do in some magical manner of her own contrivance.

In Rome, where she spent two weeks of February, she found the conditions that most appalled her, where "6000 priests, 300 monks, 3000 nuns and a spiritual sovereignty, joined with the temporal powers, had not assured for the miserable insane a decent, much less an intelligent, care." And she wrote Mrs. Rathbone: "I have not to convince officers of government alone but to make stand against *priests* who interfere with everything that is done or to be done. I never felt anything more difficult than this work in Italy." In Naples under the notorious rule of "King Bomba," in Genoa and in other Italian cities to which she presently went, she found a few admirable things but not so under the very shadow of the Vatican where the poor lunatic's lot was hopelessly wretched.

She resolved to try to see the Pope, the "Anointed Vicar of Christ on Earth," to inform him that the insane asylum of the Holy City was a scandal and disgrace to modern knowledge as well as to humanity. She realized that "the appeal to the Pope involved care, patience, time and negotiation," and she built her bridge with circumspection. One of the most conspicuous and powerful among the men in the entourage of Pius IX was the famous Cardinal Antonelli, who, but a year before, had narrowly escaped assassination because of his political connivance in the affairs of the Church. Dorothea, however, responded at once to his charm of manner, to his intelligence and extreme acuity, and she seems to have been able to overlook his lack of piety and his failure to maintain the strictly celibate existence that the rules of the Church ordain. He, on his side, steadfastly upheld her and her plans for reform, and it was chiefly to Antonelli that she owed, finally, her audience with the Pope.

This engagement with Pius IX proved a fecund one which was eventually to end in Rome's possessing a modern hospital for the insane built as an auxiliary to the General Hospital of San Spirito belonging to the papal government. His Holiness, who fortunately spoke English, had also some knowledge of hospitals, having been appointed by the previous Pope as director of the Roman hospital of San Michele. Earlier in his life he had suffered from epilepsy and he had now become a kindly, winning man and zealous churchman whose tact and piety made him popular with the people. He was compelled and moved by Dorothea's appeal and her singleness of purpose, while she "revered him for his saintliness" and knelt to kiss his papal ring.

Within the Roman Catholic tradition, a place has ever been held and a career found for the exceptional woman and, occasionally, one of these who combined mystical fervor with commanding ability has been canonized. Catharine of Siena was such a one and St. Theresa who brought to an end the Babylonian Captivity and helped to return the Papacy from Avignon to Rome. The Pope, therefore, was well versed in the particular sort of devotion that Dorothea possessed and he seems not to have demurred at her Protestant background. He recognized in her the genius of a saint: her intellectual grasp of the salient forces within ancient riddles; he felt the aura of her presence, the qualities sprung from early religious application, from her perennial battles with ill health and the healing waves of sweeping mystic fervor. And finally, he was refreshed by her womanly charm, the clarity of her speech, the expression of her eyes.

Pius IX thus gave Miss Dix his entire consideration, attending most carefully to what she had to say and, a few days after the interview, going in person and unannounced to visit the madhouse which she had so vividly described. Horrified on his own account, he sent a physician to Paris, there to study new methods, and presently the hospital was built of which a Boston friend of Dorothea, J. P. Bancroft, writing her twenty years later, said: "There can be no question that a great revolution in the care and treatment of the insane was effected by the organization of this present institution, in comparison with former methods."

And now, leaving this fresh triumph behind her, Dorothea, with the idea of taking in, en route, as many hospitals as possible, set out for Constantinople. She had heard tales of the dreadful suffering in Turkish prisons and resolved to see what could be done or undone. She sent brief notes to friends at home from Genoa, from Milan, Florence, Turin, and presently, while her steamer lay at anchor in the harbor of Corfu and after concluding her tour of inspection on the island itself, she wrote to Dr. Buttolph at the State Hospital in Trenton:

You will be more surprised than I am to find traveling alone perfectly easy. I get into all the hospitals and all the prisons I have time to see or strength to explore. I take no refusals, and yet I speak neither Italian, German, Greek or Slavonic. I have no letter of introduction and know no person en route. I found at Trieste a very bad hospital for the insane. Fortunately a physician attached to the suite of the Archduke Maximilian has promised the intervention of the government at Trieste and assured me that all the institutions of Austria shall be open to my visits if I come to Vienna.

Her method of approach appeared everywhere to be such as she describes in regard to the landing at Corfu: "When the boat arrived last night, I went on shore as early as I could do anything, took a cab and drove to the Greek institutions—*saw all!*" And if in the course of these rapid visits she was able to win to her side some official of importance, the chance of improving local conditions was thereby much enhanced. This, then, became her technique. Soon, she is writing the Rathbones from Piraeus in Greece:

I am waiting for the arrival of the steamer which comes around the Peloponnesus. I came by the Isthmus that I might land at Ancona and the Ionian Islands to see the hospitals. I reached Athens at dark last night; left at noon to resume my sea voyage. The weather is intensely cold. Mt. Parnassus is as white as Mt. Blanc. . . . This hour arrives a French steamer with the blessed news of Peace. . . . I feel that Miss Nightingale will have a great work still in the East. God bless her efforts!

As for sightseeing, the galleries and churches of Italy, the monuments of Greece, these had to be ignored whenever the alternative of new achievement arose in competition. She had now, on this far-flung tour, to mortify the mind and spirit in the same stern manner that for many long years she had mortified the flesh. And so at Piraeus, she is more concerned with the ending of the Crimean War and the labors of a fellow philanthropist than with the proximity of the Acropolis.

In April of 1856, with many stopovers as the steamer plodded on, Dorothea finally reached Constantinople, her chief objective. Writing to Mrs. Rathbone, she says: "I made the most of my landings en route. At Smyrna I found a good English hospital for sailors, and also one for the Dutch and Greeks. I found my way to these by noticing the flagstaffs before landing."

She continues with the story of reaching port at Constantinople:

Taking a boat, I was rowed to a landing at Pera, or rather Galata, and toiled over or through streets that seemed only open to serve as public drains. . . . After breakfast, I stepped into a caïque with two rowers—speaking the words "Hospital! Scutari!"—and in half an hour landed at the wharf of upper Scutari. I paid and discharged the boatmen and, inquiring of an English sailor the way to the nurses' quarters, proceeded thither. Miss Nightingale was absent, having been a month at Balaclava, where there is much sickness of the English and French troops. I went over the chief hospital, which was in excellent order. . . . There was another large establishment, but I could not walk to and over it, for by this time my feet had become too painful to allow of further exercise. . . .

One marvels at the vitality tied to a fixed idea that propelled her onward in spite of the discomforts attendant upon that epoch: the narrow, delicately made lady's shoes, the long sweeping skirts held with two hands above the filth of the streets, the cloaks, pelisses, shawls, that stood for overcoats, the lack of bathing and sleeping facilities when traveling. Her era was assuredly not designed to beckon women away from the sheltered life.

To her surprise, Dorothea found the insane of Constantinople in far better condition than those of Rome or Trieste. One hospital in particular, in the Turkish quarter, astonished her by its up-to-date care of patients, its comforts and entertainment, even to the performance of music. It had been founded by Suleiman the Magnifi-

cent, a Turk who was educated in Paris and became interested there
in the famous French hospital for the insane. On his return, he set
to work to rid a part of the city of the horrors for which it had been
notorious, establishing, instead, this near-paradise for the mentally
ill. Each of the nationalities within the city possessed its own hospital and Dorothea visited them all: Greek, Armenian, Turk, European, finding the Mohammedan better than the Christian, and
the worst conditions existing in the English prison where the doctor
in charge resented her intrusion. Other than this single unpleasant
encounter, she successfully "saw all" once again and accomplished
much, leaving behind with each superintendent written suggestions
for desirable changes.

She stayed most of the time with the president of Robert College,
Dr. Hamlin, who became her sympathetic friend and who was of
course able to give her many introductions that eased her way. He
later wrote to her biographer: "Miss Dix made the impression at
Constantinople of a person of culture, judgment, self-possession, ab-
solute fearlessness . . . and yet a woman of refinement and true
Christian philanthropy. . . . She was equally worthy with Elizabeth
Fry to be called the 'female Howard.' "

To her faithful friend, Ann Heath, on her hilltop in Brookline,
Massachusetts, Dorothea now sent an unusually long letter that
described, in May of 1856, her peregrinations through the spaces of
the East. The letter was composed on the deck of a small boat taking her up the Danube to Pesth and Vienna after she had left Constantinople:

Look on your map of Europe, and you may trace my route from
Venice, whence I last wrote, to Trieste, Ancona, Molfetta, Brindisi,
Corfu, Cephalonia, Zante, Patras, Missolonghi, Mycenae, Corinth,
Piraeus, Athens, Syria, Teos, Sangras, Mytilene, Gallipoli, Marmora,
Constantinople, Bosphorus, Varna, Salund, mouth of the Danube,
Galatz, Balaka, Assora, whence the boat is bound up this grand river to
Pesth and Vienna. . . . My usual experience attends me. People are civil
and obliging, who are treated civilly. . . . I am the sole representative of
England and America on the boat. There are . . . people of many tribes,

and persons of distant English possessions. As for speech, Babel is not illy illustrated. . . . I have resisted the very great temptation of going to Palestine . . . because I could not afford the expense, though only twelve days distant from Jerusalem. All my life I have wished to visit the Holy City and the sacred places of Syria. As yet, I have confined my journeys to those places where hospitals, or the want of them, have called me.

Following this momentary lull along the shores of the Danube, Dorothea again sprang into action as she reached Vienna where a revolution in hospital treatment engineered by Viennese doctors some years earlier had brought impressive changes that were to serve as model for future generations. Here she could learn rather than instruct, presumably a welcome experience, but she nonetheless pressed on the Austrian authorities the need she had found for a new asylum in Dalmatia. Never did it seem possible for her active imagination and her driving power to lapse into inertia. Before returning at last to England, her travels bore her through Russia, Sweden, Norway, Denmark, Holland, Belgium and a part of Germany.

She wrote, in August, 1856, from London, with the journey behind her: "I have been greatly blessed in all my travels. In Russia I saw much to approve and appreciate. As for the hospitals in St. Petersburg and Moscow, I really have nothing to ask. Every comfort and all needed care . . . very little restraint was used."

And now, at Greenbank before quitting the Rathbones to sail for home, Dorothea could take the tally of her effort in foreign lands; count the results of her copious suggestions, the careful advice that she had let fall much as rain falls on parched land. The days of wearisome study, the informing of the ignorant, the tireless distribution of pamphlets, reports—how far into the future, how high, how broad was this edifice of her creation? What following wind would carry the breath of hope and betterment into the dark corners of that closed world where were caught the helpless whom she had so long called her friends? These things cannot be specifically computed, but contagion for good is as potent as that for evil. In the course of her journey she had come on the worst and the best that Europe could offer, had worked and studied with the ablest authorities on insanity and, on the level of the simpler human exchanges, had left behind bright memories to last out the future. Ten years after her visit to Prague, a package arrived in America to surprise and please her: a box made of fine and various woods holding within a sheaf of poems, a collection of folk songs, an album of photographs, a biographical account of Dorothea's life: a gesture, in fact, of "affection and admiration," recorded on ivory "To Miss D.L.D." from the "Bohemian Ladies' American Club, Prague 1868."

Two years had passed since Dorothea's arrival in England following on the disheartening defeat of the 12,500-acre bill, and now, in September, 1856, she sailed for home. The voyage was a pleasant one, bringing smooth seas to allay fears of shipwreck, bringing land birds as the vessel neared the shore: "They are very familiar and eat from our hands. One came into the open window near me while at dinner today, rested on the table by the captain's plate, picked up some crumbs . . . and flew away. . . ." A brief moment of floating peace such as many mortals take for granted, a plateau of equilibrium between heights and depths of urgencies persisting behind and before.

Back in America, unlike the home-coming twenty years earlier when she had not known where to turn, Dorothea was overwhelmed with letters inviting her presence. Friends begged her to visit them, hospital superintendents needed her help, legislators asked her support. It was borne in on her now that a large institution, a hospital for the insane, could never achieve a fixed status, become an act of finality to be left and forgotten. The business of its functioning had also to be considered. There was always the outside public, full of suspicion, susceptible to gossip; there were the inhabitants within, "a mass of disorganized human nature unable to distinguish between fact and fancy"; there were the nurses and attendants untrained in psychiatrics, often recruited among the ne'er-do-wells who could find no other job; there were the members of hospital boards who needed reassurance and whose disputes sometimes called for intervention; there was the press to be enlightened, reporters to be properly instructed and public attacks warded off. And also there were the continued requests for larger hospitals, better equipment, greater funds.

In her customary way of allowing no single instant to elapse between perceiving the need and acting to fill it—the only way, in fact, that she knew or could imagine—Dorothea set to work. From the autumn of 1856 to the outbreak of the Civil War in 1861, she obtained larger sums of money for benevolent purposes than any single mortal in the world had yet done, heading, as she did at that time, the list of the "millionaires of charity." And her travels continued. Besides visits to existing institutions, she made a point of going into each new state as it entered the Union, believing that pioneers in material civilization should become pioneers in charity.

Quotations from a few of her letters during this five-year period tell the story: "Our work of Reform seems gigantic, and most discouraging if the whole field is taken at once; but if each does his or her part, we may hope for final success. . . ." She writes from New Orleans to Ann Heath: "I have traveled, out of ninety-three days and nights past, thirty-two days and nights, and this of necessity, so that I lie down now and sleep any hour I can, to make up lost time, and today I am feeling a good deal refreshed. I am bound from this place to Baton Rouge, and thence by land to Jackson, La., next to Bayou Sara, to Vicksburg by river, thence by railroad to Jackson, Miss., after that to Memphis, thence to St. Louis, thence up the Missouri to the State Hospital at Fulton, returning to Jacksonville, Ill., and to Springfield."

From Jackson, Mississippi, she adds: "So far as I can see, a favorable impression is made, and there is a probability that I shall get an appropriation of $80,000. I ask this winter in different States more than a third of a million." A letter to Mrs. Rathbone from Oneida, New York, in January of 1858, says: "Snow two feet deep, thermometer 27° below zero, gas-burners easily lighted by the spark transmitted by the finger."

In 1859 she spent many months in the South, concentrating particularly on Texas where the possibility of large grants of land for charitable purposes fired her imagination. Texas was then considered to be on the outskirts of civilization and conditions of travel were rude and primitive. Friends begged her to reconsider her plan for going there but opposition merely served to urge her on. Writing to Mrs. Hare of Philadelphia from Austin after two cruel days and nights of ordeal by stage, she says:

> You ask, perhaps, how I occupied myself under these adverse circumstances. Why, I meditated how poor, sick, insane people were to live in being transported such distances over such roads! I am thankful I have come, because I find much to do, and people take me by the hand as a beloved friend. My eyes fill with tears at the hourly heart-warm welcome, the confidence, the cordial good will, and the succession of incidents, proving that I do in very truth dwell in the hearts of my countrymen. I am so astonished that my wishes in regard to institutions, my opinions touching organization, are considered definitive. A gentleman in the State Service said to me, "You are a moral autocrat; you speak and your word is law." People say, "O, you are no stranger. We have known you years and years."

On a day when Dorothea was eating lunch in a roadhouse on a wide, lonely Texas prairie, she noticed that the tavern keeper, with a list of stagecoach passengers in his hand, kept staring at her. When she had finished eating and had taken out her purse to pay him, he refused: "No, no, by George! I don't take money from you; why, I never thought I should see you and now you are in my house. You have been good to everybody for years and years. Make sure now there's a home for you in every house in Texas. Here, wife, this is Miss Dix. Shake hands and call the children."

Dorothea's present tour also took her, in 1860, into the West and, to Mrs. Rathbone, in comfort at Greenbank, she sends a hasty note from Prairie du Chien, Wisconsin:

> I am writing at a side table in a telegraph office, waiting for a boat to La Crosse, after which I shall push up the Miss. to St. Paul, Fort Snelling, and St. Anthony. . . . I expect to be in the Northwest, in this wonderful country of vast prairies, wide, deep, ocean-reaching rivers, and

lakes that deceive you into the idea that you are where the Atlantic rushes in upon the resisting shores of the Eastern States.

All this under traveling conditions as difficult and uncomfortable as was usual in those days of limited possibilities. The introduction of sleeping cars on railroads had taken place some months earlier and a friend had evidently suggested to Dorothea that she could now travel in greater luxury during the night journeys. She instantly replied: 'I *saw* some sleeping cars. That was enough. Nothing would induce me to occupy one of them, they are quite *detestable*. . . . I cannot suppose that persons of decent habits, especially ladies, will occupy them, unless some essential changes are made in their arrangements and regulation."

Finally, in March, 1861, she writes Ann Heath from Kentucky: "All my bills have passed. My winter has been fully successful. I have had great cares, greater fatigues, many dangers, countless blessings unmeasured—well, and still able to work very satisfactorily.... God spare our distressed country!" This exclamation was born of Dorothea's apprehension of civil war which, during these last years, had hung over her as she moved with the compass from north to south, from east to west, hearing from her Southern friends, as well as her Northern ones, the story of their grievances.

Slavery, as a disciple of Channing, Dorothea abhorred, but as a public figure with the wide world as her workbench, she had been obliged to keep her feelings to herself, refrain from discussing issues that inflamed one set of human beings against another. As any fair-minded person of balanced judgment and warm response is apt to do, she saw the merits of both conflicting sides. She visualized, moreover, a struggle for which no sort of solution seemed probable: a kind of Greek tragedy about to be staged, a massacre of blood brothers, urged on from the wings by angry partisans while a vast audience watched in the proscenium, helpless, bewildered, heartsore.

To Ann Heath she says: "I thank God, dear Annie, I have such full uses for time now, for the state of our beloved country, otherwise, would crush my heart and life. I was never so unhappy but once before, and that grief was more selfish perhaps, viz., when the 12,500,000 acre bill was killed by a poor, base man in power."

As a matter of fact, before writing this last letter, Dorothea had already made a rather spectacular move, unknown to her friends at the time, in behalf of the Northern cause in general and Lincoln in particular. Early in 1861, before the inaugural of the new President, when several of the Southern states had already seceded, she had gone to call on Samuel Felton, president of the Philadelphia and Baltimore Railroad, sending in word when she arrived at his office that she had something of importance to say to him personally. For more than an hour she then unfolded a dramatic story which she apparently alone, as a Yankee patriot, had knowledge of in full, a story based on facts gathered on her journeys throughout the South. A plan was being organized to move on Washington, seize the archives and the reins of government and declare the Southern Confederacy to be the supreme government of the United States. The inauguration of Lincoln was to be stopped and, if necessary, his life sacrificed. Already, Dorothea informed Felton, troops were secretly drilling along railway lines between Harrisburg and Philadelphia, Baltimore, Annapolis and Washington.

This was on a Saturday afternoon several months before the firing on Fort Sumter. Felton listened and acted. Immediately, he hired detectives to mingle with the troops on the railway lines and, as a result of their reports, he was able to smuggle Lincoln safely into Washington. Writing many years afterward of this episode, Felton declared he had begged Miss Dix to allow him to make known her role in helping to save Lincoln's life, and that of the Union, but she refused to have her name connected with the story. Always, early and late, she thus preferred to slide into anonymity.

Six weeks later, following the call from the President for volunteers to defend Washington, the first of the states to respond was Massachusetts. Dorothea, resting from a recent journey at the house of Dr. Buttolph of the State Hospital at Trenton, now her headquarters, heard of the assault on the 6th Massachusetts Regiment as it marched through the streets of Baltimore. This was civil war, she instantly realized; this meant that men were to be wounded, killed. Here, suddenly, was new work for her to do. The other, the work of her choice, must await the quiet which she hoped might lie on ahead. With hair-triggered promptitude, she bade the Buttolphs good-bye, had herself driven to the station, caught the next train for Baltimore and arrived in that city of confusion soon after the riot had occurred. She writes her own account of this move to the receptive Ann:

Washington, D.C., April 20, 1861

Dear Annie,

Yesterday I followed in the train three hours after the tumult in Baltimore. It was not easy getting across the city, but I did not choose to turn back, and so I reached my place of destination. I think my duty lies near military hospitals for the present. . . . I have reported myself and some nurses for free service at the War Department and to the Surgeon General.

And so, inevitably and at once, Dorothea found herself in a position of supreme power. "She makes the most munificent and generous offers," said John Hay, secretary to the President. Serving without pay, she was appointed to be "Superintendent of Women Nurses, to select and assign women nurses to general or permanent military hospitals, they not to be employed in such hospitals without her sanction and approval, except in cases of urgent need." Orders to this effect were issued by Simon Cameron, Secretary of War, and the Acting Surgeon General.

However, the vast responsibilities thus bestowed on Dorothea Dix could not be carried out either in theory or in practice, then or later. The Northern mind took it for granted that war would last but a few months, that a quick spurt of effort combined with the staunch spirit of right, would serve soon to quash the South's illicit rebellion. With this idea paramount, there was at once a tremendous response. Untrained boys volunteered by the thousands for service, inexperienced girls offered themselves as nurses, men and women gathered supplies of food and hospital garments, shipping them by the ton to Washington where no existing place or persons were prepared to receive them: an inundation of mammoth proportions bringing dis-order, dislocation and drowning, as major inundations do. Needed immediately was a thoroughgoing organization to screen and allo-cate nurses, set up emergency hospitals, receive and distribute food and supplies. Dorothea, with her long-trained habit of answering need with action, strove to build this single-handed.

The Army's medical corps was small and poorly set up, while military hospitals were no more than post centers, amateur recep-tion rooms to pestilence and death. And, though supplies continued to pour in, they were chiefly of the wrong kind and quality. The Surgeon General was dying and the Acting Surgeon General ap-pealed to Dorothea for help: "We are deficient in lint and bandages. I would most respectfully suggest that you institute preliminary measures for those important items of surgical necessity."

Women's civilian organizations were being formed all over the country and Dorothea was quick to make use of them, setting up receiving stations for the supplies sent in, employing two secretaries to help her. She opened new infirmaries, converting churches, schools, private houses, arsenals, warehouses toward this end and equipped them with supplies as well as with nurses for whose work she alone was responsible. She was daily besieged by women volun-teers of all ages who wanted to do nursing. Some were elderly and not too strong, others were young, romantic and incapable. There were then no trained nurses in our modern sense. Only a few had had hospital experience and this of no very great extent. Knowing that an Army hospital was no place for untrained girls, and im-patient with dilettantism, Dorothea issued a terse statement in the form of a bulletin:

No woman under thirty need apply to serve in government hospitals. All nurses required to be plain-looking women. Their dresses must be black or brown, with no bows, no curls, no jewelry and no hoop skirts.

This rather arbitrary procedure seemed unnecessary to many peo-ple and did not gain her popularity. Her habit of hitting direct at the mark, tossing aside impeding obstruction, working with un-compromising speed, her aversion for the inefficient and her im-mense sympathy with suffering, made her a character unpleasant to some and droll to others. How could these amateurs and outsiders know of her twenty years' devoted labor, of her wide experience in organization, of the personal authority that had for so long been her unquestioned possession? They did not know or care about the results she had obtained, the trails she had blazed. They were un-aware that, at the very moment Miss Dix's bulletin was issued, she was, at her house in H Street, sheltering and feeding scores of stranded women who had failed as nurses, and others who had come to Washington in the hope of remaining near husbands and sons. Dr. Howe, writing to friends in Boston, said of her: "Miss Dix, who is the terror of all mere formalists, idlers and evildoers, goes . . . everywhere to prevent and remedy abuses and shortcomings."

On she went, month after month without rest, forgetting often-times to eat, traveling to Baltimore, New York, St. Louis, to super-vise new establishments, sleeping on shavings on warehouse floors, attempting to deal with lice, dysentery, measles, malaria, and the scurvy that devastated the troops. Visiting one hospital after an-other, she complained of wretched sanitation, begged for a change of diet for the wounded: more greens, vegetables, fruit to replace salt pork and hard tack. The Medical Bureau moved slowly while Dorothea never ceased to prod. She became as she did so more and more unpopular, "prying and poking about . . . exceeding her au-thority." After Bull Run she redoubled her efforts to open more hospitals, buying an ambulance from her own pocketbook, appeal-ing to the country at large for dried fruit and preserves, opening her house now to nurses who were ill and needed rest.

A day came when Louisa May Alcott arrived in Washington. She was sent to the Union Hotel in Georgetown where she nursed the wounded for six weeks before coming down herself with typhoid fever. Dorothea took charge of her then, going each day to watch the girl's progress, sending her home to Concord as soon as she could travel. Louisa wrote her family that Miss Dix had brought "a basket full of bottles of wine, tea, medicine and cologne, besides a little blanket and pillow, a fan and Testament. . . . She is a kind old soul, but very queer and arbitrary."

Later she was to write in *Hospital Sketches:* "Whatever others may think or say, Nurse Periwinkle is forever grateful and among her relics . . . none more valued than the little book which appeared on her pillow one dreary day; for the 'D.D.' written on it means to her far more than Doctor of Divinity."

But the "queer and arbitrary" in Dorothea's nature were gradually to gain the upper hand. She was, of course, in a chronic state of exhaustion. When, now and then, she was ill for a few days or weeks, she directed the work from her bed. She became more domineering, her voice more shrill, she was less and less tactful. The Catholic Sisterhoods were her aversion and she discriminated against them. She demanded that all doctors intoxicated while on duty be court-martialed and she reported every transgression large or small direct to the Surgeon General. Once, finding two convalescents punished for some minor insubordination, strung up by their thumbs from a doorway, her fury was an epic thing and the battle between the hospital superintendent and herself was decided in Miss Dix's favor by no less a person than the general in command. Such were the resounding echoes of her zeal.

Stanton had succeeded Cameron as Secretary of War and he appeared to have complete confidence in Dorothea. But by this time, many of the doctors hated and resented her, although to the men in the wards she remained, with her baskets of fruit, her flowers and her gracious mien, an itinerant angel of mercy. Used through the years to being a lonely and independent worker, far-seeing and conscientious as were few others, she had planned her own projects and deferred to no one. Now, in time of war, with disaster sweeping on unchecked, with human nature crowding human nature in a race between the noble and the base, with hit-or-miss methods a necessary corollary to the magnitude of the calamity, Dorothea's former methods could not prevail.

"This war in my own country is breaking my heart," she wrote to Mrs. Rathbone, safe in the quiet English spaces of Greenbank which, to Dorothea, must indeed have seemed remote and fair as a land of dreams.

During each succeeding year the friction burned hotter between Miss Dix and the Sanitary Commission. Nurses now were being openly engaged without her consent, pretty ones as well as plain, and surgeons were demanding the dismissal of Miss Dix. Opposition grew and finally, in October, 1863, General Orders #351, issued by the Secretary of War, turned the tide. In effect, though subtly worded, these orders abolished the office of Superintendent of Nurses, handing its functions over to the Surgeon General: a triumph for the opposition forces and a sad defeat for the redoubtable Miss Dix. Stanton had seemed to be her friend and ally. Was he then another Brutus?

In spite of a wounded heart and pride brought low, Dorothea remained at her job. Were not the wounds of gallant fighting men more mortal than her own? These men needed her. She would stay as near them as might be. By this decision she acquired the fresh admiration of the Secretary of War as well as of others in authority. But, looking back on those four war years in which she had allowed herself no single day's vacation, she was deeply saddened by what she saw: "This is not the work I would have my life judged by," she said.

Meanwhile, one more self-imposed task remained for the weary and disheartened Dorothea before leaving Washington for good, one of the tasks embroidering the borders of the flying banner that was her life. A monument in honor of the soldier dead had been proposed, at the war's end, to be erected near Fortress Monroe. The plan, however, had lapsed because of insufficient funds. To Dorothea this seemed disloyalty of a high degree. Swiftly taking to herself the office of agent, she "collected in a quiet way among her friends $8000," and, going north to spend several weeks on the seacoast of Maine, she searched for granite of an imperishable quality that it might symbolize the granite in the character of the heroes whose names were to be engraved there for posterity to see.

And now, at the end of her labors, she was asked by Stanton what form the government's appreciation of her services might take. Would she allow him to call a big public meeting where appropriate speeches might be made, or would she prefer a grant of money from Congress? "I would like the Flag of my Country," Dorothea replied, and gave the matter no further thought. To her surprise, then, having forgotten the conversation with the Secretary of War, there presently arrived by express an immense box holding a pair of the National Colors made especially for Miss Dix by the government and accompanied by an order which read in part:

> War Department, Washington, D.C., December 3, 1866
> In token and acknowledgment of the inestimable services rendered by Miss Dorothea L. Dix for the Care, Succor and Relief of the Sick and Wounded Soldiers of the United States on the Battle Field, in Camps and Hospitals during the recent War . . . it is ordered that a Stand of Arms of the United States National Colors be presented to Miss Dix.
>   Edwin M. Stanton
>   Secretary of War

The long struggle was over and Dorothea could return to the work she loved and understood, work wherein definite progress might be counted as children count beads on a talus. Thus in the year 1880, when Miss Dix had become an old lady of seventy-eight, she was able to point to 123 insane asylums and hospitals built through her efforts. She had had an active part in founding thirty-two of these, many of them enormous structures with parklike grounds, and the others had been conceived at her suggestion. Though this was but a start in searching the darkness with the growing light of humanity, a new social conscience had been awakened, new ideas set in motion.

Reaching the years of retirement for the average man and of coddled invalidism for many—the years between seventy and seventy-five—Dorothea continued her travels across the land. Asylums scattered throughout the nation's length and width became to her as children requiring surveillance and care. Everywhere on her arrival, the keys of wards were handed her and she was allowed to wander about alone.

There came the day, in 1873, when Miss Dix watched with pride as the first class of nurses especially trained to deal with mental cases was graduated and sent forth to do its superior work. She had long urged this form of training; in fact she had been steadily creating schools of trained experts to deal with all the branches of insanity. When she was seventy-five, Dr. Charles Folsom of Boston said in his book, *Diseases of the Mind:* "Her frequent visits to our institutions of the insane now, her searching criticisms, constitute of themselves a better lunacy commission than would be likely to be appointed in many of our states."

Together with her intellectual and executive powers, almost masculine in their virility and force, there was in Dorothea, also, the vein of old-fashioned female Samaritan, she who collects small bits of equipment for the ill and convalescent: toys, puzzles, music boxes, seaweed, pressed flowers, butterflies mounted on pins, eggs, birds' nests. And, "at home" in the three institutions of her choosing: St. Elizabeth's in Washington, Dixmont Hospital in Pennsylvania and the hospital at Trenton, New Jersey—her several refuges from routine—she kept in the top bureau drawer of her bedroom pins and needles, buttons, bits of cloth, half finished embroidered doilies: the paraphernalia of a devoted housewife and mother. Only, that in place of husband and children, the recipients of this woman's devotion were the helpless and the anonymous, those unable to smile or give thanks for her favors.

Public figures seem to take on the quality of marionettes, their function dependent upon a pull of the wire manipulated by the people whom they serve. Watching them, the spontaneous and the casual are rarely apparent. One cannot imagine the dedicated Dorothea Dix seated on a living-room sofa chatting comfortably with a friend. Her striking physical presence, her concentrated absorption, the high carriage of her head, the fixed and determined expression of her face, marked her as something apart from man on his everyday plane. That the weaker, more nearly human side of her nature existed, too, we know from the reports of a few who saw her when weariness and defeat had momentarily chipped the armor of her façade, when, flinging herself down in a torrent of weeping, after the usual pattern of female despair, she had amazed and softened the hearts of these onlookers. Here once again was the passionate and unruly child, the thwarted and lonely girl, she who had denied herself much that was natural to others in the attempt to make of her life an epic on the grand scale.

We leave her now, at eighty-five, alone as she seemed destined to remain. We leave her as gradually her tired body gave in to human frailty, lying in a small room overlooking the Greek portico of the Trenton Hospital. About her were a few of the mementos which rightfully accrued to her as a result of her long labors: the pressed flowers from a Southern garden with words in faded ink on a slip of paper: "In this I place a couple of Heart's Ease blossoms from our garden. They seem to me particularly *your* flowers"; with the letters from those who wrote her until her death: the Eliots of Portland, Oregon; Francis and Matilda Lieber, now in San Marino, California; and, beneath her pillow, some of the manuscript poems of her friend, John Greenleaf Whittier, who shared with her the love of heroism and faith in the common good. Almost the last letter Dorothea Dix was able to write, with unsteady pen and wandering mind, bore the caption at its head: *85 Mount Vernon Street, Boston*. This was the house of William Ellery Channing, her long-time mentor and friend—love returning love at the last.

For epitaph, in addition to the name engraved on her bleak tombstone, we might quote the letter from a doctor with whom she had worked for many years: "Thus has died and been laid to rest in the most quiet unostentatious way, the most useful and distinguished woman America has yet produced."

The ways of the unostentatious seem truly to shun the paths of fame, during many a month of days, if not forever.

II

Elizabeth Palmer Peabody

Elizabeth Palmer Peabody

Boston Transcendentalist, staunch daughter, sister, friend, companion of great men and little children, heroine of battles unafraid, Elizabeth Palmer Peabody has been maltreated by the clever. The pattern stereotyped on our minds is made of the oddities of her behavior and her appearance: the old lady buffeted by east winds, white curls flying and bonnet askew as she plods through the slush of March streets on her way to champion the lost cause, who rests from her labors in sleep upon the lecture platform, who bruises her nose against the seen but unrealized tree in Boston Common, who scatters manuscripts, railway tickets, handkerchiefs as an elderly hen scatters pebbles on the barnyard floor. This, for most of us, is the composite picture we have of her.

Studying a photograph of Miss Peabody taken in her later years, we can believe that Henry James had her in mind when he gave us the portrait of Miss Birdseye in *The Bostonians:*

A little old lady with an enormous head—a sad, soft pale face, which looked as if it had been soaked, blurred, and made vague by exposure to some slow dissolvent. The long practice of philanthropy had not given accent to her features; it had rubbed out their transitions, their meanings. . . . A discursive old woman whose charity began at home and ended nowhere, whose credulity kept pace with it, and who knew less about her fellow creatures, if possible, after fifty years of humanitary zeal, than on the day she had gone into the field to testify against the iniquity of most arrangements. . . . A formless old woman who had no more outline than a bundle of hay.

Words such as these quietly nullify a life, destroy an edifice built stone upon stone, over the years, on a foundation of love, patience,

[*83*]

sacrifice and high purpose, attributes possessed by the saints. For Elizabeth Peabody—who believed appearance and the outward manner to be of small importance, whose concentration was on other aspects of the whole—her wish to forego the aesthetic was based upon time as it took its toll in labor spent for others, labor that still lives on unto the third and fourth generation of those that loved her.

One of those who loved Elizabeth was William Ellery Channing, Unitarian divine. In a letter to her four years before his death he set down a phrase that might well have applied to her although written with others in mind: "The great is not the faultless, and is very open to vulgar criticism and ridicule; and yet with all its faults I cling to it, and care little for the hard measure meted to it by the world."

At the outset of her life, the young Elizabeth soon met rigor, toil and confusion, as they pervaded the household of her parents. Mrs. Peabody, in order to help her gentle, ineffective husband earn money, continued, between the births of her seven children, with the career she had begun at sixteen and which she had inherited from her father who himself turned schoolmaster at the dissipation of his previously large fortune. "Taking up the parlor rug" in the Salem house, Mrs. Peabody opened her doors to the school children of her friends and neighbors. Elizabeth, aged four, joined the others. There was also, among the more precocious pupils, Ebe Hathorne, daughter of a widow and recluse whose house was separated from the Peabodys' by a board fence at the back. It had taken the courage that belonged as a natural trait to Mrs. Peabody to brave an entrance to the gaunt, gray house and solicit there the favor of a new scholar from the formidable lady who lived within, wrapped in twilight, with her two daughters and the son, Nathaniel. Ebe Hathorne, at six, could read Shakespeare and it saddened and mortified young Elizabeth, as it also awoke in her the ambition for knowledge she was never to lose, that the great poet's words were beyond her grasp. It was not easy to wear defeat then or later.

Dr. Peabody, holding the courtesy title that an unmeticulous era permitted him, a teacher when he and his wife first met, had acquired his scanty medical training in order to please her. At Phillips-Andover Academy, where he taught, he had been a Latin scholar whose avocations were drawing and whittling. This was his position when he and Elizabeth Palmer, proud daughter of a once wealthy British general, were introduced in consequence of their common calling. They were married in 1802 and soon after, to quiet his bride's pleading, he left the teaching profession to become a doctor's apprentice, driving about in his master's buggy, and, in the office, stirring the brews that were later to cure their patients.

In 1804, Elizabeth Palmer Peabody was born at Billerica, near Andover, and soon after, her father and mother moved to Cambridgeport so that Mr. Peabody could attend lectures at Harvard. There, however, he decided to become a dentist in order, perhaps, to continue with the simple pleasure of using his hands. From his wife's more genteel point of view, dentistry was a humble pursuit but she capitulated to fate and went on bearing her babies. Two more daughters were born, Mary Tyler and Sophia Amelia and now, in need of greater space, they took a house in Salem, home of the Paybodie ancestors whose claim was the descent, in direct line, from Queen Boadicea.

The study of genealogy, however, did not in any way distract Dr. Peabody from the fascinations of his dentist's laboratory where he had begun to prepare the drills and the dams suitable for plugging the teeth of his patients, trying thus to circumvent the continual extractions of the day. He was not at first successful in turning the tide of long-established custom; in fact Dr. Peabody's successes seem, over the years, to have been in continual process of building and tearing down, owing to the needs of his large family and their frequent removals from one spot to another. His nature being quiet, his voice was not often heard above the more resonant ones of his womenfolk. He remains chiefly important in having bestowed enviable qualities and aptitudes on each of his three celebrated daughters. For, Elizabeth's facility in absorbing languages was surely derived from this erstwhile Latin scholar, as was Sophia's gift for using her hands, and Mary's power of selflessness and anonymity which made her later so valuable a wife to an educator and administrator such as Horace Mann. From their mother, they acquired their loyalty and sense of family unity and, in the case of the two older girls, courage in facing the unpalatable and difficult. "My mother had nothing of the martinet about her," said Elizabeth in retrospect, "she did not talk down to her children but rather drew them up to her mental and moral level."

This was the era of the fine McIntyre houses in Salem, those mansions built in elegance, many of them in splendor, as a result of the fortunes made and the sophistication acquired by the magnates of the East India trade. The beauty of fluted mantels, the height of indented cornices, the pineapples of welcome carved over entrance doors, the ornamentation worked with knife and chisel into blinds that shut out the night from beyond the wide recesses of parlor windows, the floors of tropical wood, boxes of lacquer, ivory and jade; India silk for curtains and for the ladies' dresses, painted fans and Chinese sandals—all these charming things now became, pell-mell, a part of the world surrounding the Peabody sisters' youth. They could enjoy them only vicariously, through the visits they made, attending their mother now and then when, temporarily free of a baby and with the schoolroom door closed, she could put on her afternoon dress and bonnet and go to call on her friends, on Miss Burley, patroness of artists, on Mrs. Guild, or, most intimate of them all, on the generous Mrs. Cleveland. These ladies continued to do what they could for General Palmer's daughter who, although her dress might be made of poplin and her front door bare of carving, held her head high, as she had been taught to do, and permitted no envy or false shame to make their corrosive way along the spaces of Peabody minds and hearts.

Neither did Mrs. Peabody's worldly preoccupations nor the ambition she had for her husband's career cause her to lose track of her lofty ideals in bringing up her children. She read to them from Spenser's *Faerie Queen,* from the Prophets and the Psalms, interlarding these stories with tales of noble deeds among real people. At the hours when she had to be away, she took pains to leave them in charge of some cultivated young lady who would not demean their minds. The Peabody daughters responded to this treatment rather better than did their brothers, two of whom died young after careers which were profitless as well as adventurous; and the third, who as assistant in dentistry to his father, cut no memorable swath in life.

A seventh child, a little girl, was born during the early Salem epoch but she lived only a short while. Elizabeth was fifteen at the moment of the baby's birth and she was permitted to stay at home this time to assist her mother's labor, rather than be sent off, as previously, to visit.

Things did not go as well now with Mrs. Peabody as in the past. She had not wanted this baby, but when it died she was temporarily shattered by grief and a conscience that smote. God's anger had been vented on her, she feared, for her sin in having denied the child her heart. The episode profoundly affected Elizabeth, the pain and the sorrow in childbirth, while the conversations between the sensitive girl and her mother on the topic of woman's suffering and the need for her subjection to the will of man left an impression that may have turned her permanently away from marriage. Furthermore, this was the moment of the great depression of 1818-1819 which adversely affected the Peabody income, dependent as it was on Dr. Peabody's ship-owning clientele whose fortunes were temporarily diminished.

A bad time it was, and Elizabeth was later to say of herself and her sisters: "We were first drawn together by a common calamity." It stifled much of the natural humor and mischief in the temperament of Mary Peabody, bringing her a certain dour quality along with a fervent conscientiousness, while Sophia, the youngest and her mother's pet, more sheltered and pampered than the others, took refuge in the headaches that were, until her marriage to Hawthorne, to play a large role in her life. As for Elizabeth, stirred by the presence in her world of William Ellery Channing whose sermons she had begun to absorb at the age of eight, she became, now, more than ever aware of the need to support and sustain those less strong than herself. Almost overnight, she grew into the responsible "Miss Peabody," a title she bore to the end of her life.

An uprooting of the family was presently to be engineered by Mrs. Cleveland who had moved to Lancaster. There, in order to help recoup her husband's fallen fortunes, she had opened a school for boys with Jared Sparks as master. She begged her friend, Mrs. Peabody, to follow her and open a school for girls. A pleasant, old-fashioned farmhouse with a rambling room to hold scholars was found for the Peabodys and soon the setting of the lovely Lancaster meadows became the new background for their existence. The younger girls were ecstatically happy here, picking the wild flowers, leaping the brooks barefoot, binding their hair with bright ribbon to please the boys. In the hours that unrolled for Elizabeth, by contrast, there was little time for this kind of dalliance. Her life was definitely that of a young woman of high ambition, concerned with the pursuit of knowledge and the advancement of her family. Teaching the children in her mother's school during much of the day, responsible for their progress and behavior, she also read avidly, and in any leisure moment, applied herself to the study of Greek. Thus, soon, did the law of self-discipline that commands the great of the earth, come to govern the life of Elizabeth Peabody.

And now, with the Lancaster school well on its feet, it seemed to her a propitious moment to start a school in Boston. A real academy of learning it would be, attended by such quantities of scholars that her family could eventually join her there. She proceeded with the plan, sanguine, confident, although knowing almost no one in the city, and turned over the existing school to Mary and Sophia, the latter only thirteen years old and without the zeal for teaching that preoccupied the others. One friend Elizabeth had in Boston, young Eliza Cabot, member of a family of Boston Brahmins, who set about finding pupils for the new school. Presently a nucleus was formed, but to Elizabeth's disappointment it was not substantial enough to warrant summoning the family from Lancaster. The Peabody girls, however, happy as they had never been before, were delighted with the idea of remaining where they were, and probably

Dr. Peabody was also. It had apparently not occurred to any one of them to dispute a scheme of Elizabeth's, so closely were they tied to her, so unquestionably were they the recipients of the eagerness she lavished upon them and their welfare. Though separated from her sisters now, she constantly wrote them letters of advice and admonition: to Mary on the subject of the Lancaster school, to the youthful Sophia on the improvement of her mind, recommending that she read Middleton's *Letter from Rome,* Stewart and Norton's *Controversy,* as well as "those poets with whom no one has found fault and which are perfectly moral." *Lalla Rookh,* very popular at the moment, she frowned upon as being not only frivolous but beside the point.

The point, then, for Elizabeth was Unitarianism. Spurred on by her passionate belief in Dr. Channing, she was swept off her feet by the excitements of religious discussion and the rewarding pleasures of theology. Also, she had begun reading Greek with a young scholar, so shy as scarcely ever to be heard uttering a word, but master of his subject, Ralph Waldo Emerson. He taught at a school in his mother's house in Federal Street and consented, when asked, to take on Miss Peabody as a private pupil. The shyness between them finally dissolved when Elizabeth tried to pay for her lessons. He said she had learned nothing from him, that she had already known Greek and he could, therefore, not accept her money. They made friends then and there, an example of virtue rewarded, and were to continue their association until the end of their lives. But Elizabeth's school in Boston, possibly because of such stimulating ideas in the world outside, failed as a money-maker and had to be abandoned.

So abundant an intake of learning, however, demanded an outlet and there was, besides, the question of money. Elizabeth could not remain in Boston without funds and, in Lancaster, the intellectual life was too limited to invite her return. A career of teaching was obviously the way out, if not in a school of her own, then as governess and instructor to the young in some private house. A situation of this kind was open at the moment in a big house on the Kennebec

River in Maine. It was offered to Elizabeth and she accepted it, placing her grammar books and her Greek lexicon in her little box-trunk and proceeding by small steam packet up the river. This was when she was nineteen, in 1823.

A whole new adventure confronted her now but she was neither apprehensive nor downcast. In letters to her sisters, she goes so far as to speak of a young man, also on board, as her "steamboat beau." The man—whose name was Bridge and whose forebears were from Augusta, Maine—entertained the girl by giving her the story of the great families who inhabited the large estates along the Kennebec, part of original grants of land: the Gardiners, the Hallowells and the Vaughans. Here in Maine there had been a prosperous center for shipbuilding and, deriving their wealth from this industry, the three families lived in a fashion almost feudal, each estate a kind of self-contained kingdom set in parks filled with deer and game birds. Elizabeth was on her way to "Salama," the house of Benjamin Vaughan which, with its wide lawns and its white elegance, was visible from the river. Pleasant indeed it must have been to let herself drift, idle for a moment, on a boat that labored in her behalf, allowing the world to slip by along the lovely line of the shore, while an attentive young man devoted himself with tales of splendor past and present.

The actual taking up of her duties in the Vaughan household seems not to have disillusioned Elizabeth. The head of the family, Benjamin Vaughan, a Jamaican by birth, possessed a background of cultivation and worldly importance, as also of political and religious courage. He had, as a youth, been refused a degree at Cambridge in England because of his Unitarian sympathies, but at Edinburgh he had received his degree in medicine. With plenty of money and influence he had been able substantially to help the rebellious young American colonies and he had known Franklin as well as Robespierre, who had obtain Vaughan's release from a Paris prison during the French Revolution, a sentence imposed for his activity in the interests of the people. Vaughan's maternal grandfather was Benjamin Hallowell, one of the proprietors of the Kennebec purchase, owning thirty-one miles along the river front, and it was here that the young liberal took refuge from turmoil and political stress. Elizabeth found her new employer a most agreeable man, making friends with him on the first morning at breakfast when he came upon her inquiring into the books on the dining-room shelves. She had discovered an inner row of volumes ranged behind the outer and, to her delight, she learned that he possessed, for those days, an immense library. He had brought ten thousand volumes with him to Maine at a time when Harvard College had only twelve thousand.

A stimulating employer Benjamin Vaughan continued to be for Elizabeth, pater familias of a large clan occupying on Sunday morning the four front pews of the Unitarian church which he had built, clinging to his Revolutionary garb of small clothes, wig and other exotic habits from the past: a kindly, worldly autocrat who remained her friend always. The boys of the household studied with tutors from the English Cambridge, while boys and girls alike read French with men and women imported from France. It was indeed a compliment to Elizabeth's powers of mind that she had been chosen to take on the education of the younger children. Here was a household governed by the airs and customs of a larger world than she had known, a place where provincialism did not thrive, and it helped her to acquire a wider viewpoint and gentler manners.

Meanwhile, at home, the Peabodys had returned to Salem, and Elizabeth knew from Sophia's letters—Mary being rarely given to speaking of her inner feelings—that both girls felt trapped, confined once again within the limits of city streets, the flower-strewn meadows of Lancaster become but a memory. Their older sister's warm heart went out to them and, with her usual habit of rapid decision, she resolved to alleviate their despair. She would start with Sophia, her special charge, whom everyone spoiled. She wrote inviting Sophia to join her in Maine. The position at "Salama" being so pleasant, Sophia could take it on while she herself would move over to teach in the nearby Gardiner household. Sophia, however, did not feel equal to this: "Don't you think that Mary had better come the first year and let me be older?" was her reply. So Mary arrived presently to teach the Vaughan children and Elizabeth bade good-by, quitting this hospitable house for the Gardiners' at "Oaklands."

Here was a more difficult task, as she had known it would be when she organized the transfer, principally because of Mr. Gardiner's religious and political creeds. He was a thoroughgoing Episcopalian and regarded Channing as a devil. His forebears had been among the band fleeing to Halifax at the close of the American Revolution and for Elizabeth it was almost impossible, during the discussions they carried on, not to attempt drawing off a little of the Tory blood from her irascible employer's veins. Righting the balance toward enjoyment, however, was her pleasure in the friendship that she established with Mrs. Tudor, who was Mrs. Gardiner's mother and who took an affectionate interest in the girl. She had lived for some years in France and she and Elizabeth read French together—Voltaire and also Madame de Staël—who, Mrs. Tudor assured her young friend, made no intellectual distinction between the sexes. "She knew that genius has no sex," Elizabeth wrote Sophia in high excitement, deciding forthwith that she would try, if possible, to become the great Frenchwoman's counterpart.

Mary and Elizabeth, meanwhile, were invited to join a local club for young people that met of an evening, now and then, to read aloud from the classics. Elizabeth had been learning Hebrew with the local minister and she complained to him that these gaieties cut into her hours for study. Besides, she confided, she was unpopular with her contemporaries, the young men in particular. The minister, true to his office, counseled her wisely. He advised her to keep her mind off Hebrew when she went to parties, to dress herself becomingly and to exert herself more with the young men. Ever amenable to reason she considered sound, Elizabeth took great pains with her appearance as she readied herself for the next club meeting, carefully combing and pinning her hair, putting on "one of those square handkerchiefs fastened on each side." When the reading aloud had come to an end, she went to sit in turn by each of the gentlemen who "had formerly considered themselves neglected," and, it appears, miracles were performed. So successful was she now in her role of alluring young lady that she received, by way of climax, a proposal of marriage.

Here was the culmination of her romance with the "steamboat beau" who had not allowed her to forget him. This man, whom Elizabeth referred to in her letters as L.B., seems momentarily to have reached her heart, for she writes that she "now knows what love is." But, with her scholar's mind and her catholicity of taste, she was afraid to capitulate to the masculine will, to become entirely subservient to masculine domination. Had her mother not warned her that within marriage woman must submit? This idea appalled her, she could not see herself in such a role, physically or mentally. And so the melancholy L.B. retired. Later, Elizabeth was to write her family she was glad she had refused him, that "L.B. was not sound-minded nor well-principled," a summary of character made after he had come to a catastrophic end of a sort she never disclosed.

The struggle of diverse tenets and temperaments continued, meanwhile, between Mr. Gardiner and the young teacher. He began to feel something close to aversion for the bold-minded girl who was always ready to do battle with him and his ideas. He called her "impractical" and she became increasingly conscious of his disapproval and dislike. Moreover Boston, after these months of removal from the glamor of great minds, drew her once again. And so the two young women packed their trunks, this time for permanent departure.

Elizabeth and Mary Peabody, a functioning team in education which, with intervals, was to persist until their deaths, decided upon opening a school in the suburbs of Boston, at present a part of Brookline. Here a certain number of rich Bostonians had country places and here, too, there would be the meadows and brooks so much a part of the happy school life at Lancaster. The pair together constituted an exceptional unit, Mary supplying the factual and sensible in teaching the young, while Elizabeth provided the inspiration that was a part of her being, composed as this was of philosophy, religion, moral striving and affectionate understanding. She—

as Dorothea Dix was doing at the same time—took most seriously
the state of her pupils' souls, inviting the girls to go to her in private
for talks that were intended to place them on new spiritual heights.
Also, as with Miss Dix, the aura of an unhappy love affair that
clung about her like the soft shades of a summer night, fascinated
the young and increased her prestige with them.

But Elizabeth did not stop short with the welfare of her students.
Her sister Sophia's proper development was also on her mind. Many
were the letters that traveled between them on the subject of the
younger girl's curriculum planned exclusively, though from a distance, by Elizabeth. Sophia was to study French all day twice a
week and Latin all day on the remaining days. The drawing, begun
some time earlier, that Sophia clung to with so much persistence,
was a good thing, too, Elizabeth informed her. She was to keep that
up but she should take care that the Saturday morning lessons given
her by their Salem aunt were meticulously followed. This attitude
of Elizabeth's, her approval and encouragement, were a major source
of relief to Sophia who had feared her sister might consider drawing
a frivolous pastime. Elizabeth went so far as to suggest to Sophia
that she begin work in oils, promising that she herself would pay
for the new tubes of paint. But here Sophia demurred. She believed
she had better learn to draw thoroughly before turning to paint.
And Elizabeth let her be. Perhaps she was too busy to be able to
pursue matters further at the moment.

The Brookline school was a success. But the idea of a school in
Boston proper, on Beacon Hill, had for five years been simmering
in Elizabeth's mind and now she and Mary decided to go ahead.
For Elizabeth believed, and Mary followed her, that a new age had
dawned, with Channing as prophet leading the way. She met the
"great little man" often nowadays in the houses of her pupils' parents and it brought her a vibrating excitement to be in his company.
She walked to Boston on Sundays through storms of snow, when
the streetcars did not run because of the drifts, never missing a
sermon, seeming to live on these moments of tremendous uplift. In
fact the prudent Mary became worried over the manner in which

her sister was swept off her feet: "He is too much your whole happiness," she warned.

Channing's conversations as well as his sermons stirred the girl who took long walks with him on Saturday mornings when they discussed methods and dogma that had engrossed the minds of scholars and theologians throughout the Christian ages. She wrote down his sermons from memory, sometimes while he read aloud to her in French—an exercise in concentration—so that these should not be lost to posterity; she prepared them for the press and she provided him now and then, unawares, with the text for his next Sunday's sermon, pouring out all she had ever thought or learned, in a torrent of giving. Channing was touched as well as amused and he was impressed by her remarkable memory of which he spoke to many people. This, in addition to her ardent devotion and her never-exhausted vitality, her eagerness like spring freshets forever renewed, made her not only a worthy opponent but a charming and useful companion as well. A letter from Elizabeth to her friend, Lydia Haven, written in November of 1832 sums up her state of mind just now after returning from her duties in Maine and from her romantic but frustrating encounter with a young man there. She chides herself for "brooding over the past and neglecting the blessings of the present," and she goes on to say that "when Mr. Channing had been returned a few weeks I wanted to write and tell you how much more *immortal* I found him than ever before—and how I felt my mind serene under the all annealing influence of his mind and feelings. I am at this moment writing in his study—where I am every evening. . . ."

For Elizabeth there was, over and above the doctor's noble mind and his magical personality, the solid fact of his creed that stood like some leaf-covered mountain, its peak touching the blue of heaven. It lifted her to heights she had but dreamed of before this happy alliance, so that she floated on white clouds moving across a summer sky. Small wonder that this exalted life held no place for the ordinary young man who might attempt to court her on the earthly plane. Presently, however, as these things happen when the business

and the vagaries of life step in to block the way, when the equilibrium within a friendship is somehow disturbed, Elizabeth's
meetings with Dr. Channing became less frequent, their contacts
less fruitful. But he presented her with his daughter as pupil in her
school and Elizabeth's friendship with him, as with Emerson,
endured to the end.

The school in Boston began with such a flourish, thirty pupils the
first year, that Elizabeth felt it safe, in 1832, to invite her family to
quit Salem and come to live with Mary and herself. This they did,
chiefly, perhaps, for the sake of Sophia who delightedly trod the city
pavements, going to the Athenaeum where she could study Flaxman's neo-classic illustrations for Homer and Dante, going to visit
Washington Allston at his studio. There were also the visits Sophia
received at home in the house on Fayette Street, the visit on one
glorious morning of Allston himself and, later, those of the young
men rounded up by the assiduous Elizabeth, who came to receive
instruction in painting and sculpture from the lovely invalid. As
for Dr. Peabody, in addition to dentistry, he had now taken up the
practice of homeopathy and was busy much of the time concocting
the harmless little pills with which he hoped to supplant the un-
compromising doses of physic then in fashion. Something touching
there was in the singlehearted purpose of this peace-loving man shut
away from the stress of the world with which his eldest daughter
dealt in his stead, heroically, if not always in practical fashion.

A rewarding period in many ways this was for Elizabeth who
laid the groundwork now for her life's future, making friends on
every side, continuing her studies, organizing the articles and books
she was so readily to turn out later on. Occasionally she was over-
sanguine in the matter of the human beings she chose to admire and
to trust. One of these was a suave gentleman by name William
Russell, an "educator," who became the first editor of the *American
Journal of Education.* He also taught elocution and, one evening at
a party, made bold to criticize Dr. Channing's delivery. Elizabeth
was not only drawn to this man who seemed to care so much about
the education of the young, but she was also impressed with his

poise, his apparent knowledge of the world. She therefore invited him to join Mary and herself as partner in their school, so that its tone might be heightened by the presence of a gentleman. She neglected, however, as was her wont, to draw up a contract of business with him, difficult as it was to remember during her moments of enthusiasm that there might be some flaw in the human being she chose to extol, he who stood ready to join her in the battle for truth.

Another event, forerunner of future involvement, was that of Elizabeth's introduction to Bronson Alcott. On their first meeting, the youthful philosopher did not appreciate her qualities: her manners were too offhand, she was not womanly enough. Their second meeting took place on his marriage day and occurred by accident. Coming out of King's Chapel, the family church, on Sunday morning, the Peabody girls were invited by Dr. Channing's brother, who stood outside, to linger on that they might attend a wedding shortly to take place there. Bronson Alcott was to be married that morning, he informed them, and the bridal pair would be glad to have a part of the congregation witness the ceremony. Following this, during the welcoming parties for bride and groom, the Peabodys met them often. An extract from Sophia's journal says: "Mr. and Mrs. Alcott spent the evening but Betty talked all the time and I did not have a chance to hear a word from the interesting contemplative man." Alcott, as he wrote of it in his own journal, seems to have changed his mind about Elizabeth: "Miss Peabody is certainly a very sensible lady. She has a mind of superior order. In its range of thought, the philosophical discrimination of its character, I have seldom if ever found a female mind to equal it."

This was a happy, or at least a quiescent, moment in the Peabody family history when for a time even Dr. Peabody seems to have been able to make and preserve a little money. Elizabeth, growing continually in confidence, grew also in the capacity for tenderness that she lavished on those about her, taking more and more upon herself in the organization of their lives. A benign kind of dictatorship it was, that worked toward the enhancement of the human

spirit. Small wonder that "Betty talked all the time." Her enthusiasm for the prospects and the possibilities of life were without any
earthly limit.

As for Miss Peabody's teaching methods, they seemed to consist,
in inspired proportion, of erudition and a native understanding of
children's needs. Many years later, writing her *Reminiscences of
William Ellery Channing,* she tells us of her methods in some detail. She sets them down as she gave them to Channing who had
questioned her ready faith in a child's spontaneous desire to learn:

It seemed to me that it was equally natural for children to be interested in the laws of the expression of thought, as in the laws of outward
things. My scholars have never had any lessons given them to learn at
home. My plan was to teach them how to study, by sitting down with
them and helping them to true habits of analysis, which I found made
them remember more easily than if they were called on merely to remember; for the secret of memory is accurate and lively perception.
Agonies of the will are more apt to destroy than produce it. . . . All
great acquisitions come from voluntary thought and from voluntary
thought alone.

Miss Peabody was thus almost a century ahead of John Dewey
and our so-called "Progressive System." Her method of teaching
Latin to her young students did, in fact, take for granted a great
deal of interest on their part. She began by giving them to learn by
heart *Deus creavit coelum et terram intra sex dies.* Then they were
asked to find out all the English words derived from these Latin
ones. This they did, ending the lesson with a repetition of the
sentence by each student. Next came the reading of about ten pages
of the *Historiae Sacrae* before commencing the grammatical analysis. The lesson lasted half an hour a day. By means of this system,
Elizabeth's little class was soon able to translate the Latin version
of *Robinson Crusoe,* and one of her small students actually shed
tears over Robinson's first interview with Friday. Meanwhile their
older brothers in the Boston Latin School had managed to complete
only the first year of Latin grammar, working on the language six
hours a day in school and two hours at home. Surely Miss Peabody's

accomplishment had to do more with the genius of her teaching than with any pedagogical system.

Presently, in contrast to sustained exuberance—a human law seldom transcended—catastrophe appeared, to disrupt the Peabody equilibrium. Two of Elizabeth's brothers, undergraduates at Harvard during the Kirkland era when frequent expulsions were the order, got into conspicuous trouble over some prank and were themselves expelled, leaving many unpaid debts in their wake. The unsavory nature of this affair was a blow not only to their mother and father but also to Elizabeth at whom certain unkind souls now poked fun for her high-minded ethical principles thus come to grief within her own household. And, going to the school exchequer for funds to help the boys out of this crisis, she found it bare. The money she had believed to be there in substantial quantity had disappeared. This was the work of the egregious Mr. Russell who during the school's prosperity had taken money from the till as he needed it. No accounts had been kept and no more than a verbal agreement was ever made between him and the Peabody sisters. There was nothing to do but close the school while Mr. Russell went off to Philadelphia, unchastened because Elizabeth, in her generosity, wished to spare Mrs. Russell. And once more the Peabodys returned to Salem, permanent shelter from storm and stress.

Elizabeth herself did not at once follow, or rather lead, her family into retreat. She had become engaged in a quixotic adventure of a long-drawn-out nature involving an inheritance. Two of her recent pupils, orphans, were being cheated out of funds due them, and it devolved upon her, she believed, to set things right. The girls' guardian or trustee lived in New Bedford, so Elizabeth went off to confront him there, remaining on during all of an embattled winter, laboring and striving within a situation which was, for once, not hers to command. Dr. Channing knew the world as he knew Elizabeth, and warned her in advance. He was skeptical as to the outcome of this affair. But he also recognized the spirit of Christ and His Beatitudes. How stop, in its manifestations on earth, the play of this spirit? For Elizabeth's motives were selfless and pure. But the outcome of events, ending in the abrogation of right, as Elizabeth saw it, finally forced her to withdraw. "I was unprepared and I lost," she said. "I kept stumbling over realities and still the guiding light was not."

Meanwhile, on her return to Boston, she found Dorothea Dix installed as Dr. Channing's secretary, being paid to do what she herself had in the past done for nothing. Her dislike for her rival was swift and intense and she had, furthermore, to submit to a scolding from the beloved master. She lacked order and method, he told her, at this unhappy moment in her life. Nothing to do, Elizabeth promptly decided, but to open another school, the sooner the better. Mary was sent for once again and two rooms were engaged at Mrs. Clarke's boarding house in Ashburton Place, haven for Boston intellectuals in need of shelter. One room could serve as bedroom for the sisters, the other would become the schoolroom.

Mrs. Clarke, mother of James Freeman Clarke, the abolitionist, was an outgoing, enterprising lady acutely interested in all that concerned the men and women who came to live beneath her roof, and, at her comfortable table, she saw to it that the conversation was kept at high level. "Mrs. Clarke out-talks all of us, even Elizabeth," Mary was presently to say. Elizabeth, of course, remained a stand-by for her landlady who was delighted when some subject worthy of superior minds had been held persistently aloft above the soup, the roast and the pudding. Jared Sparks was one of the boarders, the Peabodys' friend from Lancaster days who had first introduced Elizabeth to the excitements of American history. He had brought his young bride to Mrs. Clarke's in order to spare her the rigors of housekeeping and also, possibly, to provide himself with pleasant mental stimulus while writing the life of George Washington, based on the priceless letters and manuscripts with which his desk was strewn. But for young Mrs. Sparks, as for the more timid souls without the gift of communication, the dining room at Mrs. Clarke's became a kind of purgatory. In fact, the bride left the table after the first meal and never returned. Thereafter, meals were served to her in her room.

There was also, under the same roof, George Hillary who ran a Unitarian weekly and who got Elizabeth to write articles for it: *The Creation, Temptation* and *Sin.* Horace Mann was another of the boarders. He was a recent widower, engulfed in grief for the loss of his lovely young wife, and the two Peabodys found him a magnet of no small power. Elizabeth took over his reclamation, reminding him of the joys and comforts of religion, giving him the promise of meeting his beloved in another world. She read aloud to him of an evening from Constant's *Analysis of Locke,* and sat on at his side in Mrs. Clarke's little parlor after Mary had gone to bed, listening to his sighs, sighing sympathetically in return. He became for Elizabeth "dear Mr. Mann," her responsibility and her delight. Their talks on philosophy and religion, evening after evening, were not sufficient for all that she had to say, and often she woke in the night to make notes of new ideas that struck like sledge hammers along the convolutions of her brain. Elizabeth's sisters believed that at twenty-nine she was at last falling in love. But the association remained ever on the heights and if, now and then, in bidding her good night, Mr. Mann held Miss Peabody's hand rather longer than convention demanded, it was by way of gratitude to her for so much moral support. "Not that it would not be possible for Mr. Mann to make me love him exclusively," she is one day to write Mary, going on to explain, ". . . . All I want is to be *loved.* . . . I have got torrent feelings, I allow . . . but they are *feminine* and they are *sentiments* not *passion*s and they should be treated therefore with delicacy. They do not come from the blood but from the intellectual soul and they are *pure.*"

This was the era of Platonic love, friendship unsullied by lust, high-minded companionship and sacrifice to family, as young women renounced marriage for the life of devotion to duty. At bottom, undoubtedly, as in Elizabeth's case, there lurked a dread of surrender to the male animal, but in sublimation, that alternative chosen by these virgins, much was gained, in fervor and productive accomplishment, for posterity. Intent just now on establishing her own particular form of sublimation, Elizabeth seems not to have perceived that her sister Mary had fallen in love with Mann, "from the blood" as well as spiritually. There was real rivalry between the girls but conscious only as it concerned the practical Mary whose eye was always upon reality. With the arrival of Mann in Mrs. Clarke's boarding house, it had been Mary's self-assigned role to cheer the downcast man, persuade him to laughter, wean him out of the past and into a possibly delightful present. But as soon as she achieved a small success, along came Elizabeth like a wind from the east to scatter extinguishing showers on the beginnings of the new. Poor Mary was very unhappy. How rescue "dear Mr. Mann" from her sister's impassioned solicitude?

Meanwhile, with the school at Mrs. Clarke's continuing to grow and the bulk of the family living in Salem, an institution known as "The Box" went back and forth each week between the two cities. This was actually a container for soiled clothes but it was used by the inventive Elizabeth as a conveyor of presents large and small which it was her pleasure to bestow on brothers, sister, parents: books for the two older boys who at present kept an apothecary shop in Salem, paints and brushes for Sophia. Backed by Elizabeth, who sang her young sister's talent all over Boston, Sophia had had the courage to offer for sale certain of the copies she made of the masterpieces in painting that were popular just then, and she had actually gone a long way toward supporting herself by this means. Elizabeth not only obtained orders for her sister from people who found that these copies—so faithfully, so meticulously made—filled the gaps on their drawing-room walls; she also procured for Sophia's use several of the originals from which further work might be done. Proceeding one day to the studio of Washington Allston, she borrowed from the obliging man his latest canvas, "Jessica and Lorenzo," before the paint had actually dried.

But Sophia's headaches, increasing in intensity and becoming more prolonged, worried Elizabeth as they also worried Mrs. Peabody who, out of her concern and her adoration for this delicate daughter, was unconsciously helping her to become a chronic invalid. Elizabeth then made a quick decision. Sophia should be placed in a warm climate, preferably the tropics; she should leave Salem as soon as matters could be arranged. Surely a way could be found, provided a few questions were asked, help enlisted. Soon, the proposed trip was the talk of Boston. Every sort of suggestion was brought up and discussed. Finally, it was the faithful Mrs. Cleveland who evolved the plan to be chosen from among all the others. Her husband was now vice-consul at Havana. Sophia could go to Cuba, there to take up a post in some rich planter's luxurious house where the beauty and the peace of plantation life would cure the headaches in no time.

A quite perfect plan which Elizabeth instantly accepted as she set to work to collect among willing friends the muslins, the petticoats, the India prints needed for her sister's wardrobe in a warm climate. Sophia, however, petted and sheltered as she had been, begged not to be sent off alone. In thinking it over, Elizabeth decided that Mary would be a satisfactory companion and she promptly arranged this affair also.

The two girls set sail on a brig for Havana out of Boston harbor in November of 1833, soon encountering a severe storm that depressed even more the spirits of the invalid Sophia and of the lovesick Mary. For "dear Mr. Mann" was now to be left entirely in the hands of the exuberant Elizabeth and what would be the final outcome? Cuba did not beckon as an Elysium to the silent, self-effacing girl sent along as chaperon to her pretty sister. Meanwhile, contentedly unaware of Mary's inner life and pleased with the result of her latest efforts, Elizabeth now closed her school, gave up the rooms at Mrs. Clarke's and went to spend the winter with a friend, Mrs. Rice, whose children she was to instruct in return for board and lodging. Here, she was given the use of a small sitting room with a coal-burning grate where she could, in the evening, receive Mr. Mann when he chose to call.

The days were arduous now as always. At five o'clock she rose in the dark to study and write. At seven she took on young Willie Rice, giving his mind the proper slant for the day; then there was a brief time out for breakfast and conversation with Mr. Rice while his wife remained in bed. The girls of the family she taught from nine until one o'clock. Following that she was free to pursue her own course which at the moment meant writing articles for magazines, articles seemingly accepted without difficulty but with small return in money for her toil.

During this winter she published another of her series on history: *Key to History of the Hebrews and the Greeks,* which earned her nothing in the way of funds. There was a children's Christmas book, for which she received from her publisher the complete works of Harriet Martineau, and she also wrote for the *Christian Register* and the *Examiner* on subjects such as "Social Crime and Its Retribution," essays that paid her a total of twenty-seven dollars. One of the reasons for slim sales was the arid quality of her style. Now and then a friend suggested that she write articles in the same vein as her letters, gay, unstilted outpourings. But this she seemed unable to do. Not until one reads her *Lectures to Teachers on the Kindergarten,* written toward the end of her life, does one hear the real sound of Elizabeth Peabody's voice, the true beat of her heart.

It soon became unhappily obvious that Elizabeth could not live and keep her family above water on the proceeds from her writing. Something else must be found. During the last five or six years she had, now and then, given lectures under the title of "Historical School" with the idea in mind of supplementing female education beyond the point where early schooling had stopped. The lecture platform, however, was not in 1833 looked upon as a province of women and any one of them who attempted to use it professionally found herself in an unpleasantly conspicuous position. None but afternoon performances could be thought of, the idea of traveling lectureships was ruled out and the subject, as well as the house in which the lecture was held, had to be chosen with care. Previously, Elizabeth had ventured as far as Salem with her lectures but here she was not a success. Mrs. Peabody, ever given to the happy phrase in summing up a situation, said: "She is before her time in Salem, at least. People cannot appreciate her mind or mode of teaching. She will not manœuver, she will not flatter."

But presently, during her stay with the Rices in Boston, a rumor reached her that "friends were concocting a reading party." Elizabeth thought it an excellent idea and wondered who would be chosen to do the reading. The word "party" implied an evening performance. They would select some cultivated gentleman, she supposed. And so she was overcome with pleasure when these friends invited her to take charge of the evenings. She accepted with delight and felt she was "being fed by the ravens" when tickets to the course, amounting to one hundred dollars, had been sold. Difficult and most important, her initial choice of subject. She finally settled on excerpts from the works of her newly acquired friend, Harriet Martineau. Later, she had the considerable satisfaction of seeing, as one of the results of these readings, the establishment of a new set of working conditions for women at the Lowell Mills. For the two Miss Lowells, owners of the mills, were among Elizabeth's subscribers and had been much influenced by the tales of hardship in England's Manchester mills, as Miss Martineau stated them. When Dickens visited the United States, he was to announce that the Lowell Mills were a model for all the others.

Now, while her readings soon became the fashionable thing in Boston, Elizabeth was at the same time keeping in close touch with her sisters in Cuba. Letters written daily, which she called the "Cuba Journal," went out over the seas to Mary and to Sophia who were living on a plantation with an affluent Spanish family. Mary was governess to the young boys of the household and Sophia was in the process of enjoying life, drawing portrait heads of the young gentlemen who came to visit the hospitable house, walking with them, riding on horseback, waltzing. Her headaches had disappeared, to the patent alarm of Mrs. Peabody back in Salem where life offered little diversion compared to the joy of ministering to her darling. What a loss to maternal solicitude if Sophia were to return home hale and hearty like any ordinary young woman! Marriage would then certainly follow for so attractive a girl.

As a matter of fact, Sophia and her new-found liberty were to cause a certain amount of trouble even before her return to Salem.

Word reached Elizabeth, and also Boston, of her sister's flirtations out there in Cuba. One young man in particular—a foreigner to boot—was being named as the recipient of her affections. Elizabeth went into a panic. She wrote, scolding Mary, urging her to guard Sophia more closely, warning Sophia herself that her reputation was being weighed in the balance. Sophia, as an artist, was in an especially precarious position. Only an artist such as Allston, a man, and married to someone of old Boston stock, could move freely without the taint of the "Bohemian" being attached to his name. All this in a flutter of letters that showed how deeply Elizabeth Peabody was, in spite of her pleasure in woman's emancipation, a part of strict Puritan mores. She had not quite reached the all-inclusive viewpoint of her admirable Madame de Staël.

Mary's reply to Elizabeth was full of spirit. She chided her for spreading and keeping alive with too much gossip the tale of Sophia's amours which were, she said, innocent and harmless. On the other hand, Mary wanted to know, with all that Elizabeth continually wrote of Mr. Mann and his visits to Mrs. Rice's parlor, whether she was in love with him or he with her? Elizabeth's answer was to make Mary happier than she had ever been before: "It is a brother and sister's love on both sides," she says. "It is the supreme delight of my heart," she continues in her generous and honest fashion, "when one of us has a friend that the other may have the same. . . . I do not wish to be preferred, but I am rather better pleased that you should be preferred—as you are certainly preferable."

Thus she continued to send off the "Cuba Journal" and to receive a regular packet from her sisters, a packet containing letters to their various friends as well as to the family which, with the entire postage paid by Elizabeth, now and then amounted to as much as eight dollars. Such are the penalties attendant upon loving care and warmth of heart.

Notwithstanding the complexity of her many duties and efforts at breadwinning, it was not in Elizabeth's nature to be deeply satisfied unless she was running a school. In the back of her mind now was the thought of organizing one for boys "to teach them Latin and first things." She had the promise of Willie Rice as the first of her pupils and several others were already on the list. Her plan was to open in the fall of 1834. But before this date, in July, Bronson Alcott and his wife arrived back in Boston. They had come from Germantown, Pennsylvania, where Alcott had been in charge of a school of his own assisted by Elizabeth's one-time partner, William Russell. This enterprise had been a financial failure and Alcott quite obviously had returned seeking better things, seeking, perhaps, Elizabeth's firm hand to pull him up out of the misty chaos in which he found himself. Had he not said of her during the first days of his marriage: "Her notions of character, the nicety of analysis, her accurate knowledge of the human mind, are remarkable, original and just"?

And so he sought out Miss Peabody at once on returning to Boston, laying in her ample lap his ideas for the instruction of the young, presenting to her his plans for the future of mankind. He "stayed and talked like an embodiment of light, and yet calm, solemn, simple as ever," Elizabeth said. On leaving, he asked her to read some of the private journals written by his erstwhile pupils.

Alcott's ideas delighted Elizabeth. They were, in their final form, what hers had ever been in embryo. How fortunate would be the young, she told herself, who came under the influence of this great educator. Everything was here, everything needed for the future save the pupils themselves. These she must help him find. And she went back to spend the evening with the Rices, reading aloud from the remarkable journals that had, earlier in the day, so begun to fascinate her. At the evening's end, Willie Rice was an enrolled pupil of Alcott's forthcoming school and Elizabeth was making her plans to turn over to him all the others. He had indeed sought out the right person for help and sustaining power. And now he invited Elizabeth to become his assistant when the new school got under way. He offered her as salary one hundred dollars for each quarter, an entirely inadequate sum, he said, and Mrs. Alcott agreed. Her salary, however, was the last thing on Elizabeth's mind just now and she spent each instant of her free time in helping Alcott choose and furnish that portion of the big Masonic building on Tremont Street soon to be known as the Temple School. This, for Elizabeth, brought the same pleasure that furnishing her new house brings to the bride.

Side by side with Alcott she stood, when all was ready, in the great neo-Gothic room sixty-five feet long, forty feet wide, with a nineteen foot stud, and surveyed the fine table and cabinets, the row of desks, the globes of earth and heaven, the portrait of Channing, the plaster casts bought "from the Italians": Socrates, Plato, Psyche, Christ, a Child Aspiring, Silence with its Finger Raised. The room was dark, with only small slits for windows, and cold as a tomb. But there was gas for light and a "stove apparatus" for heat and just outside, in an anteroom, were chairs and table for Elizabeth and her pupils where she would teach them Latin, arithmetic, geography, during two and a half hours each day according to the arrangement made in advance with Alcott.

As had now become the established pattern surrounding Elizabeth's movements, however, no business arrangements she made with friends ever held to their original form. No one in advance, herself least of all, could foresee the amount of unpromised time and devotion she was to pour, like spring rains bringing new growth, on the enterprise she believed important, the idea she thought valuable. In the case of the Temple School, the two and one half hours of her contract gradually stretched to a full day. She became so engrossed in Alcott's conversations with his pupils, his approach to their mind and character, that in the hours between her own teaching, she sat on a bench in the huge cathedral room and made notes on his dissertations. As with Channing in earlier days, she felt that "someone should write down these immortal words." And, while the weeks went by without any seeming prospect of her being paid, she said to her sisters: "I shall give my services for the first quarter." She continued to give her services to the end.

To make some amends, possibly, the Alcotts presently invited

Elizabeth to live with them, turning over to her a pleasant room which was put down on the books as being the equivalent in value of two hours' schooling and, when the next Alcott baby was born, she was named Elizabeth Peabody. This was all very agreeable, for Elizabeth adored the baby, the future "Beth" in *Little Women,* and it was restful to be in possession of a quiet room of her own, to work at evening, keeping the records of Alcott's school, writing up her own journal. An excerpt from the journal, in 1835, is characteristic of her industry, her generosity and the originality of her approach to life:

One o'clock—I have arranged my papers and sewn them together. . . . Tomorrow I mean to look over those which are in my hair trunk. It will take me a week or two to get my study in order perhaps. I am a very orderly person—notwithstanding my habits—which have arisen from my having lived so much at war with my mental instincts. Some day I am going to sit down and think over where I ought to have drawn the line between following my own instinctive feelings and sacrifice of my objects to others. . . . While I believe obstinacy in having one's own way . . . is necessary, I have constantly allowed it to be secondary in practice—but I should grow *Dix-y* and old maidish—inflexible and hard . . . I particularly detest such a character as Miss Dix—I don't detest Miss Dix herself however. I think she is rather better than her character —if such a discrimination can be made—and this discrimination can be made—I like Mrs. Alcott very much. But I admire parts of her character still more than I do her . . . I look upon her faults also as phenomena . . . and also as *necessities.* . . . They seem the growth of the Eternal Fall of Man rather than of her own will.

There were, however, in her present life divergences from the ideal. Alcott was accustomed to giving his thoughts free verbal rein and to be listened to attentively as the words issued from his lips. Elizabeth, on the other hand, delighted in her own conversation. It was the breath of life. And, to maintain her point of view, permitting no misconception to remain in the mind of her auditor, was one of the articles of her creed. The argument between them was thus frequently pulled apart until, now and then, it was irremediably sundered. Once, after a verbal encounter of this kind, Elizabeth, in her journal, notes that on arrival upstairs after dinner she felt very uncomfortable, as if she had been treated not too civilly: ". . . I resolved that in future I would take more pains to be silent on a subject on which it is possible for Mr. Alcott to differ from me and I from him. But I think I shall find it quite a trial to my patience to sit silent under this wholesale abuse of whatever has become the order of society. . . ."

One night at the dinner table, the topic arose of Mr. Graham, inventor of Graham Flour, who claimed that the use of his process would enable a human being to live for two centuries. Alcott was impressed, while Elizabeth questioned Graham's claims, making bold to say she doubted whether such a feat would be desirable, that she would look upon it as "rather a misfortune" to live so long. Alcott, aloof and severe, said, according to Elizabeth, that: "if analysed this reluctance to live another century would prove to be a suicidal statement"; and his displeasure endured. Other beliefs of his were at variance with her upbringing: his theory, for example, that an illness of the body stems from the doing of evil. This, the daughter of Dr. Peabody could not accept, nor could she, her journal assures us, accept Alcott's disillusionment with the average professional man and his integrity. It was in Elizabeth's nature to defend the motives of all but a very few among mankind. Summing up her impressions of Alcott's viewpoint, she wonders whether ". . . the sagacity of his head would compensate for the want in his heart of that humility—and sober estimate of his own place among his fellows—which challenges respect and love." She wonders if the ardor for reform has not perhaps carried him so far that he cannot endure an opinion contrary to his own and "avoids rather than seeks any communication with persons who differ from himself."

The days spent in teaching and transcribing Alcott's conversations within the Temple School were, nonetheless, entirely absorbing to Elizabeth. She marveled at his quiet power over the pupils and his ability to hold their attention. She was fascinated by his choice of subject matter and his technique in conveying it to their youthful minds. There ensued many talks between the headmaster and his flock which he kept on the level of good-natured inquiry: talks on morality, religion, duty and the origins of body and soul with especial care, Elizabeth writes in her journal, "to bring out clearly in the children's consciousness, the perception of their spiritual existence, as being the most real and permanent." This, Alcott was pre-eminently successful in doing, to his pupils' lasting advantage. Three of the older boys, however, seated alone one day at a section of the room far from the stove's heat, briefly disrupted the usual pattern. When the question arose as to how admirable was the Stoics' idea of being able to bear pain, the boys replied they "did not think it worth while to attempt to bear the cold." Alcott cleverly brought them around to a less immediate application of the case in point but one cannot help wondering whether pneumonia may not have been the result. Indeed, one marvels at the endurance and the submission of these New England children as, unlike our children today, they put up with physical discomfort and the long hours of application that brought them and their studies to a place, by our current standards, far in advance of their years.

We have from Miss Peabody herself the account of what went on in the classroom at the Temple School, as well as Alcott's method of directing it. For she was presently to make a book from her copious notes, a book which, with its title, *Record of a School,* won her the praises of Ralph Waldo Emerson and served to renew the friendship that had lapsed since the days when together they studied Greek.

There seems to have been great interest on the children's part in all that went on and they were participants, often, in their own education. One of Alcott's theories was that teaching in terms of the children's imagination, rather than by means of set subjects, would serve to prepare them for college at fourteen or fifteen years of age. Thus he taught geography with the help of natural science and topography, illustrating his talks with descriptions of mountains and swift rivers, reading to the children from Washington Irving, Audubon's *Journal,* Cook's *Voyages,* Flint's *Valley of the Mississippi.* He constantly encouraged self-analysis, biography and journal writing—"since they bear upon the skillful use of language and are as truly the initiation of intellectual as of moral education."

Even the very small children, Elizabeth observed from her post at the back of the room, delighted in the idea of self-government, self-analysis. They wanted to find out what they were made of inside, and Alcott was kept constantly on the alert answering the metaphysical questions put to him. The children's average age was ten years, and now and then some of them became restless, moved in their seats or whispered to each other. To bring an end to this and gain their concentrated attention, Alcott described the workings of a perfect machine, saying that its proper function was always to run quietly and without friction. In studying geometry, he informed them that they were studying the laws of the universe, and that no amount of impatience or anger with the problems involved could solve them.

All went well until, after a time, Alcott began to instruct them in religion, reading to them from the Bible in the course of which, very naturally, the subject of birth came to the fore. With the vision of Zacharias and the birth of John the Baptist, questions concerning the prophet's arrival in the world had to be satisfactorily answered. Many of the children were only seven years old, some even younger, and only a few of them knew about birth "in the usual way." Alcott's explanation seemed to Elizabeth quite beautiful: "A mother suffers when she has a child. When she is going to have a child, she gives up her body to God and he works upon it in a mysterious way, and with her aid, brings forth the child's spirit in a little body of its own." A statement such as this, given orally, would have done no harm, presumably, if Alcott had not followed it up presently with a published version: *Conversations with Children on the Gospels*. His reason, he said, for setting down his ideas on the teaching of sex was that "no one should have wrong thoughts." But a fury of protest followed, among decorous Puritan parents, reaching such proportions that the Temple School had finally to be closed, the sheriff himself conducting the deposed master, a child in either hand, down the Temple steps.

Elizabeth did not witness this humiliating scene. She had left the school some time before to go to Lowell where a young woman friend was dying of tuberculosis, the husband having summoned her that she might quiet his wife's fears of death and damnation, giving her the assurance of another world wherein all was forgiveness and serenity. During a part of the time that Elizabeth was absent from the Temple School, Sophia, now returned from Cuba, had attempted to fill her sister's place and, seated on the rear bench listening to what went on, she could not help wondering, she later said, whether Alcott's conversations, as also the children's, were not sometimes "indelicate."

As for Elizabeth, as soon as she had wind of Alcott's plans for the publication of the *Conversations with Children,* she became terror-stricken and begged him to desist, going so far as to ask him not to associate her name with the book or, failing that, to make it plain in the preface that their ideas on the teaching of sex did not coincide. This, unfortunately, was not clearly explained and when the cataclysm occurred, Elizabeth was deeply hurt as well as disillusioned. She stood by the discredited schoolmaster, however, proclaiming her loyalty to him and to his teaching methods, writing an article entitled: *Mr. Alcott's Book and School.* This was published in the *Register and Observer,* and was an act of great courage. Margaret Fuller defended Alcott, and so did Emerson. Emerson, in fact, did more. In the long talks he had with Elizabeth at this bad moment, he tranquilized and restored her spirit. "I have caught his faith—or rather he has kindled mine. My prayer is, may this vision last. This is my Mount of Transfiguration."

In 1838, with Mary and Sophia once more at home, the right time seemed to have arrived for the purchase of a house in Salem. An ample one of three stories was found on Charter Street looking over the old burying ground, roomy enough so that Dr. Peabody could have quarters there for his office, and particularly pleasant for Sophia whose bedroom windows gave out onto Colonel Pickman's flower garden. It came to be known eventually as the "Grimshawe House" for the reason that Hawthorne placed the setting of *Dr.*

Grimshawe's Secret there. At the moment of the move, Dr. Peabody
was much involved in experiments with mesmerism, even though
for many Salem inhabitants it savored rather too much of witchcraft, and he had invited into partnership a young man who spe-
cialized in this subtle art, practicing it occasionally on Sophia when
her headaches became intolerable.

Sophia was busy at present making her copies of old masters, for
which she received four to five hundred dollars apiece, while Elizabeth continued to teach at the Temple School, not yet gone on the
rocks. In fact, she was just now using every source at her command
to preserve friendly relations with the temperamental, egoistic Alcott, sharing much of her life with him, taking him out to Concord
to call on Emerson that the two might meet and converse. She also
introduced Alcott to Washington Allston on a visit to the painter at
his studio. Elizabeth had been summoned there because of an article
she had written for the *American Monthly Review*—an article on
Allston that had immensely pleased him. He was, the story goes, so
flattering to her on this visit that she became flustered enough to
start for home, when the party ended, without her bonnet.

Following on a previous visit to Allston's studio with young Sarah
Clarke, sister of James Freeman Clarke, as companion, Elizabeth
writes of it to Sophia in Salem:

. . . Just as we arrived he was coming along to his painting room in
an old hat and coat—his gray locks floating over his shoulders—a sight
to behold. He went in and laid aside the old hat and then his hoary locks
looked picturesque enough—looking like a little child's. His clothes
however were absolutely ragged. [Sarah Clarke had brought him a picture to criticize] . . . he took a cigar, which he called his *tobacco spec-
tacles*, and sat down and looked. . . . Soon he said "This is *clever* . .
very clever indeed." In a minute or two more he looked round with a
quick, bright, sweet look. "You have got it *in* you," said he.

And now, with the appearance of Alcott's book and the closing
of the school, Elizabeth took up her abode at Charter Street, staying there, more or less, during the next four years. Here her sister

Mary, who had earlier refused to become professionally involved with Alcott, considering him an oversevere taskmaster, continued quietly, in a back parlor, with schoolteaching on her own. Occasionally Mr. Mann came out to lecture at Salem. Then he was easily persuaded to spend a night or two with the Peabodys in a room that Mary assiduously readied before his arrival. In fact he came often, even when there was no lecture on the boards. His presence continued to give Elizabeth great pleasure, the more so as she was temporarily without definite occupation. She had finished the generous article written in Alcott's defense wherein she said: "Never were children more independent of an instructor, notwithstanding the astonishing command he has of their attention. . . . Their young brains ought not to be exercised in chopping logic. Their pure imagination should wander free into the eternal reason."

When the article had gone to press, Elizabeth turned her thoughts in the direction of the discovery of genius as it existed in the immediate world about her, hoping to sweep it out of obscurity and into the light. Jones Very, the poet, was one of those she pushed to the forefront by bringing him into the presence of people influential in the writing world. The second of her efforts as detective and patroness of the arts was even more spectacular. This was in connection with a series of stories that had recently appeared anonymously in the *New England Magazine,* edited by one of Elizabeth's cousins. It was rumored that the author was a mysterious "Mr. Hawthorne" and, remembering her one-time schoolmate, Ebe Hathorne, of Shakespeare prowess, Elizabeth decided to call on the family who, entrenched recluses one and all, still inhabited the gloomy house in Herbert Street.

The doorbell was answered by Louisa, younger sister of Ebe, and soon Elizabeth had secured the information she needed. Her brother worked constantly at writing, Louisa said. The clue had been a good one. "Mr. Hawthorne," for the benefit of the literati, had simply added an extra consonant to his name. Miss Peabody returned home to write him a flattering letter and, in gratitude, he sent her a copy of *Twice Told Tales,* published in March of 1837.

Others besides her immediate family were thus included within Elizabeth's range of influence. But she found Mr. Hawthorne less docile than her sisters and father had been, often entirely unmanageable, in fact. She attempted, after their first encounter, to find him a position as journalist, that he might make extra money, but he told her flatly that work of this kind did not interest him. In November of that year, however, he and his sister Ebe went to call at the house on Charter Street. Sophia was in bed with one of her headaches and so their entertainment devolved chiefly upon Elizabeth. Fortunately, there was much with which to entertain the Hawthornes on that afternoon in spite of Sophia's absence. The devoted Elizabeth took up from the reading table the volume of Flaxman's *Greek Poets* lent her by Allston, drawings which had brought suggestions to Sophia for her own work, and she also procured a notebook holding Sophia's "Cuba Journal," portions of which she read aloud to the presumably delighted Nathaniel. "He is as handsome as Lord Byron," she told her sister later and, on his next coming to call, Sophia found herself well enough to descend to the drawing-room floor. She was wearing a white robe in the Greek style and must have looked like a Rossetti angel, for it appears that Hawthorne fell in love with her at first sight. Elizabeth observed the glances he bestowed on her sister and she worried lest he become a suitor. When the visit ended, she wrote him a letter in which she told him that Sophia was an invalid who should never marry. Hawthorne's reply appeared to satisfy Elizabeth, trustful as she was apt to be of human motives and the beneficent outcome of all human encounters. Perhaps there was also for her a kind of vicarious pleasure to be derived from witnessing at close hand the growth of an ardent courtship. At any rate, Hawthorne's visits continued.

A period followed wherein Elizabeth persevered in trying to manage Hawthorne, tried to improve the shape of his existence, to modify him as a human being. She wanted him to meet Longfellow and Holmes and she was heartbroken when he refused. He was too shy a factor, she believed, that might easily be swept away, granted a little will power. He preferred solitude and the preoccupation of his own thoughts, he told her. But he could not deter in her the desire to find him the perfect job. The impecunious young man, so without the ability to make his own way, should occupy some government position that would fetch him a salary, thus permitting him to take his time over the writing of his books. But Hawthorne continued to wish that Elizabeth would leave him alone while she, surveying him from without, saw how much easier and pleasanter his life would be were she permitted to do a little remolding.

How natural a desire this was, coming from a capable, eager creature such as Elizabeth Peabody whose motives were guided by love and sympathy tied to unquestioning confidence, whose thirty odd years in the world had brought her no husband to cherish, no children to guide. The practice of charity combined with hope and faith, those old-fashioned virtues, filled a heart voluminous as her gesture which included all mankind. But Hawthorne, although calling often at the Charter Street house, managed usually to evade Elizabeth's grasp. Once she succeeded in beguiling him to a party at Miss Burley's, that patroness of talent, but his shyness brought less rather than more in the way of advantage, tongue-tied as he was and aware, as though tortured in Hades, of his bodily awkwardness, the gaucherie of his manners. Salem believed that he was courting Elizabeth, unaware of the handsome young man's preference for her sister.

The day came, presently, when Hawthorne and Sophia, as a mark of gratitude for her loyalty and concern, gave Elizabeth, ahead of the rest of the world, the news of their engagement to marry. The news at first dumbfounded her but soon, with the talent she possessed for enthusiasm, she set to work to secure for Hawthorne a position in the form of a sinecure. She found one before long through Mrs. George Bancroft, wife of the historian and one of the subscribers to her "Reading Parties." This was a position as weigher and gauger at the Boston Custom House, work, Elizabeth believed, of not too arduous a kind. Hawthorne accepted the proffered job because of Sophia and their future together and, as a result, Boston again loomed large on the Peabody horizon. The family had been saddened, recently, by the deaths, not far apart, of two of the Peabody brothers, Wellington of yellow fever in the epidemic at New Orleans following the Mexican War, and George who died in November 1839, after a painful illness of paralysis of the spinal cord. It seemed now as though this might be the moment to pull up the pegs that held the family within the narrow confines of Salem, the moment to drive stakes solidly into the soil of that "Hub of the Universe," so compelling to Elizabeth. She belonged at the hub, she felt, her family also, right at the center where ideas were distilled in purest form, where the fine product of hand and soul were perennially to be found. Only, if the move were to be made, it should be into the thick of things, into the very heart of the matter, and permanently so. No more retreats from Boston's bright lights at times of stress, as in the past. They should carry with them as they went the assured sense that this establishment would endure.

The idea came to Elizabeth that she might open a bookshop in Boston, a shop which would differ as much from the ordinary wholesale place as a factory for spinning wool differed from the hand loom. Here, books would be arranged on shelves in the Peabody sitting room, a "book-room" it would be, and purchasers could sit deep in chairs by the fireside or in the sunshine of a front window to sample the wares. On the shelves customers would find nothing to shock their sensibilities but each book should be worth while and, for the added pleasure of her customers, she would stock the place with French and German classics as well as with current treatises on science: all this a great innovation.

Channing's advice was sought in the matter of the bookshop as, until now, it had not been thought the genteel thing for women to compete in matters of trade. The needle-and-thread shops for gentlewomen were all that had so far been attempted. His reply set Elizabeth at ease. He sent his blessings to her and to the shop with the words: "The business seems to partake of the dignity of literature." What better than this? But, kind friend that he was, he went on to warn her of her haphazard business methods, her enthusiasm so often ungrounded. And then, to finish the matter, he deposited at her request sufficient funds with his London publisher that she might have a reserve to draw on there for the purchase of English publications. Allston did the same thing with the firm supplying his art material, advising Elizabeth to stock the new bookshop with paints, brushes, varnishes. She thus became the "sole agent in New England" for these London organizations.

The shop opened in a house at 13 West Street in July, 1840, when Elizabeth was thirty-six years old. Dr. Peabody, as usual, had been given a corner in which to manufacture his bright-colored liquids and he now had his son Nathaniel as permanent partner. Their remedies were once in a while sold to Elizabeth's book-loving customers as were Sophia's drawings. Mrs. Peabody's rocking chair was placed in a front window for her use in the few free moments between cooking, tending house, and helping to sell books. More and more, she contrived to share in this last occupation, knowing intimately many of her daughter's customers and their tastes, able to advise and to guide their choice of reading. On Wednesday afternoons, chairs retrieved from closets and cellar were set up within the library and ladies came in numbers from Cambridge and Brookline, as well as from Beacon Hill, to listen to Margaret Fuller's "Conversations." Here was another of Elizabeth Peabody's generous impulses bearing fruit, for no charge was made to Miss Fuller for the use of the room and she as much as Elizabeth seemed to take it for granted that these lectures had permanently succeeded the earlier Peabody "Reading Parties." The Wednesday afternoons, however, were not entirely disadvantageous to Elizabeth and the shop. The lecture ended, Mrs. Peabody, Mary and Sophia managed all three to make many sales while Elizabeth, her psyche knot slipped to one side, excitedly discussed with clients the points Miss Fuller had scored.

And now another of Elizabeth's dreams could enter reality: she would become a book publisher, bringing forth, through the medium of the press, the wisdom and beauty set down by the hand of man, in such a way that the writer might benefit as well as the middleman. This was a moment when ethics in the publishing

world were often equivocal. Elizabeth's methods were to be above-
board and honest, the printing to be done by jobbers and sold at but
slight profit to the West Street shop. Once again Channing was
consulted, once again he made the deciding gesture forward, giving
Elizabeth a pamphlet of his own to print on the subject of "Emancipation." It sold with gratifying results, bringing her success in her
first venture. But, soon after, the customary pattern established itself and the publishing project was forced to an eventual stop. For
the abolitionists had approached Elizabeth with a series of articles
which she agreed to print at cost. Profits thus were too negligible
to make the business worth continuing. However, this was a happy
and fruitful period and, before the press at West Street closed for
good, it was to publish three books by Hawthorne, several of Margaret Fuller's translations from the German and, during two years,
it brought out *The Dial,* organ of the Transcendentalists.

The Transcendental movement came into being in 1836 at a discussion club or symposium assembled for the purpose of talking of
the French and German philosophers as expounded by Coleridge
and others. The original members—Emerson, George Ripley,
Hedge, Alcott, Convers Francis, James Freeman Clarke and Thoreau—presently expanded to include Margaret Fuller and Elizabeth
Peabody. This was a great concession to the feminine mind and a
most unusual gesture on the part of New England gentlemen at
this epoch of history. Miss Fuller was said to be a "terrible antag-
onist" when she gave battle in philosophical argument and Elizabeth, according to Emerson, had a "beneficent" influence upon her.
Elizabeth herself was able to stand firm on the subject of "perfectibility" and other matters close to the hearts of this learned company, for had she not had her initiation in girlhood with Channing
as docent? The aim of the Transcendentalists was to break with the
formalism of Calvinist and Unitarian theology and to encourage a
widening literary outlook in the public mind. Presently, in 1840, the
quarterly magazine, *The Dial,* was issued in order that ideas gathered during meetings might reach a larger public. The movement
actually brought a real stimulus, during the several years of its in-

corporation, to ideals of human behavior and it aroused much of the impetus, locally, that culminated in the abolition of slavery.

The failure of sporadic attempts by an outside press to publish *The Dial* was the reason for Elizabeth's taking it over. Here again, she had first applied to Channing for advice. His reply was all that she had hoped for. "Nothing," he said, "terrifies me in these wildest movements. What has for years terrified and discouraged me is apathy." For one of the early issues, with Margaret Fuller as editor, Elizabeth wrote an essay entitled *A Glimpse of Christ's Idea of Society*. Her own Christian spirit showed itself at that particular moment in her guarantee to Margaret Fuller of a hundred-dollar salary as editor, before any profit accrued to the publisher. Unfortunately, the salary was not forthcoming and soon Miss Fuller resigned. Of the seven hundred copies issued each quarter, only three hundred were paid for by subscription and Elizabeth was finally obliged to tell Emerson they could not continue, while he signed the back notes that had accrued.

On Wednesday evenings, Miss Peabody remained at home to her friends in the West Street shop and they came in quantities, enjoying the warmth of atmosphere, with the books as background, the stimulating talk, the diversity of company. The shop was headquarters for those Harvard professors who came there to purchase their foreign language books, as well as for the Concord philosophers. Hawthorne dropped in to listen to the plans for Brook Farm and so did a group of young Harvard students of theology who were fascinated by Ripley and his faith in regeneration even though their professor, Andrews Norton, considered Ripley a heretic. Thomas Wentworth Higginson was one of this company and often they talked well on into the night, arriving just before the shop closed its door to the public.

During the great depression of 1840, when women went forth to beg in the streets, the advocates of Brook Farm proclaimed that in a world of their planning, wherein all work and wealth were equally shared, mankind would be spared such suffering and ignominy. Each man and woman, within their Utopia, would contribute to the others in substantial labor and forward-looking ideas, thus ensuring a perpetually renewed vitality. Elizabeth lived ardently within this dream. She visualized as part of the society a new and glorious kind of school to be called the "Brook Farm Institute of Agriculture and Education," where boys and girls would be taught by the brilliant men and women members of the community. What a fine universe they would begin to build!

Hawthorne believed in the plan, too, for a while, seeing in it a means for supporting Sophia, with plenty of time left for his writing once the communal labor was discharged each day. He joined the Brook Farmers therefore in 1841 when, along the meandering brookside acres in Roxbury, the colony was first established. He wore the blue linen smock that was the order for the men, and he worked hard at pitching manure, contributing with intelligence and fortitude to the company's plans. But there proved to be less and less leisure for him and for his writing, too many high ideas joined to babbling voices, no hours of quiet reflection. And so he left the group as, sadly enough, little by little, many of the others did also. The time had not yet come when men and women could depart from the multitude, setting up a world which, even though founded on the heights, was yet but a dream.

The West Street house was the scene of two marriages within two years. The first, in July, 1842, was the marriage of the lovely Sophia with Hawthorne. James Freeman Clarke performed the ceremony in the small parlor off the book-room and his sister Cornelia helped the bride fasten pond lilies in her hair. The wedding journey under the afternoon sun, recently emerged from behind storm clouds, was the carriage drive from Boston to Concord, to the "Old Manse" where the bride and groom were to live for the time being. On one of her visits to Emerson, Elizabeth had made the arrangements for the Hawthornes and she had asked Thoreau to dig and plant a garden for the young couple, giving them thus a little push into their first summer together. Mrs. Alcott, who with her family had moved to Concord, went over on the wedding morning to decorate the house—a truly pastoral scene. The Hawthornes spent a summer of bliss along the meadows and river of the old town, taking small heed of Mrs. Peabody's injunctions regarding health, and managing to escape from Elizabeth's friends who came out from Boston to call on the bride and groom.

In the spring of the next year, it was Mary Peabody and Horace Mann who were married in West Street, sailing on the same day for a trip to Europe that was to combine a honeymoon with the business of investigating school systems in foreign countries. To Elizabeth, the announcement of Mary's engagement had come with rather an unpleasant awareness for, after all, it was to her that "dear Mr. Mann" had first belonged, her in whom he had first confided; she it was who had begun to awaken his interest in education, bringing added zest to his ideas on the teaching of children. Their intimacy had never lapsed and, while she had not wished to marry him, it seemed that he belonged in good measure to her. It would be an irreparable loss were this marriage to wrest him permanently from mind and heart. But here they stood, these two whom she loved, wrapped in a happiness which was the legitimate right of man and woman on their wedding day. How could she begrudge them this? She must be happy too. All unconsciously, Elizabeth had mastered the lonely art of sublimation, and she derived, perhaps, from the union of her two sisters, a kind of vicarious pleasure not far from a marital bond of her own. At any rate, it was with relief that Mary, bidding her good-bye at the ship's side, observed that her older sister seemed "perfectly satisfied."

With two more members added to the family, Elizabeth set cheerfully to work in their behalf. She concentrated principally on Hawthorne, convinced as she was that he should find lucrative work to supplement the meager dollars brought in by his writing. On leaving the Manse in Concord, he and Sophia had returned to Salem where Hawthorne broke down for a time after the death of his mother whom Sophia conscientiously tended in her last illness. Elizabeth had gone out to look after the children during this crisis and she was pleased to find on Hawthorne's recovery that a pro-lific writing period was upon him, for he was composing *The Scar-*

let Letter. But she could not keep from suggesting that he plan his tales on a cheerful rather than a tragic note in order to please his readers, thereby increasing the sales. Hawthorne, by way of reply, took to avoiding this irrepressible sister-in-law. But she seems not to have been aware of his displeasure. Her fervor, her tremendous powers of affection, were the dominant drives in her life and she could not contain them even though, now and then, they were overlooked.

With the Manns, also, a certain amount of back pedaling was forced upon Elizabeth. On their return from the wedding trip, with Mary already expecting the birth of her first baby, Elizabeth attempted to regain the old footing with Horace, referring as in the past to his early sorrow on the loss of his young first wife. This Mary could not tolerate and she wrote in stern words to her sister bidding her change her attitude: "There is such a thing as being sympathized with too much. It is the last touch of delicacy which sees this," she said. Elizabeth, apparently, desisted. But her talks with Mann on education and politics were to continue as often as they were together, neither of them wishing to forego the pleasure brought by a shared desire to right the world's wrongs. Mann reported to Elizabeth now on the details of his European reconnoitering, on the struggle, among other things, for independence in Hungary, an event which so fired her imagination that she wrote a book about it and did much to help one of the unfortunate sisters of Kossuth, Madame Meszlenyi, who later sought refuge here.

Meanwhile, at the West Street shop, business had begun to slacken and it seemed necessary to Elizabeth and Mrs. Peabody that they let out their extra bedroom to a paying guest. The popularity of the Old Corner Bookstore, Boston's stand-by, was one reason for the falling off at West Street, for it was more conveniently situated, and also, possibly, a more neutral place in which the public might choose its reading matter. Channing continued to come to West Street, however, to look at the daily papers and he enjoyed being called now and then by his protégée, Miss Peabody, when someone worthy of his attention waited there to converse with him.

With the shop's affairs slowing down and her efforts at giving assistance to Hawthorne and Mann seemingly superfluous, Elizabeth was much in need of an object or a cause to take up the slack in her energies. She presently found this in a young theological student at Harvard by name Greene, a former lieutenant in the army who concentrated now on religion and philosophy. An ex-soldier, handsome and well set-up, he was considered by Elizabeth entirely worthy of her assistance when he had come into the shop seeking for further information on Kant, and soon she was appealing to Channing to help set Lieutenant Greene on the right track. The result was a series of conversations at the shop, dealing with metaphysics, conversations between the two men that wafted Elizabeth heavenward. How find greater pleasure than in watching the beneficent effect wrought on the self-assured, dark-eyed youth by her lifelong friend and mentor, the great Channing, who had begun to influence her as a child in Salem when her mother had taken her to hear him preach in the big chilly church. She so well remembered his first appearance, a small, eager man standing in the pulpit wrapped in a "traveler's greatcoat—slowly lifting up his large, remarkable eyes, with the expression of seeing something." She remembered how her attention had been "fixed by that look" which she "always associated with the one recorded of the martyr Stephen." She remembered also the question that had arisen to plague her mind as a child, a question connected with Jesus' spiritual discipline that she had longed to put before Channing but dared not, realizing she was a "stranger and interloper hardly thirteen years old." She had had to defer it for ten years. And here they were united, these two men, her old love and her new, objects, both, of her vivid enthusiasm, for did not one of them exemplify perfection on earth, as nearly as this is vouchsafed to man, while the other, still within the malleable state of youth, represented the hope of the future.

Dr. Channing at this particular moment continued to come to the shop partly because of his pleasure in theological argument—for Lieutenant Greene had brains and vitality—and partly to prevent Elizabeth from falling too much a victim to Greene's charms. "I observed yesterday great solicitude in your manner as your young friend was conversing," he said to her one day. And a little later, in his study, packing his books while Elizabeth watched, for what was to be his last summer journey away from Boston, he warned her of the dangers of an alliance between a young student and a thirty-eight-year-old woman. Had she forgotten the lesson he had taught her years before and that she was, later on, to speak of with so much gratitude? "I largely owe to him the salutary conviction that nobody believes what is false because it is false, but because it seems to be true." Well for her to remember this in her dealings with the smooth-spoken young Greene. Channing begged her now to write him often as the summer unwound, to make him "partner" to her new thoughts. For, during many previous bookshop summers Elizabeth had written copiously to him, letters he and she called his "newspaper." But this time she made no promise. Something, perhaps an unspoken disapproval on the part of her old teacher, held her back. "I do not know, sir, I have hardly learned to clothe my thoughts in words," she answered, and, although he smiled benignantly when they parted, she failed to write.

This was to be a long farewell, for Channing died in October, "peacefully gazing on a beautiful sunset sky." Elizabeth heard of his death one morning by letter, and, while her eyes were yet full of tears, Washington Allston came into the shop. There, the news given him by Elizabeth was almost too much for his strength. He stepped back and sat down: "Dr. Channing was a good man, an excellent man! I loved him," were the words he uttered. And leaving the shop to go home—as Elizabeth later heard—he was long in recovering his equilibrium. When his strength returned, he set at once to work designing a monument for his old friend whom he was so shortly to follow.

A story written by Elizabeth toward the end of her life and called *Last Evening with Allston,* describes the visit she made to the painter's studio not long after Channing's death. Obviously, she did not intend to allow this friendship to end in a sudden wrench between the living present and far eternity. With Channing, new influences that momentarily engulfed her had kept them apart at the last. She would regret it always. This time, no such thing should occur.

She found Allston, she tells us, working as he had for many long years, and in spite of his feeble condition, on "Belshazzar's Feast," an immense canvas immensely conceived but difficult to execute. He laid down his brushes on her arrival and taking out his portfolio showed her then "enough sketches and work planned for one hundred years to come." It seemed to Elizabeth a great pity that these ideas should remain dormant, should not bear fruit, that Allston's influence as painter and teacher should not be more assured.

"Let me tell that in Boston," she exclaimed, and on the instant made plans to go forth shouting his name aloud, gathering in pupils whom he could train after the manner of Michelangelo's apprentices. Boston, thus, might become the art center of the world.

"Drawing is the first thing, drawing is the second thing, drawing is the third thing," Allston said to her, and she wondered why it was thought that he had done little work of a brilliant kind since he left England. She herself, after viewing a Boston exhibition of his painting in 1839, had written: "Almost all communion of one mind with others is partial. You are made aware of different depths at different times. But here, at one glance, you take in the whole of a great mind and are rendered silent in reverence. You feel anew how great a thing one human mind is. You see how it may be a mirror of the whole race, of nature, of something above nature."

Allston's conversations also were "immortal," no doubt of that. Each of them "had the beauty of a work of art." And Elizabeth admired his poetry, too. Listening to him as he read aloud to her on that day of her visit, she took the book from him, briefly to memorize and then recite one of the poems it contained. This touched him and made him happy. They went on to speak of "dying saints and the smiles of children, who always met death quietly and gladly." And then she bade him good-bye.

Returning from a short journey three weeks later, Elizabeth was told that Allston was dead. "Seldom have I felt the dreary pain, the sense of what Byron calls 'obstruction's sway,' that answered to the sudden announcement made to me—'Allston is dead.'" She could hardly contain her emotions and, believing it to have been an oversight on the family's part that she was not invited to the ceremony, she went to the house in Cambridgeport on the day of the funeral. Standing beside the deathbed, she spent long hours wrestling with her soul, feeling unworthy of being in "so grand a presence." In moving words she describes the scene: "Again and again everybody went and looked, as if the eyes could not be satisfied with seeing. But at dusk the procession could be delayed no longer, and the fatal lid was closed."

They walked through a golden twilight and came presently to Cambridge under a moon partly obscured by clouds. Then in deep darkness, lighted only by students bearing torches, Allston was lowered into the grave. Just at the last, the moon briefly reappeared, speaking to her of the "triumphant wings of faith."

In retrospect, Elizabeth was to say of Washington Allston that he had been a true solitary when at work or when weary, but that whenever he entered a room filled with people, even of his family and intimates, "he was in full presence." He circled about shaking hands with each "in delighted recognition." When he bade his family good night, "it was done with so much sensibility that it would do well for the last time." Thus it was he had said good night on the final evening of his life.

A sensitive, gentle man of poetic impressions, he had been an imaginative boy, Elizabeth wrote of him, and, in the woods of Carolina where he first played, he composed miniature landscapes about the roots of trees, cottages of sticks shaded by tiny branches made of suckers. Sometimes he transformed ferns into small men and women by twisting the stems with colored yarn, and he listened with passionate interest to the slaves' tales of wood witches and sprites. Taken to Rhode Island at the age of seven, he spent his early youth in the state that sheltered Gilbert Stuart, Malbone, the miniature painter and William Ellery Channing, before he went to

England to live and work there for twenty years. Then, after coming to be widely known abroad, he had returned to Boston.

With two of Elizabeth's old and wise friends gone from her forever, she attempted to fill the existing vacuum with her customary hard work tied to a discovery of the new in ideas and the human beings who held them. Lieutenant Greene, for some time a boarder at West Street, was now planning a trip to Europe and his departure further diminished the Peabody resources. Elizabeth had recently taken a position as teacher in a school for boys run by a Hungarian, Dr. Kraitsin. She had also published a pamphlet of his, *The Significance of the Alphabet,* as well as treatises on new methods of learning German that for a while were popular with Harvard undergraduates. Dr. Kraitsin and his ideas became for a time one of Elizabeth's enthusiasms, so much so that Mrs. Kraitsin, before she was finally put away into an asylum, created enough of a furor to cause Miss Peabody to resign her teaching post. Elizabeth's mother, ever loyal, took her daughter's part: "All she has had to do with the affair does honor to her head and heart and has been full of her self-sacrificing spirit," Mrs. Peabody proclaimed. And a little later, Mary Mann was to say of her sister: "It is refreshing to see her elasticity and perennial faith and trust in her fellow mortals." A grandly united family, the Peabodys were, the women conspicuously so, in appreciation, in striving, in sympathy.

The Dial had ceased publication in 1843 and Elizabeth meanwhile brought a new magazine into the field, *Aesthetic Papers,* becoming its publisher and its editor, as well as a contributor. The first issue appeared in 1849. It included a story of Hawthorne's called *Main Street,* which Elizabeth wished might have been more cheerful in tone, and an article of her own, entitled *The Dorian Measure,* that caused a good deal of excitement in Boston with the apparent suggestion that dancing in the Greek mode should be taught in the public schools. Carried away by the vision of balance and order in Greek life within the Dorian State, she dwelt on the benefits that would accrue to the young of her day were they to be disciplined in like manner.

Another piece from Elizabeth's pen at this moment was an essay on *Language*. "The human mind," she wrote, "is in relation to nature as the stonecutter . . . to the quarry; and language is at once the representation and vehicle of all that has been quarried." Important and individual, many of these ideas, but too few subscriptions were forthcoming to warrant a continuance of the magazine in spite of, or possibly because of, its high moral and scholarly tone. With sorrow, therefore, Miss Peabody relinquished one more plan. Subsequently *Aesthetic Papers* became a collector's item but this in no way benefited Elizabeth and her shrinking budget.

Her next enterprise was in connection with the student charts of Joseph Bem, a Polish general who had contrived a method for learning historical dates by means of a series of printed squares to be colored according to topic and period. Elizabeth believed the idea foolproof as well as an immense aid to study and she was confident that the Boston public school system could do no less than order these charts by the hundred, other cities following in its wake. To prepare for these extensive sales, she labored on the squares in advance, sitting up far into the night to color them, thus doing serious damage to her eyes. At last, she told herself, the Peabody family would come into their own financially, enjoy some of the luxuries they had always been without. But Boston turned down Bem's charts and a new approach had to be thought of. Here, Horace Mann lent a helping hand, giving Elizabeth introductions to normal and private schools throughout the country.

She spent, during the coming year, much time on her travels, selling the charts as she went, making enough money to add substantially to the support of her parents, who were now growing visibly older. She had published a book of her own to accompany the charts, a book on Universal History, and people listened fascinated to her talk as she radiated her confidence in the joys of learning, her belief in progress. Moreover, she made many friends who were to stand by in faithfulness when later she again toured the land on behalf of Froebel's kindergartens. Mann said of her: "She always finds enjoyment in her path, for she always makes herself so agreeable that she is in the greatest demand everywhere and the object of the most devoted attention."

More than this, Miss Peabody made her impress easily and without question wherever the welfare or the training of children was under consideration. She knew them and she cared for them so entirely that she convinced her audience as a matter of course. Channing, who himself had so much enjoyed the society of children and who had said, "A child's little plan should be respected"; Channing, whose pleasure in bathing at Newport was enhanced by a long line of children hand in hand with him, at the center, as focal point, had once given Elizabeth his reasons for leaving his daughter Mary in her charge: "You have, I think, a true perception of what is good, pure and divine in human nature, and especially in children. You have a true respect for the mind of a child. You would not for the universe injure the young mind for the sake of making a show of it and building up your school or your reputation."

Lecturing presently to teachers in training, Elizabeth told them that "in the majority of cases moral discouragement is the secret of children's naughtiness; and as Dr. Channing used to say, 'There is nothing fatal to child or man but discouragement.'" On the other hand, she assured them: "If you respect the individuality of a child and let it have fair play, you gain his confidence. Nothing is so delightful as to feel oneself understood. It is more delightful than to be admired."

The moment had arrived, she now realized, for giving up the shop. Several reasons there were, pressing with such force as not to be denied. Neither of her sisters was any longer present to bring intelligence and vigor into the business of bookselling and Mrs. Peabody had become too frail to labor in the shop's behalf. Furthermore, West Street was at present lined with shops, making Number 13 a less agreeable place than it had been, while the magnanimous patrons of earlier days, led by Channing, had departed on errands from which they would not return. And so, the day thus came when the setting for ten years of concentrated effort, the nursery for ideas that had grown there like plants in organic soil, the repository for hope and tears and trust and turmoil, closed its entrance door to further patrons. Elizabeth packed her books, her pamphlets, the old issues of *The Dial,* storing them at the rear of her brother Nathaniel's apothecary shop, and said her quiet farewell to this pregnant portion of her past, alive now, in its vacant resonance, with the vivid voices of the great who had spoken there.

But, as balm to her spirit, tiding her over this bad moment, there was preciously preserved, whenever she cared to look at it, a letter from Channing who had never failed to see and to sustain: "Mary tells me your shop disappoints you. You are indeed called to suffer disappointment; but be of good heart! A large share of good has fallen to you. How many noble minds have been open to you! How few have sent forth their sympathies as far and as joyfully as yourself!"

For the present, her mother and father were living on the farm she had found for them near the Manns in West Newton, and, while she herself continued to travel, her handbag filled with the cardboard charts that had become her present livelihood, she relinquished entirely the kind of existence the shop had provided. But her ideas for mankind in its growth toward the light she would never relinquish. She would never lock the door on enthusiasm even though this other, this tangible one, had had to be closed.

Meanwhile, with the Hawthornes at Concord again, and Nathaniel the recipient of fame, he and Sophia drifted steadily farther from the Peabody and the Mann families. For one thing, they took no part in attempting to improve the lot of man, and to Mary and Elizabeth it seemed that their ideas were not sufficiently antislavery. Hawthorne was a friend and supporter of Franklin Pierce and had dedicated a book to the man whom the abolitionists regarded as their enemy. He had even issued a short biography of Pierce to be used as political provender when Pierce was a candidate for the Presidency. Elizabeth had tried with all her might to influence the Hawthorne point of view and bring to it a greater magnanimity, but she had been rebuffed. And so it seemed wise to leave them to themselves. In fact there was nothing else to be done. Then presently, as a reward for his services, Pierce appointed Hawthorne to the consulship in Liverpool and the ensuing geographical space between the families accentuated even more, and in final fashion, their points of view.

But Mary and Elizabeth continued to see alike. Horace Mann was now a Congressman and his wife, alone in Newton much of the time, with her small children, decided to take in as paying guests Mrs. Clarke and her daughter Sarah with whom she and Elizabeth had boarded long ago, in Somerset Court. Elizabeth returned now and then to West Newton from her tours across the country, her clothes "all tattered and torn," her body and mind in need of repose. During these interludes, the ladies gathered at Mary's house to sew and gossip and to talk of times gone by while they repaired the damages to Elizabeth's wardrobe, patching, darning, even quilting her a new petticoat. Very pleasant and heart-warming it was. But the day came when Mrs. Peabody fell ill, when to draw a tranquil breath became for her a difficult thing to do. Elizabeth, fortunately at home, nursed her mother, taking turns with Mary, helped by her father, until, one night, watching by her bedside they saw her die as though, deeply tired by life's long journey, she had at last turned quietly away and gone to sleep. Sophia Hawthorne, in Lenox, was at the time awaiting the birth of a new baby. She had made the journey to Newton when first her mother had been taken seriously ill. Later, Mrs. Peabody had begged that her youngest daughter remain at home to nurse herself for the sake of the coming birth. And so we have Elizabeth's letter to Sophia written on January 11, 1853:

So very gently she passed at last that it was a quarter of an hour that we were in doubt. . . . . Last night we put her to bed at ten o'clock and I as usual lied down at the head of the bed and she slept more peacefully than for a long while till two . . . and then she roused and got up for a short time . . . then she lay in my arms three or four hours during which time I thought she would go. . . . We had been dreading a final struggle between her tenacious life and the death angel—but no, *her life went out into the free spaces.* . . . We are all at peace-peace-peace! This sentiment in me shuts out all realization that the only being in the wide world whose affection for me knew no limit has gone out of it, and it seems to me I never shall feel separated. . . .

And now, in the presence of eternity, her first-born daughter reflected on the precepts she had learned at life's beginnings from this generous and true parent: ". . . the inspiring love to God, the all-conquering duty to posterity . . ." those things which had made, along with "the idea of personal freedom and independent action," an ineffaceable mark on the child's imagination.

There was at present Dr. Peabody to consider in particular and, as heretofore, Elizabeth took the problem on herself. She gave up her traveling lectures and accepted an invitation to teach at "Eagleswood School" in Perth Amboy, New Jersey, so that she could have her father with her, spending evenings with him, reading to him while he sat deep in a comfortable chair. This had been her principal motive in joining the colony at the large stone house on Raritan Bay where Eagleswood School, and the community surrounding it, was a part of one more venture in ideal living so much the fashion with humanitarians at the middle of the nineteenth century. The community here was modeled on Brook Farm and Thoreau had been requisitioned to make a survey map of the region. The school was headed by Theodore Weld of Boston and his wife Angelina Grimke who was one of the fervent abolitionist Grimke sisters. Weld believed that the cultivation of the body went hand in hand with the cultivation of the spirit, and the school curriculum therefore combined calisthenics with Shakespeare. But, along with the romantic plans of other reformers in the past, Eagleswood did not fulfill its promise. The water supply was precarious, there was insufficient heat and the interior gas light envisioned by the colony's benefactor, Marcus Spring, failed to cast its glow upon the work-driven teachers and their students. Mr. Peabody was wretched, unoccupied as he was, uncomfortable, rootless, his hands empty all the day. He missed his grandchildren, the young Manns, now at Antioch in Ohio where their father had become president of the new college. Impossible to send him on the long journey there; he was too old. It was obvious that he must return to Massachusetts where his life had been spent, and Elizabeth, in her dilemma, wrote Hawthorne in Liverpool asking for money to go toward his care. Hawthorne responded somewhat indirectly to this appeal, having an aversion to being commended for such acts of beneficence, but Dr. Peabody was nonetheless grateful for his assured place at home during the brief time left him on earth. He wrote to thank his son-in-law for the draft from England, but his letter was followed soon after by one from Elizabeth announcing her father's death.

While the Hawthornes were at an English seaside resort, their daughter Una recovering from an attack of Roman fever and Sophia regaining the strength she had lost during her arduous nursing of the girl, Nathaniel finished writing *The Marble Faun*. Soon after the book's completion they sailed for home saddened by the news of Horace Mann's death from overwork at Antioch. To Sophia, deeply in love as she was with Hawthorne, it seemed impossible that Mary could face life alone. She found her sister stoically calm, however, when they arrived back in Concord, and occupied with the business of installing herself and her sons in a comfortable house there, a solid and cheerful house with a wing at one end suitable for a schoolroom should the occasion arise for teaching, as indeed it almost certainly would arise.

For Mary realized, in her courageous way, that life must go on and in no niggardly fashion, that her boys' education should be of the best, that she herself must remain involved in work worthy of her standards and tradition. And so the house she chose was ample enough to include not only a schoolroom, but it could also provide a home for her sister, now fifty-six years old. Quite wonderful, it seemed to Elizabeth, to have this new base after the recent years of journeying to and fro. Here in Concord, with Mary and the nephews, she had at last a grandly spacious room, truly one of her own, where trunks and boxes could be unpacked and material properly organized. "I may *do something* satisfactory to myself and friends which I have not done before," was the idea she held buoy-antly in mind.

In her customary way, Elizabeth began her new life in Concord by working to extend the life line of others. She became an assidu-ous supporter of Mary's new school for the very young. This was at once a great success, run on lines so modern as to be a precursor of the German kindergarten, with manual training and singing games and "the kindly Mr. Thoreau" to take the children on nature walks. It had been opened as a feeder to the school for older boys and girls belonging to Frank Sanborn, once ally and supporter of John Brown, who had narrowly escaped deportation from Massachusetts when the United States Senate had voted his arrest. The citizens of Concord, then, in bold alliance to keep Sanborn among them, had defied Congress and the intruding warrant servers, and now the two schools proceeded quietly with their work in educating future Concord citizens.

Also close to Elizabeth's heart was the possibility that Mary should begin work on a life of Horace Mann, and she gathered to-gether the letters written to her by the great man during their youth, handing them over to her sister, going off one day to Boston in the grip of her excitement at this new idea and returning at evening with the promise of a publisher for the book. Then there were the Hawthornes to aid and abet, young Una and Rose in particular. For the family had settled in Concord on their return from Europe and now in 1860 the three Peabody sisters were together again in close proximity, reunited after the long years of separation. Some-how, the solid, sunny quality that Mary's house gave out made these occasions particularly pleasant. But it was not easy for Elizabeth and Mary to remain patient with Sophia, the baby of the family whom they had helped to rear, their once pliable darling who was now a sophisticated woman of the world and whose ideology was little more than a graft on the roots of her husband's personality.

In 1860, high-minded ideology was given over to antislavery and here the Hawthornes did not follow the two older sisters, both ardent workers for emancipation. Sophia believed in allowing the waters of abolition to seek their own level; she disliked vehemence and the recounting of unpleasant tales—horror stories of the slaves' mistreatment—especially into the ears of her sensitive daughter who had been so ill in Rome, the lovely Una, her Aunt Lizzie's favorite. A letter written when still in Europe by Sophia to Elizabeth tells us of the mother's feelings toward Una, now going on fifteen: "I wish the 'summer of golden charity' to reign on Una's 'sweet lips' during this blossoming into womanhood and tender spring green of judgment. And you would display before her great innocent eyes a naked slave girl on a block at auction."

The death of John Brown had shaken Concord, divided as it was between the pros and the cons. A crowd had thrown mud at the windows of a house where an antislavery meeting was in progress, while at the Alcotts', John Brown's widow and daughters had briefly been given shelter. Elizabeth was much involved just now with the welfare of Brown's followers, the six men on whom he had chiefly depended and who had been imprisoned after his death. People overlooked them, she averred, and she hurried about collecting money to aid in their rescue. Presently four of the men were hanged and it shocked her that so little attention was paid to their death and to the families they left behind in the living world, a world which seemed already to have forgotten Harper's Ferry. Of the two men still alive, one, by name Aaron Dwight Stevens, was imprisoned in Virginia and Elizabeth traveled to Richmond to appeal to the governor for his reprieve. Governor Letcher disliked all antislavery enthusiasts and Miss Peabody, who had come to call on him, with her Northern accent, her assured manner—unlike that of a Southern lady—her hair carelessly worn and her shabby clothes, did not enhance the cause. Impossible it was to turn the governor from his preconceived notion of the prisoner as "reckless, hardened and dangerous to society." Stevens thus went the way of the others and Elizabeth returned sick at heart to Concord, knowing that one more martyr had given his life to the misunderstanding and the brutality inherent in man.

Antislavery meetings in Concord and in Boston were now frequent occurrences and Elizabeth rarely missed one, going to them usually with Lydia Maria Child, Julia Ward Howe and Maria Chapman. One meeting in particular in January of 1861, a large one at Tremont Temple, was memorable for its speakers and for the possibilities it brought of lurking danger. On arrival, Elizabeth was taken in charge by a corps of young men whom she recognized as former pupils. They ushered her inside the hall, forming a protective cordon until the speakers, Wendell Phillips, James Freeman Clarke and Emerson, were finally shouted down and the meeting broken up by the mob that surged toward the platform. Then Elizabeth, surrounded by her bodyguard, was hustled away to safety. Here, indeed, was bread returning on the waters of her past.

At the onset of the war, when New England women flocked to join Dorothea Dix's nursing service, Elizabeth had not applied. She decided that Miss Dix, a rival long ago for the sweet guidance and gentle favors of Channing, would consider her too old to tend the battlefield wounded. Instead, in Washington, appalled by the influx of Negro children—refugees from plantations, separated from their parents, wandering homeless and starving about the streets—she set to work to organize an orphanage to shelter them, seeking out William Francis Channing, whom she had once tutored in Latin, to further the project in his office as Congressman. This was presently done, the bill was passed and the construction of the orphanage begun, whereupon Elizabeth returned to the North to raise funds and enlist teachers for the school that should, she felt, be an accessory to the new home. Two of her nieces volunteered, daughters of Nathaniel Peabody, whose education she had aided and supervised and, in spite of the fairs held everywhere for Miss Dix's popular sanitary commission, Elizabeth managed with her sister Mary's help to organize a sufficient number of supplementary benefits to raise for the colored children's school $1100.

In 1864, on a driving tour with his friend Franklin Pierce along roads lined with spring's green meadows and blossoming trees, Hawthorne died. Sophia, bereft of her love, was consoled a little in believing that, ministered to by the angels of heaven, he rested now from his long labors which, toward the end, had brought him only frustration and haunting pain. She remained on at Wayside for the time being in the house her husband had bought for her, and here she based her life on concentrated preoccupation with her three children. Una continued to be her Aunt Lizzie's chief concern. The girl had evidently inherited the Peabody family bent in dealing with the young and she wished now to leave home in order to train for a teaching career in Boston. Elizabeth warmly approved of Una's desire for independence and tried to help her. Indeed a durable bond existed between the aunt and this niece who seems to have been a faithful correspondent of Elizabeth's throughout the years. In June, not long after her father's death, Una wrote: "This is the first time I have written to you my regular Sunday letter since Papa died. . . . He almost always asked me on Sunday 'Have you written to Aunt Ebie?' and very often liked to read my letter. . . ."

Sophia, however, continually came between them. Her beloved Una, she believed, was made of different fiber from Elizabeth whose books and letters she intercepted, returning them to Mary's broad house on Sudbury Road. Una, nonetheless, did not entirely relinquish her intimacy with "Aunt Ebe," going to visit her when Elizabeth was away from Concord, poking gentle fun at her eccentricities.

A letter sent by Una to her sister Rose from Salem during the autumn after Hawthorne's death gives us a picture of the relationship between the two. A fire had broken out one Sunday morning in the woods near the house of Mr. and Mrs. Cole, friends of Miss Peabody in Salem. It was at a moment when the family was attending church: ". . . but Aunt Ebe immediately sent for them, and Mrs. Cole said when they came home they found her lustily at work with water and a hoe. What she was doing with the hoe I cannot imagine, unless she was casting up an earthen redoubt round the house . . . Yesterday Aunt Ebe got up at an astonishingly early hour, in consideration of my departure, and I read her a good deal out of Spenser. His *Shepherd's Calendar* and *Mother Hubbard's Tale*. I enjoy these old poets excessively. They are so simple and true and say with such sweet eloquence all the best things that we read in these latter days, in a much less attractive form. . . ."

Just now, the only way in which Elizabeth was permitted to deal with the unhappy fortunes of the Hawthornes was in connection with their finances. For there had arisen difficulties with Ticknor and Fields who were Nathaniel Hawthorne's publishers. Mr. Fields had been a great friend to Hawthorne as well as a business counselor and his wife, the charming Annie, Boston's consummate hostess whose salon was modeled on those of the French eighteenth century, had become an intimate of Sophia. And yet the settlement of Hawthorne's estate seemed to leave far less money available to his family than they had been led to expect. The cost of adding to and refurbishing "Wayside" on their return from Europe—Hawthorne's study built at the top of the house, a glass-bound minor Gothic tower, the library thrown out into the meadows at the back, the bow window swelling toward the sun where, touchingly, Sophia instructed her Sunday school class in the uses of the Bible—all this had cut deep into their funds. But it had seemed easy enough at the time, for Ticknor and Fields had been quick to forward the money owed to carpenter or painter, and they had been generous, too, in their promises for the future. Now, however, the specter of insolvency arose to confront the widow and her children. Elizabeth, of course, bestirred herself promptly—for Sophia was no business woman—consulting the Hawthorne lawyer as well as George Putnam, her publisher cousin in New York. The bare facts in the case seemed clearly to warrant a lawsuit but this the timorous and stubborn Sophia would not tolerate. She had always turned her back on the unpleasant as it pressed in from the world without, and she did so now. Gathering up her children, she engaged passage on a steamer bound for England and sailed away to live in a small house in London until her death three years later, a final release which surely she could not have wished to postpone.

Life, for Elizabeth and Mary Peabody, was without enhancement unless they were engaged intimately in molding and guiding the young. They returned now to this pursuit, concentrating on a kindergarten school, the first of its kind, on Boston's Pinckney Street. Begun some years earlier by Elizabeth on the pattern of Froebel's classes for little children, it became instantly popular with a large enough quota of pupils to make necessary an assistant to the directress. One of the pupils was Maud Howe Elliot who remembered that "Miss Peabody was an angel," and that the children in that beginning class stood high on the roster of fine human beings. The sisters remained loyal in their teaching to the ideas of Channing and Mann but they now widened their scope to include Froebel whom they knew only through his books. More than any other educator, Froebel was presently to influence Elizabeth. He became the epitome of all that she had believed and tried to formulate.

There were many questions, however, on the practical side as the months passed, that demanded answers, questions having to do not only with the training of teachers but dealing with a wider establishment of kindergartens. Did not the children of the very poor, for instance, subsisting under appalling conditions, need, as did the more favored ones, a solid base at the outset of their lives? And what of the country at large? How proceed with a task which might well become Cyclopean? Besides, Elizabeth longed to meet this great German ally, grasp his hand, become his friend.

Finally, in 1867, there was found to be enough money in the school treasury to pay for a passage to Europe. Elizabeth decided to make use of it for this purpose and, to her great joy, friends banded together to raise an additional sum, proffering it to her with the excuse that it would not fail to serve future generations. Also, a new friend, Charlotte Cushman, the actress, whose nature was all bounteousness, now presented Elizabeth with an entire wardrobe from among her own things for the journey ahead. While a few of the dresses with their lively color and passementerie trim were better suited to the giver than to the stocky, energetic traveler, Miss Cushman's gesture touched Elizabeth's heart.

She sailed at last on her first trip away from the shores of America and went immediately to Germany. Here she presented the letters given her before leaving by Carl Schurz and his wife, converted kindergarteners both, letters that opened the doors of those "transcendental Jews" who were the Schurzes' friends in the old country. A fine antidote these intelligent people were, Elizabeth wrote in her letters home, to the "rather fanatical and bigoted Lutherans" whom she saw elsewhere.

In Berlin she went at once, taking little time out for the usual sights of the city, to the "Kindergarten Seminary" run by the Baroness von Marenholz Bülow, Froebel's star pupil, who had begun life as a rich invalid but who had been converted to the teacher's career when, in an obscure village of Germany, she had accidentally come on Froebel as a young man conversing beneath a roadside tree with a group of children. She had stopped to listen and had been so captivated by his mode of approach to the child mind that she lingered on. She it was who succeeded later in removing the ban placed on kindergartens in Prussia and she had founded a school for teachers in Berlin as well as the *Jardin des Enfants* in France. Because of her charming presence and superior intelligence, the Baroness was able to win over many fine minds to the cause of young children, men such as Michelet, Lamarck and the cultivated Abbé Miraud. She labored all her life to keep the kindergarten the pristine thing it had been as Froebel first conceived it, free of the impairment caused by regimentation wherein children were given set pieces to copy rather than being allowed to contribute to their handiwork through their own imagination. This was to be another of Elizabeth's battles of the future, the battle against uninspired teaching.

There in Berlin, Elizabeth delighted in the equipment and procedures of the Baroness' school, the gay, bright-colored cubes, the balls, the pegboards and the music. Children sang their prayers and they played singing games based on folk tunes and folk ways, and everywhere she found an atmosphere of simple joyousness. One of the teachers she met, Frau Kriege, Elizabeth liked so much that she persuaded her to go to Boston, taking her daughter as assistant, to begin work there in the Pinckney Street kindergarten at present in charge of Mary Mann. This the two Krieges did forthwith, rather sooner, possibly, than Elizabeth had expected, and, arriving in Boston, they took over the Peabody kindergarten so entirely, in thoroughgoing German manner, that Mary thought it wisest to retire. Back in Cambridge, she then applied herself to publicity for the establishment of kindergartens in general, thus furthering not only Froebel's cause in America but that of the Kriege ladies locally. How altruistic was the Peabody vein!

Elizabeth returned home by way of England, lingering there for a period at the end of her trip which had lasted for rather more than a year. She was given enthusiastic co-operation in establishing the English Froebel Society and now her chief task would be with the Froebel Union in the United States, a network of Children's Gardens which, as she pictured them, were to be planted and cultivated in all the various soils of the land. She arrived back in time to help Sophia Hawthorne in her complex dealings with Ticknor and Fields, and, finally, to see her sister off for Europe. She did not of course realize that this sailing away was to be an everlasting farewell. The two had more or less planned to meet soon in Europe, in Dresden possibly, where Elizabeth hoped Sophia might establish herself. They would spend many happy, quiet hours together there. But Europe was not again to shelter Elizabeth Peabody nor would Sophia ever more see the elms and the church steeples of her native New England.

At last the stage was set for Elizabeth Peabody's lifework, the work for which she was to be remembered, seeking its direction as she had when, in Concord, after her parents' death, she unpacked her possessions in Mary Mann's welcoming house. She began now to organize a training school for kindergarten teachers that there might be a whole corps of fine young women equipped to deal with the highly special task of preparing children for the way in which they should go. From this moment on, whenever she saw an attractive girl she would stop her and say: "My dear, you must take up kindergartening." And she persuaded several young war widows into this rewarding career. From Frau Kriege's first training class in Boston there were only two student teachers graduated, but one of them was Lucy Wheelock, soon to be the founder of the famous school which for many years was to have so widespread an influence. In 1873, a kindergarten was established in St. Louis, and at about this time young Kate Douglas Wiggin, author of *Mrs. Wiggs of the Cabbage Patch,* organized another in San Francisco. At the Philadelphia Exposition of 1876, there was a display of kindergarten work that helped to spread the idea of its value so that more and more of these schools for youth opened their doors.

Whenever a new training school was under contemplation, Elizabeth was asked to lecture to prospective teachers and to return there as often as might be in order to inject and pervade the experiment with her vitality. Here, the friends she had made in other years, on her travels with Bem's Charts, eased her way. Those who had earlier heard her impassioned pleas for the mind of youth came to hear her again, responding with enthusiasm to this new idea which she presented so forthrightly, so movingly, in behalf of the German Froebel.

In her lectures she stressed the religious and spiritual side of the matter, telling her listeners that a lofty and benign influence during extreme youth would forever after hold a human being to the right path. And she gave as example an anecdote concerning a small boy with whom she had had much to do during his mother's protracted illness. She had spent some time of each day reading to him from the Bible, from the Songs of David, and he delighted in these, singing his own prayers as David had done. "The thing we ought to do in the religious nurture of childhood is to preserve a faith which comes from the child's seeing God even more clearly and certainly than it can see outward things." This, then, was Elizabeth Peabody's creed, one that never failed to move her hearers, and she was apt to end her talk by reciting verses from Wordsworth's *Ode to Immortality,* verses read aloud to the young girl by Dr. Channing when first she came under the great man's spell.

But the standards Miss Peabody set for teachers and teacher training remained consistently high and she was as little tolerant of the amateur spirit and of sentimentality as Dorothea Dix had been in establishing her nursing services.

Whoever proposes to become a kindergartner according to the idea of Froebel must at once dismiss from her mind the notion that it requires less ability and culture to educate children of three than those of ten or fifteen years of age. It demands more; for, is it not plain that to super-intend and guide accurately the *formation* of the human understanding itself, requires a finer ability and profounder insight than to listen to recitations from books ever so learned and scientific?

Thus, in finding the logical outlet for her faith and enthusiasm, Elizabeth Peabody was "really doing something" for posterity. No doubt of this. And her pleasure was assured when she was able to arouse devotion to the cause among prospective teachers to whom she addressed herself. She was fond of spurring them to high effort with a sermon of her own contriving, one that seemed to give no choice but to follow it:

We are always either educating or hindering the development of our fellow creatures; we are always being uplifted or dragged down by our fellow creatures. Education is always mutual. The child teaches his parents (as Goethe has said) what his parents omitted to teach him. . . . Those persons who feel that education is wearisome work have not learned the secret of it. I have never seen a good kindergartner who was not as fond of the work as a painter of his painting, a sculptor of his modeling. Teachers who are not conscious of learning from their pupils may be pretty sure they teach them very little.

In 1870, Elizabeth succeeded in collecting the funds necessary for the opening of the first public or free kindergarten in the United States, dedicated to Boston's poor children. During seven years it was supported by private gifts until at last the benefactress tired of so prolonged a demand. Mrs. Pauline Agassiz Shaw then took it over and continued to run it, and several others, with Miss Mary Garland as her assistant. Miss Peabody went on with the role of organizer, smiling upon new establishments, signing the diplomas of teacher graduates, and she was particularly pleased when the moment come to bestow the graduating diploma on Lucy Wheelock.

Following on the effort of seven more crowded years, at seventy-three, Elizabeth had a slight stroke. She did not allow it to interfere with her work, however, rising from her bed rather more stooped than before but with her courage, to balance matters, at even higher peak. In 1878, in New York, she attended a large meeting of the Froebel Union with Miss Wheelock going along as companion to watch, tend and guide her through the complexities of city traffic. But Elizabeth managed to break bounds early one morning before breakfast and contrived to find her way alone to the church where the meeting was to be held in order, she said, to see that all was well with the arrangements. Also, on the big evening, she failed to change into the sober black silk dress of Mary Mann's providing and instead wore the once gaily concocted hand-down from Miss Cushman, which the years had reduced to a comfortable neutrality.

Meanwhile, one last imposition of doubtful nature was to be laid upon the stalwart shoulders of Elizabeth and her sister Mary. An Indian woman, "Princess Winnemucca," so-called, came to Boston in search of a patron. She found this twice over in the Peabody sisters who jointly took her in charge. Elizabeth hired a hall and lectured on the wrongs of the Paiutes, the tribe to which the Princess belonged, on their need for schools and a more ample life. The Princess appeared on the platform in full regalia. Mary wrote a book, giving the claim of authorship to the appealing Winnemucca. It sold well with its title: *Life Among the Paiutes; Their Wrongs and Claims.* The result of all this was the return of the Princess to her tribe with a substantial sum of money and a promised allowance of one hundred dollars a month which was sent her for six years. Presently the fund ran out, the Princess protested, and an investigation of matters in the West revealed that the new schools for Indian children had barely been started. People laughed at Elizabeth and her interminable gullibility. But unabashed, and now well over eighty, she boarded the train for Washington where she personally appealed to Congress on behalf of the unfortunate Paiutes. Their cause remained a just and urgent one, she averred, even though they might have been deceived by an unscrupulous member of the tribe.

The year 1887 brought the death of Mary Peabody Mann, and a gentle but persistent sorrow to her sister Elizabeth: Mary, who had been the ballast of the homemade wagon the sisters had for so long driven side by side through pioneer land; Mary, who with modesty and humor and delicate tact, had maintained her courage and her capacity for work during arduous years. As editor of the *Kindergarten Messenger,* and anonymous supporter of Elizabeth's spectacular campaigns, she had written: "I visit kindergartens, and tell stories to the children, and think about it and write about it and wonder when the world will be better." This was a summary in symbol form of a quiet and good life, the life of a woman who had ever managed to "think about and write about" others than herself.

And now, bereft of her steadfast companion, her unassuming alter ego, bewildered and off center as she must have felt, Elizabeth withdrew more and more into a new kind of privacy and began, in a tranquillity she had never known, a fresh period of writing. Her *Reminiscences of William Ellery Channing* had appeared a few years earlier, but there was the book on Allston, and other friends whom she loved, to be given to the public, old essays to be reorganized. She set to work on *Last Evening with Allston and Other Papers,* which included the *Story of Brook Farm* and an appreciation of Hawthorne. She had not been able, always, to help this brother as she had wished, to get to the core of the man, distill his essence to scatter it at the feet of the world. Here was an opportunity to reach a larger audience with her praise. Thus appeared, in a new edition, essays previously published in *The Dial,* in *Aesthetic Papers* and other magazines.

The essay on Hawthorne, retrieved from the *Atlantic Monthly,* dealt with *The Marble Faun.* Here, Elizabeth places Hawthorne "with the highest order of artists. For it is not the material in which a man works that determines his place as an artist, but the elevation and fineness of the truth his work communicates."

The *Reminiscences of Channing* dealt with the pattern of his life, his utterances, his far-seeing advice, the wisdom of his restraint, the might of his exaltation. A journey into the past its composition had been for Elizabeth, but a journey unaccompanied by bitterness or nostalgia for the moment lost. Pure pleasure it was to be able to dwell on the "wonder and glory" she had received at Channing's hands. Moreover, the writing had seemed to put the right perspective on what had gone before, to show her at last that she had deserved his watchful care, his tolerance, his amused beneficence, and that she had herself succeeded in giving more than a little in return. There it all was in retrospect as she reread her journals, notes, letters, scattered everywhere about her, read of her eager labors in Channing's behalf: the early copying of his sermons, the long walks and the arguments on theology, her inquiries in Maine, as a young governess there, relative to the quality of the preachers, that Channing might be properly informed; her reports on Father Taylor, that sailors' snug harbor and rock of granite; her steady rounding up of news, of personalities that stimulated and nourished; her efforts, toward the end of his life, at relieving fatigue and heavy care, when Mary consented to be drawn into the "conspiracy of repair," going to the Channing house in Mount Vernon Street to sing in her sweet and simple way those airs that restored the spirit.

Thus reassured as to the validity, the actuality of things remembered, she could set them down with the gusto that was her forte. She tells us that her object in writing was "to make a clean script of the impressions Dr. Channing made on my mind in the years between 1816 and 1842; for he seemed to me a fixed center around which was much revolution of thought in Massachusetts."

He had assuredly been a fixed center for her. She thought again of the first burdens he had put upon her, a trying out, an ordeal by fire, it almost was, when inscribing from memory with pen and ink she wrote, one by one, fifty of his sermons, writing at top speed, pausing only occasionally to rest her hand while, "raising his large, devouring eyes to see if it was taken in," he read aloud to her, during the weeks and months, "several volumes of Plato and the whole of de Gérando's *Du Perfectionnement Morale.*"

She thought of their talks at the luncheon table in those early days, the lingering on long after the meal had ended; she remembered the protracted silences that were often formidable for Channing's guests, as for herself, before she understood that these were due to something being said that really arrested his attention. She remembered the "tone and phraseology" of his prayers, so different from those used in conventional public or family worship and, hearing him, she tells us that "this was the first time I realized that any man now, like a prophet of old, conversed with God as friend with friend." She remembered his saying: "He would have us forget ourselves in the glow of goodness displayed in others; it is the *glow* He wants, and not the homage to Himself." Of words such as these, in retrospect, she says: "It was delicious to me to hear him say these things."

According to Elizabeth, Channing had "a singular directness and transparency that harmonized with the candid simplicity of children, but often was oppressive to frivolous, commonplace and conventional elders, who felt themselves solicited by his intensity. 'Dr. Channing asks you how you do,' said a brilliant lady of society, 'and when you say you are well, he replies, *I am very glad,* as if it were of real importance to him. And when he says, *It is a beautiful day,* you think of the morning of creation when the sons of God shouted for joy.' "

When, during the latter part of his life, Dr. Channing requested Elizabeth to go to hear a sermon of Father Taylor, the vehement preacher whom Melville celebrates in *Moby Dick,* she complied cheerfully and with thoroughness, hearing him not once but several times. For she was a wonderful go-between in the case of human beings who held her imagination, a creative quality in itself. In the *Reminiscences* she describes Father Taylor and his reaction to Channing. Taylor was a Virginian "of untraceable lineage who early went to sea and did not learn to read until much later when he was a prisoner at Dartmoor, in the War of 1812." In prison he began to read the Bible and then and there underwent a conversion to its doctrines and its beauty, spending the remainder of his life in the attempt to draw men away from evil and into salvation. His congregations were made up chiefly of sailors and inhabitants of the waterfront. Elizabeth reported in detail to Channing on Father Taylor's sermons, his eloquence and his stamina. He preached morning, afternoon and evening for as long, oftentimes, as an hour and a half, preached with passion and a wonderful intensity that drove his beliefs deep into the souls of those who heard him. She marveled at his power and at his gargantuan generosity. Meeting him presently, coming to know him, she wrote that Taylor had a "joyous temperament. . . . He enjoyed the exhilaration of seeing young people in any . . . large gatherings . . . even in those at horse races in Virginia, the whale-fishery in the Pacific Ocean, in Labrador which he called the reservoir of nature overflowing with animal life, especially with birds." Taylor seems to have shared with St. Francis this love of wild creatures.

As for Channing, a summary of his feeling for Elizabeth Peabody, a kind of leave-taking, came to her in a letter he wrote her from Saratoga Springs where, in 1840, he had gone in search of health:

> . . . I am truly gratified by the freedom with which you consult me as a friend. During my long acquaintance with you, I have felt an increasing interest in your happiness. I have honored you for the noble spirit with which you have passed through sore and peculiar trials. I have not looked with indifference on your enduring trust in God and the human soul. . . .

What more, after all, could she have asked for, what finer tribute than this? It was her privilege to dwell on it now, permit herself this luxury, alone as she was with her past, her work almost ended.

The book was published in 1880 and sold well, thus bringing Elizabeth a little money for the comforts that an old woman nearing the age of eighty might well desire. A little money, a little leisure was enough, too much, perhaps, for Elizabeth Peabody to whom sharing with those less fortunate than herself, to whom activity and accomplishment, meant life and liberty and happiness.

Of Bronson Alcott she felt less disposed to write, intimately connected though they had once been. She may well have believed that the best had already been told in her *Record of a School,* written when they were at work together, a book which had brought Alcott fame in the years of his beginnings. He lived near by in Concord, directing there his "School of Philosophy," and, although Elizabeth attended the meetings throughout the seven years of its being, she was not at first asked to join the faculty. Their far-away alliance in disaster had evidently not been entirely forgotten. However, an entry in Alcott's diary for December, 1865, says:

E. P. Peabody spends the day with me. Still the same sympathetic, serviceable and knowing woman whom I have met from the first. The good purposes that she has furthered and brought to consummation during the last thirty years, who shall find out and celebrate? I think her one of the most generous souls that I have known, and a part of the life of New England.

When, finally, Elizabeth was invited to lecture at the "Concord School of Philosophy," she read a paper on Milton and, although very nervous, she was a great success. In the year that followed she appeared again on the platform, this time speaking on *Paradise Lost,* and there was one more lecture on the *Philosophy of Education* which Lyman Abbott published in the *Christian Union.* Now and then she went to sit with Emerson whose loss of memory saddened her, so that his death in 1884 she accepted rather in gladness than in sorrow. That summer the Concord School gave itself over entirely to Emerson. Everyone who had known him well was asked to speak of him. Reporting the proceedings, the daughter of Julia Ward Howe, Mrs. Anagnos, said of Elizabeth Peabody: "She was listened to with tearful interest." So long were her memories, so deep her love.

During these final years at Concord, Elizabeth was the last of her generation. But self-pity did not find its way into her heart for the reason that it was already crowded with the life that still pulsed within it, the affection she had for young people, the excitement of new ideas, the joy of learning. Presently she moved to Jamaica Plain, there to be near her favorite nephew, George Mann, and from here she set out on a series of excursions in the neighborhood. Near by were the meetings on Woman Suffrage, many of which she went to with Julia Ward Howe as her companion. Then there were the meetings organized to further World Peace or to set up an International Board of Arbitration. All manner of causes to fight for in the year 1893. Further afield, she went to call upon various rich business men, taking it upon herself to ask that they leave their money to sundry worthy causes she had consistently fostered. A few of these men did change their wills in answer to her pleas. One remembers Dorothea Dix, advanced in years, accosting strangers, advising, exhorting. Such is the power and the habit of solicitous love in those whose lives have gone to this end.

One of the gentlemen approached by Elizabeth was Robert Hall Gardiner, her old-time Maine acquaintance who had said of the young girl that she was "wholly devoid of common sense." Now, changing his views of her not one whit and adding, apropos of Brook Farm, that "she had once been a member of a communist society in the neighborhood of Boston," he nonetheless arranged for an annuity to be placed in her name. Such is the spirit of the indedendent "down-easter": rigid, gruff, but susceptible to tenderness.

The moment came at last when Elizabeth, during the first days of January, 1894, did not, as was her custom, quit her house to engage in her usual errands. Instead, she lingered on in bed, a truly astonishing occurrence to those familiar with her habits. And then, four days after the New Year had been rung in, she was dead. Mary Mann's young grandson, Horace, thirteen years old, was taken to see her in her coffin, and his exclamation stands as a more suitable epitaph than any that an adult might devise. "Why, my Aunt Lizzie was beautiful!" he said.

The funeral was held in the Church of the Disciples, a liberal church founded by James Freeman Clarke. Several friends spoke at the service, among them Frank Sanborn and Mrs. Ednah Cheney, novelist and educator. It would have delighted Elizabeth to know that a woman had been permitted to stand within the chancel, as it would have pleased her to learn how live her spirit seemed in death. She would have been happy, too, to know that they buried her in the Sleepy Hollow Cemetery at Concord, in eternal alliance with many long-loved friends.

A fund was raised to place a monument over her grave, but a simple stone seemed best to those who knew her, and the money was given instead as a foundation for the Elizabeth Peabody House on Charles Street in Boston. There, year after year, teachers and young children and the thousand people of all nationalities who enter its doors each week, carry on the reality that once had been her dream.

III

Catharine Maria Sedgwick

Catharine Maria Sedgwick

In 1789, thirteen years after the birth of our nation and three days after Christmas, a little girl, their sixth child, was born to Judge Theodore Sedgwick and his wife in the southwest bedroom of their house in Stockbridge, Massachusetts. It was a night of bitter cold and the baby had arrived two months before the appointed time, but she was "fair and handsome as a London doll" and, in the capable, loving hands of the chief household retainer and ex-slave, Mumbet, was warmed into well-being and placed squarely on the path of life. All that winter the baby, sleeping in her mother's room, a mother too delicate to nurse the young Catharine, was given the bottle by her oldest sister, Eliza, who arose in the chill night of an unheated country house to perform this act of devotion.

Devotion, indeed, to one another, was the characteristic pattern of Catharine Maria Sedgwick's family, a quality imbibed, it would seem, with the air fresh over the mountains, with the sound of the Housatonic winding through the meadows below; imbibed perhaps as well from the devoted care of Mumbet herself, Mumbet with her dark skin, whose clear sense, love of justice, high intelligence and downright honesty made her an unconscious moral teacher of the Sedgwick children. She gave them tenderness and she taught them truth, courage and loyalty as she taught them to face tragedy with calm dignity. When at the age of seventeen Catharine wept passionately for the loss of her mother, Mumbet spoke to the young girl: "We must be quiet," she said. "Don't you think I am grieved? Our hair has grown white together." And Catharine wrote later to a member of the family: "Even at this distance of time I remember the effect on me of her still, solemn sadness." When Mumbet herself lay dying, she said to her mistress: "It is the last stroke and it is the best stroke."

The story of their friendship, that of the well-placed young woman and the older one brought up in slavery, ends only in the graveyard, in the widespread, tree-shaded Sedgwick plot at Stockbridge where engraved headstones form concentric circles about the monuments of Judge Theodore and his wife; and where Catharine's stone, a cross carved with tendrils of ivy, stands between that of her brother, Charles, "the beloved Benjamin of his father's flock," and, on the other side, a stone inscribed: "Elizabeth Freeman, known by the name of Mumbet."

It was Catharine Sedgwick's allegiance to her family in all its ramifications, to her friends of every kind wherever they might be, that marked her as a woman of imagination and fortitude, one who possessed the genius for bestowing grace along her path. This talent, rather than her achievement as the author of her many books—perhaps the most popular novels of her time—should enable her to hold a lasting place in the memory of man.

William Cullen Bryant said of her: "Admirable as was Miss Sedgwick's literary life, her home life was more so. . . . Her unerring sense of rectitude, her love of truth, her ready sympathy, her winning and gracious manners, the perfection of high breeding, make up a character . . . I would not exchange for anything in her own interesting works of fiction."

Now and then, a free rein given a child in his upbringing, an unconventional approach to education, be it tempered with moments of salutary control, make for impetus in the future, an originality of viewpoint, a life untrammeled by decorum. This was the kind of upbringing bestowed of necessity on the young Catharine, cut off much of the time from her father who spent his middle years 280 miles away from Stockbridge as member of the Congress in Philadelphia, and from her mother, a victim of severe melancholia, a disease requiring not only the constant and tactful care of

Mumbet—the one person who could calm and reassure the invalid's spirit—but oftentimes necessitated prolonged absences from home when she was committed to the care of a doctor living in a neighboring town. The child was left, therefore, in the somewhat haphazard charge of her older sisters, Eliza and Frances, and brought to task now and then by her brothers, Theodore and Henry, until they were sent away to school.

A third brother, Robert, a few years older than Catharine, soon became her close companion and protector, saving her life once when, searching for eggs in the barn, she slipped beneath a mass of hay and would have suffocated had he not heard her faint cries and brought their father to the rescue. With even more gratitude did Catharine remember a day, when, five years old, ill in bed and alone, for her sake Robert gave up going out to play in order to lie beside her on the bed to comfort her. "How early we are impressed by love and disinterestedness!" she writes of that faraway time. Such things are "small matters . . . but are the cement of household loves."

Catharine's tender feeling for her mother and her affection for her father were nothing short of precocious. Among her earliest impressions was that of wanting to please her father. "Papa's coming home!" and the joy that swept the household; "Papa's going away!" and the sadness that ensued. And well she remembered the arrival of the weekly coach from New York bringing letters from this wonderful parent.

With her mother she seems early to have grasped the unhappiness of that self-sacrificing spirit. Only seldom, she tells us, did Mrs. Sedgwick try to alter the course of the Judge's life, to tie him closer to his family. "Pardon me, my dear Mr. Sedgwick," she wrote on one occasion, "if I beg you once more to think over the matter before you embark in public business. I grant that the 'call of our country,' 'the voice of Fame,' and 'the Hon'ble,' 'right Hon'ble' are high sounding words. 'They play around the head, but come not near the heart.'" She tells him that his children and she, in particular, need his attention. "I have not a distant wish that you should sacrifice your happiness to mine. . . . Submission is my duty and, however hard, I will try to practice what reason teaches me I am under obligation to do. . . ."

The Judge, a staunch Federalist, chose public office and duty to his country but not without a struggle. "You can imagine," he writes his older daughters, "how much the conflict between a sense of public duty and private inclination affected my spirits and temper while I was at home. . . . The struggle was painful and severe." He then adjures them to take good care of their mother, for "She possesses all the softness and tenderness which renders woman so amiable and she has a greatness and nobleness of mind which I have hardly known equaled by her sex. How dignified, how exemplary in all her sufferings!" But the Judge sets out nonetheless on the difficult journey that in winter takes five or six days, and once again Catharine is told that "Mamma is sick and sent away to a good doctor," while we hear of Theodore Sedgwick dining in 1792 with President Washington who puts him at the head of the table, and, later, on the last day of that administration, begs the Judge to remain on in Congress, saying the country is in need of such men.

During the weeks when Judge Sedgwick was at home, he used his paternal authority to good effect and then it was that young Catharine learned the salutary necessity of intensive effort to counteract the easygoing tenor of her habitual rearing. He kept her up until nine o'clock at night to listen while he read aloud to the family: Hume, Shakespeare, *Don Quixote* or *Hudibras*. The small girl did not understand the purport of these major works but she did acquire, through her father's "magnetic sympathy," the love of reading that became her true education. At the age of ten she remembers her passionate absorption with Rollin's *Ancient History;* she found rather dull Mrs. Barbauld's *Economy of Human Life,* but she felt a strange charm in Rowe's *Letters from the Dead to the Living.* Beguin's *Children's Friend,* translated from the French in four volumes, was a great favorite, while for Sunday reading there were the Bible and a book of "good old sermons."

In contrast to these arduous mental labors, the balance for Catharine was struck by an entirely haphazard attitude toward school

and toward life in general. Everything made way for the girl whose
father was so important a person, whose mother's family were members of the "River Gods," as the Hawleys, the Worthingtons and
the Dwights of the Connecticut River were called. Indeed, Colonel
Dwight and his wife, who became the stately "Madam Dwight"
after her husband's death, had been opposed to the marriage of their
only daughter, Pamela, to Theodore Sedgwick, an unknown young
country lawyer and widower. Pamela and her brother, Henry, were
closely related to the Hopkins and Williams families, later founders
of Williams College, and Colonel Dwight himself was one of the
leading men of Massachusetts. Besides so much security of family
background, there was also in the foreground of young Catharine's
life the devoted and eager service of the colored servants whom
Mumbet headed: "Lady Prime," a runaway slave; Agrippa, once the
body servant of Kosciusko in the army of the Revolution; and several others. They saw to it that the child had all available luxuries,
among them an ample lunch to carry off each morning to school:
cakes and cold sausage, nuts and apples that she munched in solitude, between the morning and afternoon sessions, as she lay hidden
on the floor beneath a desk, reading of the glories of Cyrus.

Here in the district school there was little variety in instruction;
lessons were in reading, spelling, geography, the first four rules of
arithmetic and the art of parsing. Catharine had a persistent desire
to head her class and this she usually did. No one, however, supervised her studies or overlooked her progress. The return home after
the daily session was on the back of "Old Rover," a superannuated
horse brought to school by one of the Negroes. Catharine placed
her favorite friends up behind her and galloped them home in turn,
one after another, while the boys cheered. The days of summer she
spent in berrying, nutting, wading in the Housatonic, which flowed
through her father's meadows, swimming by moonlight. On Satur-
days at school, two girls swept the schoolroom floor after the others
had left, and these two were permitted to choose a third. Catharine
was the favorite choice because of her unlimited credit at the store,
enabling her to leave while the others swept, and return with a

bottle of Madeira wine, sweets and raisins. Writing of these child-hood things years later, to a small great-niece, Catharine tells of the day of reckoning that finally came when, with the semiannual bill in hand, her father summoned her. "My dear little girl, this must not be in the future," were his words; mild but effective reproof, she tells her niece.

Judge Sedgwick was richer than his neighbors, though no pluto-crat, his income barely adequate to the needs of a careless household and to wide-flung hospitality. No money was spent on mere style, Catharine tells us. A large family, they lived in a rambling frame house of small rooms heated only by open fires in the drawing room, kitchen and master bedroom. The other rooms were cold or warm according to nature's progress along the turn of the seasons and the children were far from being pampered in the modern sense of the word. It was the duty of Catharine's brothers to fetch the cows from pasture one mile away and there were errands innumerable to be run, a constant borrowing of tallow candles, dressmaker's pat-terns, staples, physic. Remnants of patriarchal life clung to the household. Judge Sedgwick raised sheep and, after the shearing, the women gathered up the fleece to spin and weave it at home. Servants were clothed from the wool, the boys' overcoats were made of it, woolen sheets for the stoveless bedrooms and "carpets perdurable and well-looking." Not until she was fourteen did Catharine own a silk dress. In winter crude "stuffs," in summer calico or muslinet were the rule. As often as she liked, she ordered a pair of calfskin shoes. One winter, the village cobbler reminded her later, he cut and stitched fifteen pairs, one after another, as preceding ones were discarded because of being water-soaked or run down at the heel.

The careless, impulsive girl was somewhat controlled by her fa-ther's "awful frown." He made use of this at the table to dispel any querulous tone or the beginnings of ill feeling. The children were taught: "As God is love, so love is God, is life, is light." Love was the habit of the household; they met it at birth; it was their in-heritance.

When Mrs. Sedgwick became too ill to keep her place at the head of the table, the Judge called in a widowed aunt to fill her position. Hilarious comedy ensued as the widow, conversant with small economies, tried to reorganize the casual philosophies of young people and servants left heretofore to themselves, "with streams of expense flowing out on every side." Retrenchment invaded such items as the boys' clothes, and young Robert, on a trip with his father to New York, was made to travel in coarse, butternut-dyed pantaloons, while for best he was equipped with a suit of broadcloth handed on from brother Theodore, remodeled and worn so thin as to give way with any sudden motion. "There they go," Robert would say as he sank into the armchair of a New York drawing room. A great joke.

After Catharine had spent a summer in working a sampler and doing little else of an instructive kind, she was sent away to school in New York. She went when she was eleven years old and there she learned to read French, as also she took dancing lessons three times a week with a Monsieur Lalliet of the old tradition. Besides these enhancements to education, there was, for Catharine, the tremendous excitement of going for the first time to the theater, of seeing Cooper and Hodgkinson in *Macbeth*. She looked forward in a dream of delight to the performance. But, as the bloody tale unfolded, Catharine begged her brother to take her away. "I know it is not real," she implored, "but they are really enraged." Other plays there were that delighted the girl, and all her life the smell of a newspaper drying at the fire brought back the excitement of drying out the damp sheets, as she had that winter, to find the playbill.

At the dancing class in Broad Street, she first met Susan Ridley, presently to marry her brother Theodore, an elegant young lady much admired by the somewhat envious Catharine, and sent to school by her uncle, Brockholst Livingston. Two years later they met again at Mrs. Bell's boarding school in Albany. Mrs. Bell was Irish and had been much in the society of clever men. She had a cheerful disposition and great social talent. Catharine, who "lacked order and system," already possessed a social facility of her own and she found little at this school to awaken the reasoned knowledge she was more in need of. Mrs. Bell affected invalid habits, rose late and was much away. But when at times she put in an appearance she had a knack of inventing conundrums and poetic riddles that charmed the girls, while she loved romance and was drawn most toward those of her pupils who were clever and attractive socially. Theodore Sedgwick, Catharine's oldest brother, was responsible for introducing his sister to Mrs. Bell. He later reproved her for her "little dot of a courtesy" in face of the "sweeping courtesy with which she was received." Miss Ridley, however, on graduating, had managed to become an accomplished young woman who was entirely to Theodore's taste.

At fifteen, Catharine went, for six months, to Mrs. Payne's school in Boston where her father's friends opened their doors to her. Already her qualities, combined in unusual degree, served to endear her both to teachers and to the world outside. She was attractive in appearance with large, expressive eyes and a quick smile; she was also mature for her years—adapting easily to older people; she was romantic, ignorant of the world, enthusiastic and loving. People were delighted with her spontaneous and affectionate nature and she was admired and flattered, spending the winter in a bewildering gaiety which she thoroughly enjoyed. In fact, she appears to have established during those six months a new record for charming the difficult Bostonians. Three years later, her brother Harry writes Catharine in Stockbridge that his Boston friends received him most cordially but chiefly, he found to his mortification, because of "a little chit of a thing about nineteen years old—a little thing in petticoats called a sister, merely because it happens to be pretty, amiable and accomplished!"

Back again at home, Catharine was prodded by her conscience, in spite of her father's geniality and absence of reprimand, and she set to work to study French during the early morning hours before breakfast. In a few weeks, on this regime, she found that she had learned more than during the long school winter. But she never ceased to regret those wasted months and the lost opportunities for learning. With this experience, her formal education ended.

Meanwhile her life had become increasingly entwined with those of her brothers. Theodore she had been thrown with little, but with Henry and Robert she was intimate, while a younger brother, Charles, was petted by them all. This boy, so puny at birth that he was considered by Judge Sedgwick as scarcely worth saving, was saved nonetheless by Mumbet's homely powers. He had not been sent off to the smart schools of the day, nor to college, as were the older ones, possibly because his father, growing older, could not bear to part with him. He seems, at a young age, to have shown the sweetness of disposition, the gentle, humorous, self-immolating spirit that immensely endeared him to his fellow men. His modesty, indeed, was so pronounced that for a time it was believed his mental equipment was not up to that of his brothers. Later in life, as often happens in connection with true worth, his powers became apparent to everyone, but the enterprising, the acquisitive, the competitive, those qualities inherent in many Americans, he was without.

The first tragedy of Catharine's life was the marriage of her sister Eliza, that sister who had so faithfully taken the place of a mother to the child. The wedding ceremony in the Stockbridge house was interrupted by Catharine's sobs, violent, uncontrollable. The little girl, aged seven, would not be comforted. Away in the East Room with Mumbet and the servants, the bridegroom tried to reassure her but she pushed him off in a fury of hatred. For two days her grief held her chained, and from then on all weddings, for Catharine, were times of sadness even though she gained new and dear friends from them. As for Eliza Pomeroy, who had long nursed brothers and sisters, she eventually produced twelve children of her own, remaining throughout her arduous life "calm, patient, reserved, sternly, scrupulously true, dutiful in her affections."

Catharine's other sister, Frances, who was married later, was rather more volatile in disposition, as indeed who might not be, excitable, imaginative, and immensely generous. She was an addicted reader of poetry, fervent in her enthusiasms and affections but unstable and easily depressed. Frances and Catharine in their youth were closely joined by their intense love of nature, taking day-long walks of exploration together during the years, and also by their magnified devotion to their father.

There is recorded in Catharine's youthful journal the fact that once, on the Judge's arrival home from attending Congress, she was asked what her father had brought her. "Nothing," she replied, "but he called me his dear little lamb and sweet little bird." Words such as these the wise parent had been able to make seem more important to the child than any tangible offering. Ordinarily generous to a fault, the judge had apparently wished to lay all stress, during these occasions of reunion with the family, on the affections. And his youngest daughter remembered and acted on the example all of her life.

Judge Sedgwick held firmly, also, to the tenet of hospitality. His public office and frequent residence in town brought him a wide acquaintance which his warm nature changed often into friendship. Gentlemen, then, traveling in their private carriages, spent the nights with friends, and Catharine recollected that their house was a kind of "general depot," the great gate continually swinging open, more like a hostelry of olden times than the quiet house it later became. Here, the Judge gave shelter not only to the gentleman in his coach but to those "in chaise or on horseback . . . to the poor lame beggar that would sit half the night roasting at the fire with the Negro servants."

The fire, it appears, was magnificent. "As the short winter day closed in, a chain was attached to a log and that drawn by a horse to the doorstep and then rolled to the fireplace, shaking the house at every turn. Then came the magnificent 'fire stick,' then piles on piles of wood." Hospitality was a large part of the children's education. Uncles, aunts, cousins, spent summers and winters in Stockbridge beneath the roof of the distinguished relative who headed the family. Regard for others and daily sacrifices established a habit, as did the faculty of going without minor comforts and indulgences. These sacrifices became a part of life rather than a duty. They took their toll, nonetheless, of the housewife in charge of the establishment, of Mrs. Sedgwick while she lived, and of Catharine later when, during the interim between Negro and Irish servants, she was obliged to do much of the work herself.

The Judge, whose house was one of the few in town where servants ate at a separate table, where tradespeople were expected to use the back door, was well aware of the honors due him by the rank and file. His attitude, however, was always considerate. In fact, by his native courteousness, he is said to have reformed the manners of the bar, to have brought a closer union between bar and bench. Though a stern Federalist, he was ever on the liberal side where it concerned the emancipation of Negroes and autonomy for independent sects such as the Shakers.

Early in life, the Judge's heart had been brushed by sorrow, something to implant tenderness within its deepest recesses for all time. He had married young Eliza Mason at the outset of his career, had loved her with all his heart and lost her within a year. She had died of smallpox contracted, it was believed, in combing her young husband's hair which he wore long and tied in a cue, he who had but recently returned to her arms from the "pock house," a small shanty where in isolation he had fought his own bout with the dread disease. He never forgot his girl wife and her apparition pursued him in quiet moments bringing a sense of her living presence. Catharine tells us that she well remembered the "sweet, tender expression of his face when he said: 'I have had my dream.'" And Catharine tells us also, a happy ending to the tale, that her mother, Pamela Dwight, whom the Judge married within a year following his Eliza's death—an unselfish, unjealous woman—had insisted that their first daughter be named for the departed.

Politically, as long as Judge Sedgwick lived, there was little choice possible to the daughter who was so close a companion to her father. How differ from a man whose warmth and generosity, whose popularity and assurance, whose august position in politics and the world made him a paragon so easy to worship and to follow? A true Federalist, Catharine explains, "believed Jefferson to be false, the type of all evil"; a Federalist dreaded the influence of

France, felt an enduring tie to Britain and hoped to maintain a strong aristocratic element within the government. Bitter hostility followed the rise of the Democratic party. "The whole nation from Maine to Georgia was divided in two parties. The federal stood upright, with their feet firmly planted on the rock of aristocracy— honest and noble men." So felt the Sedgwicks "who believed that all sound principles, truth, justice and patriotism were identified with the upper classes."

As a child, Catharine was certain that every democrat was grasping, dishonest and vulgar, an enemy to his country. She shared the faith of a staunch old parson who in a sermon one Sunday morning announced to his congregtaion: "I don't say that every democrat is a horse thief but I do say that every horse thief is a democrat!" And, when very young, visiting cousins at Bennington, she had walked the boundaries of the big square family pew while her uncle made the "long prayer" in the chancel above, to right a small gold eagle, emblem worn by the Federalist ladies, which had inadvertently stooped its head in the bow of her aunt's bonnet.

There was the trip that the thirteen-year-old girl made one summer with her father, a journey of a week from Albany to Canandaigua. All through her life Catharine was to enjoy travel, dwelling on its pleasures, accepting its vicissitudes with a light heart as she first learned to do, presumably, on this occasion. They traveled in a phaeton of English build belonging to the Judge. It was "high and easy" and the horses were good, while for their added comfort the house servant, Cato, accompanied them. They stopped at excellent taverns and at poor taverns, they encountered old friends and made new friends and for Catharine there was a delightful novelty in each day. The first half day they spent toiling through the sands between Albany and Schenectady. There, an old gentleman, a fellow Congressman, dined with them at the inn and the men lingered over their wine and cigars till the heat of the day had subsided. Then Catharine and her father drove on to a small Dutch inn on the Mohawk a few miles farther. They sat on the back stoop at evening and looked out on the meadow that sloped to the river. There was a moon and hundreds of fireflies sparkling in the grass. Her father was close beside her with his cigar, "giving out an effusion of affection that was his magnetism." This was an episode to be remembered always.

The final journey made by Catharine with her father was in 1813 when she accompanied the Judge and his new wife, Penelope Russell, a Boston woman of an "agreeable exterior and an attractive vivacity." This lady had been married to the Judge about a year after the death of Pamela Dwight. Catharine was eighteen and her brother Charles sixteen at the time and there seems to have been the classic aversion to their stepmother on the part of these two young people, an aversion made the more intense for the fact that the new Mrs. Sedgwick was apparently untrained in country life and domestic cares. Catharine and Charles went so far as to say that Penelope's attempts to shine in Stockbridge were "ludicrous." These attempts, however, were short-lived as, four years later, a month after the Judge had died, she returned to live in Boston.

It was during the journey to Boston with Judge and Mrs. Sedgwick that Catharine was called upon to tend her father in his last illness. Lying in bed on an afternoon when his wife had gone out to walk, he confided in his daughter that were it not for disturbing the feelings of the minister and their friends in Stockbridge he would like to go over to the faith of William Ellery Channing, that if he properly understood Channing's belief, it suited him better than any other clergyman's. Catharine at once suggested sending for Channing that he might administer the sacrament and guide her father in the new faith. "Not at present, my love," he answered, "for, if it should please God, I wish to do it in the face of the World." But on the day of January fifteenth, Channing was finally sent for. "He came to visit Father," Catharine writes her sister Eliza, "and administered holy sacrament in the most solemn and affecting manner." Ten days later, the Judge lay dead.

Catharine's religious direction now became definitely oriented toward Unitarianism. The fact of her father's conversion allied to the prevailing magic of Channing's personality caused her to main-

tain close contact with him and the various members of his family after this first meeting with him at her father's bedside. The
little minister at home in Stockbridge had never served to compel
her as purveyor of the Gospel and she had instinctively revolted
from the strict New England Calvinism that he preached. For sixty
years the good Dr. West, "stern as an old Israelite in his faith, gentle
and kindly in his life," stood up in his pulpit and, step by laborious
step, expounded the whole moral creation of God, while the town,
in obedience to the law, conscientiously continued to pay him his
salary. Five feet high, in well-fitting clothes and shining black shoes
with silver buckles, hair cut à la Cromwell, he went at regular intervals to call on Judge Sedgwick. His knock at the east door was
as recognizable as his voice and on entering he "saluted each member of the family . . . with the exact ceremony and something of the
grace of a French courtier." He walked to the table, placing his
gloves in the three-cornered beaver and his silver-headed cane in the
corner; then, after smoothing his "numbered" locks with a little
comb from his pocket, he sat down to enjoy the social hour "enhanced by a good glass of wine." Later in Dr. West's life, he was
unjustly accused by a jealous colleague of drunken orgies with his
wife in their home. A solemn trial by jury followed the accusation
when "the little doctor," as Judge Sedgwick called him, stood up
manfully in his own defense and, being duly cleared, preached a
sermon on the ensuing Sunday, dealing with charity and forgiveness, that moved the congregation more than any other during those
long sixty years.

As far back as 1810, when she was twenty-one, Catharine wrote
a confession of sorts to her sister Frances as to the part religion
played in her life, Frances who was, to the last, an unswerving dev-
otee of dogma. Her heart, Catharine writes, "is not filled with
that entire reverence and love" that God requires from his creatures. She has not a fixed belief on some of the material points; she
is, now and then, drawn to serious things but a change of scene
induces her to shake them off as constraining her vivacity. No true
Puritan, this. And so it is not surprising that ten years later we find

her formally renouncing Calvinism and, with her brother Harry
and his wife, joining the Unitarian Church in New York soon after
its founding there.

Meanwhile, keeping up a continuous correspondence with Dr.
Channing, she confides in her brother Robert that she has terrible
doubts as to her capacity for dealing with this great man who had
thrown himself in all generosity and imagination into her life.

I have been trying for two days to answer Mr. Channing's letter but
I cannot make out anything that satisfies me at all. I know this is very
foolish for a grown-up woman and one that has been grown-up so long,
too. . . . But I shall write. . . . I had rather submit to any intellectual
degradation, in Mr. Channing's opinion, than to have him think me
insensible to his great kindness.

Yet it is not without a struggle with her conscience—in the form
chiefly of her two sisters—that she renounces the church of her
youth. She writes Frances on the eve of joining the Unitarians telling her that it has not been an easy step, that to cut herself off as
she has recently done from "the privilege and happiness of church
membership has been a subject of continued anxiety and pain. . . ."
She hopes her sisters will not disapprove. "Anything is better than
insincerity, than feeling ourselves obliged, from prudence, to con-
ceal our sentiments." Feeling, in that era, ran so high concerning
actual forms of worship that Catharine felt it necessary to summon
every argument to her aid. An aunt of hers wrote when she learned
of her niece's conversion to the Unitarians: "Come to see me as
often as you can, dear, for you know, after this world we shall never
meet again."

Catharine's intimacy with her sisters was continually fed by her
love for their children, her visits to them and their visits to Stockbridge. Back in the days when she was but a girl of eleven, she was
already writing her father of the arrival at Stockbridge of Eliza with
her babies who drove up in a sleigh late one afternoon, making her
"almost too happy" after the long wait for them in bad weather. A
year later she wrote her father again saying she believed she would

not be able to leave her parents in their old age; happiness enough to try to make up to them for what they had given her.

Thus, love and concern for her family in its every branch became, more and more, as her life went on, a pattern drawn into mind and soul. At sixteen she speaks of her joy in having her sister Frances' children with her and reports that they are "obedient and quiet." Indeed, how could they be otherwise, basking in their aunt's continually renewed powers of gaiety, enjoying the wonderful stories she tells them night after night when it is time to go to bed, stories without a fixed stopping point that sprawl and sparkle by turns, forever looking toward a happy ending. Writing his mother of her "darling boy," Catharine wonders "if you love him more than I do. Is it your habit and delight to think of him every night and wish for him every day?"

With such an avalanche of affection poured onto sisters and their families, one marvels that an equal amount, perhaps more, was left in reserve for bestowal on the brothers. After Judge Sedgwick's death and the departure of the "wicked stepmother" to Boston, Catharine became housekeeper for these brothers at Stockbridge, eagerly and capably ministering to them as often as they were able to be there. Summing up her feeling, she writes Robert in June of 1813: ". . . There is an activity in the principle of love that, like the impetuous element of fire, brightens and purifies every object it touches." And again: "I am satisfied by long and delightful experience that I can never love anybody better than my brothers. I have no expectation of ever finding their equal in worth and attraction. . . ." Robert's reply was: "Your letter . . . has just reached me; my very soul thanks you for it. . . . I can never be sufficiently grateful to my Maker for having given me such a sister. While we remain on earth let us never waste a particle of that invaluable treasure which we have in each other's affections." As for Charles, the most cherished of the family, it was with pleasure touched with consternation that Catharine received the news of his engagement to marry Elizabeth Dwight of Northampton. She unburdened herself to Robert: ". . . Charles! Charles! I have hardly been able to think of anything else. It does appear to me that there has hardly ever been anything so bright and soft in moral beauty as that which this union presents. . . . I do not think that we shall any of us lose any of his love."

Marriages within the Sedgwick family had now become the rule. Of the brothers, Theodore was the first, marrying the stately and accomplished Susan Ridley as soon as his law practice in Albany was on firm ground. Harry followed in 1817, taking as his bride Jane Minot of Boston. This marriage was a boon to all the Sedgwicks because of the bride's "rare sweetness and strength of character and piquant originality of mind." It was an especial boon to Catharine for an intimacy was born and throve between the two women which lasted for forty years. The various houses in New York City lived in by Harry Sedgwick and Jane, first in Greenwich Street, later in Warren Street, became beacons to draw the family and their many friends. As the years went on, Catharine spent month after month with them there and it was Harry who became Catharine's literary agent and docent when she began to compose her novels. As far back as 1812, he had written: "In looking over my letters, I found a delightful scrap of yours on the sacred character of a pastor. I believe I shall insert it in the *Messenger,* that you may enjoy the novel pleasure of seeing yourself in print." In those days, whenever the family were gathered at Stockbridge with distinguished friends from home and abroad, we are told that it would have been difficult to find a household with more good sense, culture, more ease and freedom, or more gaiety and affection. Catharine, with her lighthearted unconventionality, her sense of the ludicrous and her intellectual keenness, was the central figure of the group. Everyone loved her, increasingly so as the years passed, within miles of Stockbridge and Lenox.

Robert, the last of the brothers to leave home for good, married in 1822 Elizabeth Ellery of Newport and, striving to be magnanimous in the face of growing solitude and a poignant sense of loss, Catharine said of the bride:

She is certainly a great provocative to the imagination. . . . She has a very bright and intelligent face, without being handsome. Allston has selected her for a picture of the prophetess, and it has the expression of a seer into futurity. . . . For my own part, I have tasked myself to the duty of resignation. . . . I am through the worst of it.

Thus did their sister relinquish her hold on those who had been closest during the years of her life. She had begun, she says, as "the primary object of affection to many," and she became "by degrees to be first to none, while still to have my love remain in its entire strength, and craving such returns as have no substitute." Substitute her love never found, except in sublimation, for although the suitors for her hand were said to have reached the number of twenty-four, she continually turned them away, one after another and, in her letters and journal, does not bring herself to mention them.

Yet, in her young thirties, Catharine Sedgwick was an attractive and appealing woman of slight and graceful figure with an expression that charmingly combined bright intelligence, humor and a kind of pathetic tenderness. She had a freedom, an ease, almost an abandon of manner although she never lost the dignity and delicacy native to her, a kind of "Southern flexibility not often seen in a New England woman," as her friend Dr. Orville Dewey, clergyman cousin of Emerson, described it. Her movements were remarkably light and elastic, and the stranger instinctively turned to look at this young person of buoyant step, wearing the long natural curls of an unstudied headdress, bonnet untied and as often in the hand. Furthermore, she had strong sense and a large heart and gentle and captivating ways, so that if she could have brought herself to bestow these qualities on a husband, the marriage might indeed have prospered.

Meanwhile, the isolated village of Stockbridge was gradually turning its face toward a larger world. In 1814, the turnpike had carried a stagecoach on only three days of the week, taking three days between Boston and Albany. A few years later a daily coach reached the town, arriving on the middle of the second day from Boston after traveling most of the night. It was Catharine's brother

Theodore who was first to conceive of a railroad to be built over the mountains between Boston and the Connecticut River, but for long the idea was considered grossly impracticable. Travelers to New York in Catharine's youth took carriage or stage to Kinderhook and embarked there upon the Hudson to finish the journey by boat. A letter from a young friend of the widow Dwight, Catharine's grandmother, who sailed up the river with the old lady in a sloop, describes the end of the journey and her impressions on arrival:

We stayed at Kinderhook till the wagon came for us from Stockbridge. . . . The distance was thirty or forty miles, a day's journey. It was twilight when we reached Stockbridge. . . . When, on the morning after our arrival, the window shutters were opened, the Valley of the Housatonic, softened by wreaths of vapor rising over the mountains under the beams of the rising sun, seemed to my enchanted vision like fairyland. I exclaimed, "O, Madam Dwight! It looks like the Happy Valley of Abyssinia. There is the river and there are the mountains on every side. Why did you not tell me of this beautiful view?"

Catharine herself was always to agree that Stockbridge held the magic of the Promised Land and, furthermore, that her upbringing in a country village was a most fortunate thing. No barrier existed there between her and the neighbors while the high and the low met at weddings and funerals, in sickness and distress. For a time, after the disappearance of the old, well-trained Negro servants and before the advent of the Irish, the sense of equality in the village held one and all. Difficult, because of this, to secure servants of any kind. Catharine remembered going to call on a native woman whose daughter she hoped to lure away and into service. The girl's mother objected to the social implications. "Now, Catharine," she said, "we are all made out of the same clay, we have got one Maker and one Judge and we've got to lay down in the grave side by side. Why can't you sit down to the table together?"

And so for several years Catharine did much of the housework herself. She was a good cook and delighted in her talent for bread making. Then came the Irish to take over as servitors to the rich and to bring, along with their attachment to those they served, a sense of security that can best, perhaps, be appreciated in retrospect. Catharine, more aware of their qualities than many other mistresses, was grateful to the Irish "with all their Celtic infirmities—their half savage ways—their blunders—their imaginativeness—indefiniteness —and curve-lines in every way." And she looked ahead into the future to try to find what might be the effect of wholesale immigration on American society:

An amalgamation of various elements, the cold, calculating, intellectual Anglo-Saxon, the metaphysical, patient German, the vivacious, imaginative, indefinite, changeful, uncertain Celt, the superstitious Northman, the fervent children of the south. A strange compoundment [will] come out of this . . . a 'De'il's bro' it will be, or ambrosia for the gods, a perfecting and consummation of the species.

As for the practice of democracy within Stockbridge village and its effect on the quasi-feudal families in possession of the larger estates, her point of view was more than a century in advance of her time: "We were vexed and fretted, and thought people presuming, impertinent, stupid; but stupid they were not, and we were not philosophers. They used their power; they had something better before them than domestic subordination and household service. Their time had come."

The years of Catharine's youth slid by, the members of the family her focal point, as they visited Stockbridge where small matters of immense import concerning day to day events served as handle to turn life's crank. "The roads are intolerably bad . . . you can hardly conceive of the mud one day and the elevation of the hubs the next." Their fireside "if not brilliant has been uniformly animated with good humor." She has been reading and sewing with the grandchildren and "enjoying the brilliant Harry's conversation." When Theodore and Susan come to stay, Catharine sends word to Frances in New York: "Susan has heard that there is an India ship arrived and she wishes you to select from its cargo cambric of the quality you sent me, enough for two coat dresses made to wrap, with trimming of the same." Also "one yard and a half of fine book muslin for handkerchiefs. . . . I wish there was some philosophy in vogue that would free us from the slavery of these petty wants. . . ."

The cares of the householder did not stop here, for she writes from Albany: "As to candles, I think, on the whole, Maria had better make some. I believe there is some cotton wick in my closet. If not, you can get Tabor to spin some. Candles are 22 cents per pound. . . ." One day, she informs Robert, his letter was brought in "when the winds howled and the rains beat violently. . . . If anybody wants to know the worth of a letter, let them *wait* for one ten days in an easterly storm. If there is any fresh tea arrived, do send and charge to me six pounds. That which I bought tastes just like Windsor soap suds."

And yet Catharine remained faithful to home. In another letter to Robert, from Albany, she told him of a dream she had had, of falling into a reverie at sundown and hearing a cow beneath the window.

For a moment I thought I was at Stockbridge; and when I fairly opened my eyes and saw the beautiful new moon shining on these brick houses, I could have cried because I could not see her silver beams playing on our little stream and shining through the naked branches of the trees. I sometimes think my love for that spot is . . . too much like that of the savage who thinks heaven is to be one great hunting ground. There I have located my heaven.

After Charles' marriage, he and his wife moved in to live for two years or more in the old house—a great delight to Catharine who, in addition to their society, had the pleasure of welcoming two babies born of their union, the eldest a little girl named for her aunt and destined later to fill the role of daughter to her. However, Charles' business as Clerk of the Court took him more and more to Lenox, still a bare, ugly village perched on a hill and a great contrast, for Catharine, to the luscious valley of the Housatonic. It made her very melancholy. "My dear brother Charles has entered upon the duties of an office which confines him at Lenox, six miles from us. This is a sad privation to us. There is a sunny influence in his presence; like the light of heaven, he brightens every object around him. He is felt in all. . . ."

And to Robert she complained: "This place is dreadfully changed without him . . . the house is so still and solitary. . . . I have never felt so oppressed by the changes in our family. . . . The country is *perfectly beautiful.*"

When in 1821 Charles and his family moved to Lenox for good, the Sedgwick house was taken over by the eldest son Theodore and his wife. It now became Catharine's habit to pass her summers there and to be in New York with Harry and later with Robert during the winter. But before she settled into this routine, perhaps to console her for Charles' loss, a trip was planned for her that included the Theodore Sedgwicks and Robert, (a year before the latter's marriage) the classic trip to Niagara Falls and Canada. From her letters one gathers that Catharine enjoyed it immensely and that it did indeed brighten her spirits, as these journeys are intended to do.

They left on a day in June "all well and in fine glee" for Albany, engaging extra post coaches for Utica "at the very moderate price of thirty dollars." At Schenectady Catharine went for a walk before breakfast—a habit of hers on her journeys—and she was awed by the multitude of men she saw at work on the Erie Canal: "We are told that one thousand are between this place and Albany." She believes that, completed, the Canal "must be one of the most stupendous monuments of enterprise, industry, resolution and art of man." She was all the more absorbed in the Canal's progress for having seen it in its initial stages with her father when she was a child. "I recollected with gratitude the patience and interest with which he explained to me the construction and operation of the locks."

From Brutus on the Canal, she writes Jane Sedgwick: "The boat is drawn by two fine horses; the hindermost has a rider. They go on a very fast walk, at the rate of four miles an hour. . . . We passed six locks during the night and we all joyfully left our hot little cabin, where I had spent all my time in fanning away the mos-

quitoes, to enjoy the novelty of mechanical rising and falling. Sue
sat near the bow of the boat. She reminded me of some of the
heroines of song as we waited, in these walled inclosures, the opening of the immense gates . . . which looked like a portcullis to an
ancient castle. . . ."

Another habit of Catharine's on her travels—most useful to the
writer she was presently to become—was that of talking with the
people whom she encountered as she went. Her manner was apparently both sincere and charming, for always she managed to
reach the essence of the human being she confronted. On the
Niagara journey there were a quantity of these: a poor clergyman
at Oneida descended from a daughter of Parson Williams of Deer-
field and thus connected by blood with the Sedgwicks. The daughter
had been captured in an Indian raid and brought up by them. She
married an Indian and this man was their son. Along the Niagara
River, later, Catharine came on an encampment of fifty Irish im-
migrants who had entered the country at Quebec, all happy to have
arrived in America. This, in spite of seeming tragedies on ahead.
For one woman with a sick baby in her arms "hoped" to find her
husband in Mercer, Ohio, and a man with ten children had lost
his wife on the way over. Catharine asked how he liked the country.
"Och, ma'am, and we could not miss liking it, we find the people
so free and hospitable." Of a young girl, gone from her family,
Catharine inquired how she could bear to leave them. "Sure it is,
ma'am, if it thrive well with me, they will all come after." Close
to the rapids, Catharine found a Yorkshireman and his wife living
in a stone cottage. He "gave us a piteous account of his trials: he
said when he lay in his bed he could never tell when it rained nor
when it thundered, for there was always a dripping from the damp-
ness, and the deafening roar of the fall; and then his poor cattle in
winter were always covered with icicles. *'Il n'y a rien de beau que
l'utile.'*"

Back on board, Catharine spent her time in procuring laudanum
and camphor for a woman suffering from a toothache, and sitting
on the roof of the ladies' cabin watching the new moon over the

far-flung Thousand Islands: "some stretching for miles in length, some so small that they seemed destined for a race of fairies." She and the captain made friends and he fired his signal gun several times that they might hear the reverberations amongst the islands. "Don't they hollow well?" the mate asked, and the captain ordered the signal to be given to a fisherman on shore who answered it by kindling a bright torch that lit up his small cabin. He then put out in a canoe filled with a catch of fish to exchange his haul with the ship's steward in return for gunpowder and whisky. Snuggled inside of Robert's great coat, Catharine was happy. "Kate, we shall remember this a great while," he told his sister.

During a storm, the party was put on shore for the night at a wretched tavern where Indians, emigrants, boatmen, "lounged on the beds, swearing and drinking, the house cluttered with spiders' webs and blackened with smoke and all manner of defilement." Catharine and Robert went forth in the rain to explore a French village somewhat inland and here they discovered an *auberge* soon to be vacated by some English "milords." This was welcome shelter for the travelers. Waiting for the milords' baggage to be removed they continued on, stopping in at the huts of various peasants. There girls who spoke no English worked on their weaving, the older women spinning, "occupied as in our farmers' houses." At Quebec they landed beneath the battlements at twilight, but, even though next day they were shown the Falls of Montmorency by the officers of a British regiment, Catharine was not charmed by the precipitous Quebec, much preferring the smaller town of Trois Rivières where they obtained a pass from the *Grand Vicaire* that enabled them to visit the convent. Here, one of the nuns touched Catharine's heart. She was an American girl from Hanover, New Hampshire, gone from her home to dedicate her life among strangers.

Arrived back in Stockbridge, it happened that, involuntarily and almost by accident, Catharine stumbled upon her career as a writer. During the February preceding the trip to Niagara, Theodore had encouraged his sister to enlarge and print as a tale a tract she had recently composed on the general subject of the religious attitude

toward life, on the joys of freedom from Calvinism and the release
of the spirit into brighter fields. But she was skeptical as to her own
talent. "My brother Theodore makes a most extravagant estimate
of my powers. It is one thing to write a spurt of a letter, and another
to write a book." However, true to her role as docile and loving
sister, she did as she was told and in 1822 *A New England Tale*
appeared signed, boldly for those days of sequestered ladies, by
Catharine Maria Sedgwick. It soon found its way into the loving
hands of a public who, trained from infancy in the sharp demarca-
tions between black and white, between good and evil, took pleasure in a story wherein the young heroine emerges triumphantly
from beneath the burden of long persecution while those who had
sought to injure her are irrevocably routed.

This heroine is, of course, a saintly character, an orphan obedient
to the whims of a ruthless aunt, one who nurses the sick, lays out
the dead, is patient with the vagaries of the village madwoman, re-
sists the wiles of the wicked villain and ends by marrying a widower
much older than herself to live out her life in quiet and blissful
companionship: gratifying reward for unalloyed virtue.

Three aspects of *A New England Tale* save it from being no more
than the tract it was intended to be in its initial form. First, the authentic quality of the tale's setting within the New England woods
and mountains that Miss Sedgwick so well knew as she also knew
village customs and the manners born of these. Second, her introduction into the story of the madwoman, a local phenomenon, of
whom in her preface to the first edition she says: "The writer has
attempted a sketch of a real character under the fictitious appellation
of 'Crazy Bet' "—a poetic portrayal done with a touching simplicity.
The third saving grace bestowed upon this story, and one that lives
in all her writing, springs from the author's sincerity in depicting
her heroine, in making her credibly synonymous with things good
and true. Sentimentality, and plenty of it, notwithstanding, there
is in every one of her books the portrait of a woman who has the
courage and intelligence to stand morally on firm ground and, in

doing so, to combine her goodness with a kind of feminine charm that does not fail to hold the reader, being derived, obviously from the nature of the author herself. One cannot help falling in love with Jane who moves so genuinely unscathed through the pages of this book—her meeting, for instance, with Crazy Bet beside a grave at midnight in a lonely wood clearing:

A stouter heart than Jane's would have quailed at Bet's appearance. She had taken off her old bonnet and tied it on a branch of the tree that sheltered the grave and twisted around her head a full-leaved vine by which she had confined the bunches of wild flowers that drooped around her pale brow and haggard face; her long hair was streaming over her shoulders, her little black mantle thrown back, leaving her throat and neck bare.

"Oh, Bet," said Jane, "if you love me take those greens off your head. They make you look so wild."

"Child, you know not what you ask. Take off those greens indeed! Every leaf of them is a prayer. . . . There is not an imp of the evil one that dares to touch me while I wear them. . . ."

"It is a beautiful spot," said Jane; "I should think all obedient spirits might worship in this temple."

"Say you so; then worship with me."

The maniac fell on her knees. Jane knelt beside her. . . . The singularity of the situation, the beauty of the night, the novelty of the place on which the moon . . . poured a flood of silver light, all conspired to give a high tone to her feelings. It is not strange she should have thought she had never heard anything so sublime and striking, woven together by her own glowing language.

Catharine's brothers were delighted with their sister's performance. Theodore said: "I have read one hundred and thirty pages of the book. It exceeds all my expectations, fond and flattering as they were. I can not express to you with what pride and pleasure my heart is filled." Harry wrote in May from New York: "Jane had a large packet of letters today from Boston, all of them praising the tale. What is much better . . . increased orders from the booksellers. . . . I think, dear Kate, your destiny is fixed."

Bryant wrote in his review of the book that this was "the first time the beautiful valleys of our country had been made the scene of the well-devised adventures of imaginary persons," and the English *Westminster Review* said: "She is the most popular writer, we believe, in the United States. . . . Her works have warmed the national heart. . . ." She was treated less kindly, however, by Edgar Allan Poe. He later composed an article on Catharine Sedgwick for *The Literati* in which he said: "She attained reputation at a period when American representation in letters was regarded as a phenomenon." And although he refers to her excellence of style, he finds fault with a discrepancy in her books between the words and the character of the speaker. "She has marked talent but no genius."

The author herself seems to have been little impressed, then or later, with her success and to have been unaware of occasional adverse criticism. "I hardly know any treasure I would not exchange to be where I was before my crow-tracks passed into the hands of printers' devils. I began that little story for a tract, and because I wanted some pursuit and felt spiritless and sad, and thought I might perhaps . . . lend a helping hand to some of the humbler and unnoticed virtues. I had no plans and the story took a turn that seemed to render it quite unsuitable for a tract, and after I had finished it I was persuaded to publish it."

But there must have been more than an ounce or two of satisfaction for this authoress in embryo. We find that she stays on at Stockbridge steadfastly preparing her next book and writes to put off her friend Mrs. Frank Channing who suggests a trip to Europe.

I am not at all prepared for many of the advantages that might be reaped from a voyage to Europe, and as to happiness, I have had such an old-fashioned bringing up that there is no equivalent to me for the pleasures of home. . . . There is nothing distant and foreign that has such charms to my imagination as the haunts about my own home, a chase along the banks of our little stream with the children, breaking willow sticks for the boys, helping the girls to get the flowers, and devising and leading their sports. . . . My brother and sister are *good company* for anybody. Our dear Charles, you know, we look up to as one of nature's chefs-d'oeuvres, his wife is a very fine and charming woman, and their little girl seems made "to envelope and contain celestial spirits." . . . And we have Colonel Dwight who is *au fait* in all the arts and graces of the beau monde, and an East Indian philosopher, a man of genius. . . . Besides all this galaxy, we have just now a wandering luminary from England, a gentleman of science, who travels with a fine telescope . . . and with whom the family are up all night star gazing. . . .

And in October of 1823, Catharine tells her sister Frances with evident pleasure: "I have received a very gratifying letter from Miss Edgeworth. This is quite an episode in my humble, quiet life."

Two years after the publication of the *New England Tale,* Miss Sedgwick's *Redwood,* her first long novel, appeared. Harry, in New York, who was now her business manager and literary agent, sent her word: "*Redwood* sells very well, about 1100 are gone. The sale is constantly increasing. . . . I have no doubt that your fourth work will go off as well as any of Cooper's or Irving's. I think better. Professor Everett wrote the article in Hale's paper concerning *Redwood.*"

The book was immediately reprinted in England and translated into French for publication on the continent. And less than a year after its appearance, Maria Edgeworth wrote of it to a friend of Catharine's:

Redwood has entertained us very much. I am so flattered by the manner in which my writings are alluded to in this book, that I can hardly suppose I am an unprejudiced judge, but it appears to me a work of superior talent, far greater than even the *New England Tale* gave me reason to expect. It is to America what Scott's characters are to Scotland, valuable as original pictures, with enough of individual peculiarity to be interesting . . . with sufficient also of general characteristics to give them the philosophical merit of portraying a class.

Another plum was dropped from the hand of Mrs. Barbauld in Paris, affording Catharine "pure delight": "You Americans tread upon our heels in every path of literature, but we will not be jealous of you, for you are our children and it is the natural wish of parents that children should outstrip them in everything good and lovely. . . ."

To cap the triumph, Harry Sedgwick was told "that there was a dispute in the Paris newspapers whether *Redwood* was or was not written by Mr. Cooper." But, delighted as she undoubtedly was, on these occasions, success seems to have changed very little the pattern of her existence.

During her winter visits to New York at this period of her life, Catharine reports off and on by letter, principally to Mr. and Mrs. Charles Sedgwick at Lenox, telling them of the people she has met. She has seen Bryant, an old family friend, and "never saw him so happy, nor half so agreeable." She hopes he may be able to carry on, there being an ever-increasing demand for native literature. Harry Sedgwick is a faithful ally of the poet and continually pushes his cause. At a party given by the Sedgwicks a lady, becomingly dressed for a grand ball to which she was later going, recited her favorite pieces, among them *The Waterfowl* and *Thanatopsis*. Bryant's face showed his pleasure. At a later date Catharine writes: "I went to Mr. Sewall's in one of those horrid fits of depression when one would cut one's throat if (as Jane said about killing the chicken) it would not hurt. But when I got there I found the rooms full of agreeable people, and before the evening was over I thought this quite a holiday world."

At another party, this time at Mrs. Schuyler's, Catharine had "the pleasure of sitting for five minutes next to Mr. Webster and talking with him for half that time." Her letter to Charles is then interrupted next day by a summons to the drawing room below where Mr. Webster, making his morning call, awaits the ladies. "A very agreeable call," she says it was. "He talked of birds and beasts as well as La Fontaine himself. His face is the grandest I have ever seen. It has all the sublimity of intellect."

Quite obviously, Miss Sedgwick had made a charming impression on Daniel Webster for, during the following Bunker Hill Day celebrations in Boston, she was invited to join the Webster party to hear him address 15,000 people. At a reception at Mrs. Quincy's, on this occasion, she met General Lafayette: "It is a pleasure certainly to grasp a hand that has been the instrument of so noble a heart, but the pleasure is scarcely individual, for the hand is extended with as little personal feeling as the eyes of a picture are directed."

Contacts such as these, with the great of the world, were not, however, continual. Often the tenor of existence was low-swung and without remarkable incident: no morning calls, so much in fashion, and few evening parties, her most assiduous occupation, just then, being that of attending the Athenaeum lectures. She reassures Frances who fears that her younger sister may be straying into ways of frivolity:

> I am, it is true, in a city where fashion maintains her empire . . . but if I was with you in your house, or with Charles in his blessed retreat, I should not be more independent of fashion than I am now. Our visiting is all of a familiar and domestic kind. . . . I have been a few times to see Kean. . . .I have not had the satisfaction I should have had from his wonderful exhibition if I had not been sure that this was a right indulgence. If I had been sure it was wrong, I think I should not have been tempted to go. . . .

And, with the threat of Calvinist hell fires forever erased, safe within the fold of the gentle Unitarian faith, she is impelled to write Dr. Channing not to miss "the unrivaled Kean" in *Lear,* his greatest character. She goes on to tell him that she has just laid her hands on *Kenilworth,* which she salutes with as much enthusiasm as a Catholic would a holy relic.

Channing's gifts, his mental superiority, his spiritual grace, his talent for imparting the secret of serenity, the fervor of hope, to his disciples, held Catharine at his feet as it so held the young Dorothea Dix and Elizabeth Peabody. In December of 1826, Catharine describes for her sister Frances' benefit a recent stay in Boston:

> I think I have never enjoyed five weeks of my life so much as the last five. I have been much with those who *dwelt in light.* I have seen and heard Mr. Channing a great deal in public and private. I have received

the emanations from his holy mind. There should be quickening influence from them. . . .

And to Charles, her most sympathetic listener, she pours out her heart:

One of the greatest pleasures I have had here, or could have anywhere, has been seeing Mr. Channing. I have twice dined and spent the evening in his company, and sat next to him all the time. There is a superior light in his mind that sheds a pure, bright gleam on everything that comes from it. He talks freely upon common topics, but they seem no longer to be common topics when he speaks of them. . . . It seems to me that it would be impossible to live within the sphere of Mr. Channing's influence without being in some degree spiritualized by it.

In connection with the Boston visit, Catharine was also much thrown with Eliza Cabot, intimate of Elizabeth Peabody, and soon to marry Dr. Follen, the Swiss divine and companion of Channing. Catharine speaks of her as her sweet friend and dwells with pleasure on her elevated mind and benevolent purpose "purified from the dross of the world. I have been with her during the week preceding her marriage and have seen her character come out like thrice-refined gold."

The solace Catharine derived from this religion of human understanding plus the power she had of flinging out her affections like some bright, broad banner, held her safely poised at this critical moment of her life when, nearing the age of forty, without husband or children of her own, sensitive and often sad, and curiously subservient to the mandates of her brothers, she might otherwise have suffered prolonged unhappiness. A recent report that she was about to become engaged to marry a man whom Theodore did not approve was the signal for a letter from this brother in which he begs her to remember how "singularly happy" was her present situation, how "sincere, tried and devoted" is the affection of her family, how the "admiration and respect" of her large circle of friends confine her "within that circle in which all these blessings are enjoyed." And lastly he tells her that he looks forward to the exertion of her literary talents "as a great national blessing," that he believes there should be no possible contingency that would deprive them of it. Relentless, these brothers of Catharine Sedgwick appeared to be, in their instinct for possession.

A confession of sorts, written several months after the arrival of the letter from Theodore, tells the story of her inner feelings, suggests the extent of her struggle in giving up for always the thought of marriage:

> Again the spring is here, season of life and loveliness, the beautiful resurrection into life eternal. . . . Alas! I find there is no longer that capacity for swelling, springtime, brightening joy that I once felt. All is not right with me, I know . . . the best sources of earthly happiness are not within my grasp, those of contentment I have neglected. I have suffered for the whole winter a sort of mental paralysis and at times I have feared the disease extending to my affections. . . . It is the necessity of a solitary condition, an unnatural state. He who gave us our nature has set the solitary in families and has . . . secured this sweet social compact to his children. From my own experience I would not advise anyone to remain unmarried, although my experience has been a singularly happy one. . . . There has been no period in my life to the present moment when I might not have allied myself respectably and to those sincerely attached to me, if I would. I have troops of friends . . . and yet, the result of this very happy experience is that there is no equivalent for those blessings which Providence has placed first, and ordained that they should be purchased at the dearest sacrifice. I have not set this down in a spirit of repining, but it is well, I think, honestly to expose our own feelings. . . . They may serve for examples or beacons.

Meanwhile, there was in preparation a family bereavement following several years of an illness which Catharine had seen at close quarters during her childhood. Harry Sedgwick, the brilliant Harry, had lost his reason in the course of severe pressures of various kinds that included financial failures and waning eyesight. He and Robert had, not long since, taken up the cause of the Greeks against the "imputed frauds of some New York merchants." Harry had labored continuously, meticulously, attempting to right the wrongs, as he saw them, of an innocent people exploited by the robber barons of his country. Catharine, for some time past, had feared for her brother's eyesight as she had also feared for the collapse of his hopes in connection with speculation in the coal mines of Rhode Island where he believed he would make a fortune. Of the Greek affair, she had been outspoken in her admiration for his generosity, stating, in one of her letters, that he was generally regarded, especially among the élite of Boston, "as if he were a real Greek hero."

Of the speculation in mines, however, one of the many wildcat ventures of the epoch, she said she had little faith in any of their name becoming rich, that as a family she believed there would ever remain "something ahead we think reasonable to ask." In any case, she was averse to great wealth as bringing unseen balancing evils and she prayed, rather, for "contentment and gratitude." As it turned out, the vision of wealth, altruistic labor and all the rest were to be buried in the ashes of a mind extinguished, "a mind once so powerful, so effective, so luminous, [become] darkened, disordered, a broken instrument. . . ." And Catharine, suffering once again as she had when she watched her mother's mental inconsequences, loving yet helpless, turned now with added application to her career of writer and, in the spring of 1827, published the first book written and produced without her brother's aid.

Hope Leslie was received with acclaim, the book upon which her reputation was chiefly based, and deservedly so. Much careful study of early New England life had preceded the task of writing, as had a study of North American Indian tribal customs and rites, which the author presents with beauty and a moving sense of reality. Indeed, the reader is drawn to these Mohawks who behave with so much dignity and nobility of restraint, in spite of massacres and sacrificial ceremonies undertaken, it is implied, in retaliation for barbarities inflicted by the whites. Here, the blond, seventeen-year-old heroine, open, fearless and gay, becomes an ally of the red-skinned Magawisca, a somber girl, just and true, and they stand side by side to fight the rigid code of the Puritans as personified in Governor Winthrop. They go together to visit their parents' graves.

"There lies my mother," cried Hope. "She lost her life in bringing her children to this wild world. . . ."

"And here," said Magawisca, "is my mother's grave; think ye not that the Great Spirit looks down on these sacred spots, where the good and the peaceful rest, with an equal eye; think ye not their children are His children whether they are gathered in yonder temple where your people worship, or bow to him beneath the green boughs of the forest?"

The trial of Magawisca before Governor Winthrop's advisory council is a most picturesque occasion with its confusion of formality and spontaneity: the solemn deputies, magistrates, elders, and the Governor himself, all unction and gravity, in contrast to the impulsive behavior of the trial witnesses who move at random beneath the dais, and that of the interested spectators who have a part in the proceedings—the kind of trial a group of children might devise for entertainment on a rainy afternoon.

Here again, and most appealingly, the heroine endears herself to him who reads the story, one set amidst bloody scenes and furnished with improbable heroes and villains. Nevertheless, Hope Leslie, the petted lamb of the fold, wins her battle, winning us, too, as she fights against the harsh and the bigoted in Puritan dogma.

It must have brought satisfaction to Catharine Sedgwick to set down in black and white scenes from the background of her forebears. After all, the years had not been excessive, two generations only, since her mother's people had dealt directly with the Indians, dealt in intimacy as a part of the daily routine. Mrs. Sedgwick's half brother, John Sergeant, had been an Indian missionary, in charge at Stockbridge of a school for Mohicans and Mohawks, and Catharine, as a small girl, must have been steeped in Indian stories. And, as a family characteristic, one inherited from the Judge, there lay in her heart, as in her brothers', a need to support minority races. These things, then, she had accomplished. Satisfaction came also with the reviews and letters that overwhelmed her after the book was before the public. "I hear from all quarters what honestly seems to me very extravagant praise of *Hope Leslie*. I trust I shall not be elated by it." And she goes on to tell us that Lydia M. Child had decided to give up a tale of her own on the fortunes of John Smith because of her friend's book: "Alas for my Pocohontas! . . . However, I give her up with less reluctance than the artist whose labors of fifteen years were destroyed by the French troops in their invasion of Italy, for I love my conqueror." The last phrase gave an especial pleasure to Catharine.

There was for her the added joy of establishing new and rewarding friendships in the course of her growing reputation. Chief of these was with Sismondi, the Italian-Swiss philosopher to whom she had sent a translation of one of his essays as well as a copy of *Hope Leslie*. She received, in reply, a warm letter of thanks and, then and there, a correspondence began that lasted for many years. Various visits and excursions were, furthermore, the result of her now enviable place in the world of letters: a trip to Salem, Massachusetts, for instance, to attend the city's Two Hundredth Anniversary, where she dined with Judge Story, the speaker of the occasion, and sat at table with Dr. Holioke, "past his 100th birthday, walking firmly and erect and looking like the representative of far-gone ages." Another trip took her to Philadelphia. There, she received "civilities enough to turn a younger head than mine. . . ." She found it a delightful place and she "saw probably the very best aspect of its society; the cultivated, enlightened and accomplished. . . ." On the way home, she spent a day at Burlington with Mrs. Bradford, "the daughter of Elias Boudinot and once the companion of George Washington and all that coterie. . . ." Mrs. Bradford had known Judge Sedgwick and she kept up all the stateliness of the old style, gracefully combining it with "the comfort and ease of modern times." This was in 1830.

Best of all, however, was the return to hearth and home, to Robert and his wife in New York, to Charles and his family at Lenox where more and more she felt herself to belong. It seemed that she could never press enough affection within the wide arc of her extended arms, never satisfy her desperately loving heart. Young Kate, grown now to an age of awareness, writes later of this period:

One of the most vivid recollections of my childhood is of her agony of grief (this is not an exaggerated phrase) as the time of her leaving us approached. Before the day of railroads she went to Hudson by stage, and thence by boat to New York. She always delayed going till the very last boat, and sometimes stayed too long, till the ice had blocked the river, and she had to make a long, circuitous land journey. A deep gloom hung over her spirits, and she used to take leave of us as if she should never see us again. . . .

When away from Kate, the aunt was ever aware of her niece's education and there was a continuous correspondence between the two:

Your sweet letter, so neatly written, gave me great hopes. . . . Letter writing is one of the accomplishments I hope you will excel in. . . . Letters should be affectionate, natural and graceful—almost anybody can get as far as that—then make them witty or sensible or in any way agreeable as you can. . . .

And now, three years after the appearance of *Hope Leslie,* another novel, of three-volume bulk, was ready for the public: *Clarence,* the only one of Miss Sedgwick's books whose characters were placed against the background of New York as she knew it. Here, once more, is the heroine turned out according to the pattern of virtue unscathed, the didactic pattern of the "Annals" of the first half of the 1800's. Moving though she does along the dangerously unobstructed highways of wealth and social position, she remains nevertheless untouched by any worldly taint, and her warmth of heart and generosity—bestowing a part of her wealth on a less fortunate friend to enable her to marry a poor man—brings her at last to a deservedly happy haven within the hero's arms. The story is laboriously complex and difficult to follow with its changing scenes, (the method of Dickens, overcharged), plot within a plot, its multiplicity of characters, its thirteen-page letters couched in the sentimental, ornamented language of a rapidly vanishing day:

How do you like my hat? [a middle-aged lady inquired of a friend], You see it is a demi-saison, the reign of summer yielding to winter,

and then observe how happily it is adapted to the demi-saison of life—
alas the while!

And the virtuous, indigent young man, a model son, writes to his
inamorata:

It is, I believe, canonical to answer first the conclusion of a lady's
letter. . . . My mother! I never write or speak her name without a thrill
through my heart. A thousand times have I blessed the adversity that
brought forth her virtue in such sweet and beautiful manifestations. It
was there like the perfume in the flowers, latent under the meridian
sun but exhaled by the beating tempests. . . .

But there is a good amount of dependably built furniture placed
among the bric-a-brac that awkwardly adorns the book: the deeply
realized sufferings of the poor, the satire on the consequences of
wealth, the sketch of the supercilious English visitor of the period:

It makes no difference with such travelers. They come predetermined
to find fault, to measure everything they see by the English standard
they carry in their minds and which they conceive to be perfect. . . . I
think he is about as well qualified to decide our country and judge of
its real condition as the fish are to pass their opinion on the capacities
and habitudes of the birds.

There is also in the book a passage concerning mental stress that
is entirely modern in its viewpoint, one that Catharine undoubtedly
learned for herself in the course of sad association with the illnesses
of mother and brother. A doctor attending a man on his deathbed
says: "If Mr. F. has quieted his mind by the communication he has
made to you, he may again have an interval of consciousness. The
mind has an inexplicable influence on the body, even when to us
it appears perfectly inert."

This book, so long and difficult in the process of writing and preparing for the press before the days of the typewriter, tired its author
and brought her temporary discouragement:

Of all the labors that I have undertaken, copying is the severest. I
have now nearly come to the end of my first volume and hope to finish

it on Tuesday, so that it will be completely ready for the printer, and the rest I shall do without the painful sense of being hurried. . . . Robert sold the copyright of an edition of 2000 to be printed uniform with *Hope Leslie* for 1200 dollars. I am quite satisfied with this. . . . I am not satisfied with *Clarence* and never shall be with anything I write. . . . I miss excessively the light and repose of dear Harry's criticisms. I felt a reliance on him that I can never feel on another. . . . To balance this I have more experience and consequently far more self-confidence. . . . I have tasted the pleasure of reputation and know what it is worth, and I know it is *not* one of the ministers of the inner sanctuary. . . .

Accordingly, a trip was organized among various members of Catharine's doting family and she was borne off on one of those journeys that so delighted her, that required so much physical fortitude, and that she so well describes. This time her correspondent was young Kate and the first letter is dated from Baltimore:

We left New York at seven this morning; came as far as Amboy in the steamboat; then we mounted into wagon boxes set on sledges, and were seated on our baggage dos-à-dos, like an Irish jaunting car, eleven in our sleigh. . . . We arrived safe in Philadelphia at eleven that night. We traveled yesterday pretty much in Jonah's fashion, shut up in a stage-sledge. . . . We crossed the Susquehanna at Lancaster. . . . Fancy a lumbering stage-sledge on a covered bridge, hail and rain beating against it, the passengers with a lantern walking a mile and a quarter (the length of the bridge). Yesterday we rode eighty-five miles, today forty-eight, without any discomfort. . . . Everywhere we find civil landlords, good taverns (last night there were warm baths in the establishment), sober drivers. . . . We have been terribly incommoded with turning out in the deep snow for the transportation wagons. We passed more than two hundred yesterday. This (Barnum's) is a most excellent house. We have a parlor and bedrooms on each side. We have just supped on canvas-backed ducks. . . .

Arrived in Washington, she informs her niece:

We went into the Supreme Court. Your father will tell you that it is the most dignified body in the United States. . . . It looks like a handsome cell in a monastery. The ceiling is like a scallop-shell. All in marble. Chief Justice Marshall was presiding and reading an opinion. His voice is feeble. His face has a fine union of intellect and tranquillity, the seal of a well-spent life upon it. . . . Judge Story came down to speak to us and told me that he had promised Judge Marshall to come with him to see me. If he does so, it will be a great gratification to me to see face to face one of the most venerable and honored men our country has produced. . . . When we entered the House there was a debate relative to the reduction of the duty on salt. Some Southern members spoke with great vehemence but nobody on the floor paid any attention to them. They spoke of their oppression—of being goaded to rebellion, of the time being near when "vengeance should stalk about these halls." It was melancholy to see such feelings aroused among our countrymen and more painful to see them quite disregarded. . . .

These words, written thirty years before the Civil War, show a sensitive perception shared, presumably, by few of Miss Sedgwick's contemporaries. There follows an inventory of her social engagements in Washington that included a call on Andrew Jackson:

Began with visitors the moment breakfast was carried down. . . . Went to the House. . . . Hurried home to keep an engagement with Mr. Van Buren who had offered to call to take me and introduce me to the President. He came in his beautiful coach, servants in livery, elegant horses, and two most beautiful dogs. We drove to the palace, entered a large, cold saloon and then a drawing-room in which is a fine full-length portrait of George Washington. When the British came here in the last war the President was obliged to fly. His wife, Mrs. Madison, cut the picture from the frame and took it with her—the only article she took. The President . . . was very courteous and quite plain and pleasing. He has a wooden face but honest and pretty good.

In August of that same year, 1831, Catharine dates a letter to young Kate from Newport, amusing because of the vast contrast to the Newport of the nineties: "We have an apartment that has no view but of potatoes and ragged syringas. . . . Everything is in such rude and homely style compared with our other watering places." However, they find "pleasures and comforts developing. . . . There is no ceremony, no fuss about dress." The walks and drives are mag-

196] Three Wise Virgins

nificent and the bathing superb: "We are droll figures when we are rigged . . . portly old ladies and slim girls, now and then a beautiful young creature whose head looks like a mermaid . . . nurses and children and strapping black women bathing their over-delicate young mistresses. . . ."

There followed, for Catharine, "days of sorrow—wintry days," when her brother Henry lay dying in the Stockbridge house after the long-drawn siege with insanity: "Day after day Jane and I watch over him but we can convey no feeling of ours to his mind; we can get no intimation from that silent prison house. We look on the features that have always been the medium of kindness and ardent affection. They are the same: intelligence, composure and deep seriousness. . . ." Finally, two days before Christmas, he died. And his wife, with the gallantry habitual to her, returned to New York to live out her life with her children, one of whom, a daughter, was eventually converted to Roman Catholicism and later built a substantial stone church, a monument to her faith, in Stockbridge.

Recovering gradually from her grief, Catharine continued on with her writing and, a surer means of contentment, drew more and more of her nephews and nieces about her. She became the core of their lives, their inspiration and their rallying point. She supervised their development and organized their pleasures. One of her older nieces wrote her later: "I never went into your room in one of my saddest moods that I did not come out with a smile that you had conjured up, and most mysteriously, for I am sure I could never account for it; and when I have thought of the change in my feelings in going and returning from you, I have been almost disposed to believe in fairy work."

To the younger ones she told stories, lying beside them at the day's end when they went to bed, stories never finished, continuing on from night to night while, in the drawing room below, their elders waited impatiently for her appearance that dinner might be served. One of her nieces recollects seeing her down on the floor at seventy-five, playing "hunt the slipper" with a crowding cluster of children.

In the three years between 1834 and 1837, Miss Sedgwick published a whole bevy of books. *The Linwoods,* the most important, is a novel of the type that she began with *Redwood,* constructed with an intricate complexity of plot wherein figures appear and are extinguished with the regularity, almost, of the sun, where actions for good and evil are brought sharply into relief and later rewarded or punished with inevitably meted justice, where the depiction of female character is appealing and true. *The Linwoods,* set against a background of Dutch colonial New York, was written, Miss Sedgwick tells us in her preface, to encourage in the young fidelity to the free institutions of our country following on the sufferings of their ancestors in the battle for emancipation. This book and *Hope Leslie* seem best to represent their author in her larger works.

In his article in *The Literati* Poe speaks favorably of *The Linwoods,* saying that "the family of the widow Lee throws quite a charm over all the book" and "Bessie Lee is one of the most effective impersonations to be found in our fictitious literature and may lay claim to the distinction of originality. . . ." In spite of a bewildering design, the use of stilted language and an undercurrent of homiletics, the reader, as in the earlier books, cannot fail to be won by the lovable and intelligent heroine, in this case Isabella Linwood, and he finds his attention irretrievably held as he presses on to ascertain the story's outcome. Was not Catharine Sedgwick, one asks oneself, writing, though perhaps not consciously, for those nieces and nephews she loved so well? And had she not, over and above the moral she wished to point, learned during those snatched half hours at their nightly bedside, the engaging talent for dealing with the ever-recurrent question: "What happened next?"

Among the other books of this period was a trilogy of tales written deliberately for doctrinal purposes. *Home* has for its theme the relationship between parents and children, and the reader is given a practical and plausible chart of ideal family life. *The Poor Rich Man and the Rich Poor Man* is a picture in contrasts wherein Hogarthian caricatures of worldly, urban sophisticated existence are placed against the pastoral scene, its simple joys leading to domestic felicity and to warmth of the affections. Included in this tale is a frank appeal for better housing on behalf of the poor and at lower cost. Miss Sedgwick's social conscience seldom drowsed. The third volume of the trilogy, entitled *Live and Let Live,* draws up a plan for improved understanding between the mistress of the household and her servants, whether these be several or only one, and contains the simple and rather touching love story of a young servant girl, thus relieving somewhat the clinging aura of the tract. Here the author speaks out boldly for the right of every woman to lead an independent and self-respecting life and she makes, by implication, a plea to employers for patience in dealing with the newly arrived Irish peasant whose poverty and lack of training is the basic cause of his ignorance—a timely intervention on Catharine's part at this moment of wholesale immigration.

A warm response from clergymen and teachers, from employers of servants and, now and then, from servants themselves, greeted these books. A country doctor tells her he has "put more than fifty volumes in circulation" and has got "our Unitarian minister to say he will give a copy of *Home* to every couple he marries." And the great Dr. Channing writes her three years before his death:

> I can not without violence to my feelings, refrain from expressing to you the great satisfaction with which I have read your *Live and Let Live.* Thousands will be the better and happier for it; thousands, as they read it, will feel their deficiencies and resolve to do better.

A more generalized approval came from Chief Justice Marshall through the medium of their mutual friend, Judge Story: "Tell her I have read with great pleasure everything she has written and wish she would write more. . . ."

Catharine, genuinely modest in the face of so much adulation, sums up her point of view in a reply to Channing:

> I thank Heaven that I am not now working for the poor and perishable rewards of literary ambition. . . . With the great physical world to be subdued here to the wants of the human family, there is an immense moral field opening, demanding laborers of every class and of

every kind and degree of talent. . . . Such a Godspeed as yours, my dear friend, gives me heart and courage to proceed. . . .

Miss Sedgwick's writing brought her many friends from Europe. Her correspondence with Sismondi continued; a warm relationship sprang up with Harriet Martineau; and she became affectionately involved with Mrs. Jameson. Another European, Fanny Kemble the actress, she met at about this time. They were instantly drawn each to each and the friendship that followed became a lifelong bond. Recently, also, there had arrived in New York a band of Italian political refugees but lately released by the Austrians from the fearful Spielberg dungeons on condition of permanent exile from Italy: Confalonieri, Maroncelli, Foresti, Albinola, Castilla, Argenti and others. Catharine and her brothers were among the first to welcome these pilgrims of misfortune, who brought an introduction from Sismondi, inviting them to Stockbridge, spreading word of their plight, of their need for help. Catharine describes them as having "great earnestness of manner and stately appearance, though some of them were crippled and aged by long imprisonment. . . . They were men of superior intelligence and education, honorable gentlemen, true-hearted, loving men, ingots of gold that had contracted no alloy in the subjection of their country."

She set at once to work in their behalf, obtaining pupils, securing hospitality of a substantial kind, seeing to their general welfare, so much so that her friends complained she had turned Italian. The whole Sedgwick family, including nephews and nieces, began to take lessons in Italian of one or another of the refugees while one of them, Castilla, intending to spend a week in Mrs. Harry Sedgwick's New York house, stayed on for years. Another, Foresti, forty-five years old and a native of Ferrara, was as Catharine describes him "a man of perfectly original character, an independent thinker, modest, with a strong love of justice . . . a melancholy man who reminds you of suffering and wounded affection." The leader of the group, Confalonieri, was "the most distinguished man among them." He it was who had sacrificed most to the cause of Italian

freedom, endured the most with dignity and gentleness. "I have
never seen any man who has so realized to me my beau ideal, the
dream of my youth and the *sane* portrait of my maturity. . . ."
Later, when Catharine went with the Robert Sedgwicks to Italy,
the hospitality at present bestowed upon these unusual men was to
be repaid in agreeable fashion.

Catharine now spent the chief part of her time at Lenox. She was
happiest there and radiated an aura made of beneficence that
wrapped itself about family and friends. With young Kate she became more and more sympathetic and for her she planned picnics
and excursions as she organized evening parties and tea drinking
for the elders. In summer she spent whole days "rambling over the
hills and by the riverside"; in winter she rose at dawn by a fire, "a
roaring one, not one imprisoned by a stove," and took a fair two-
mile walk every day. "Do you know what it is to face a winter's
storm, to beat against the gusts that sweep over the hills, to plow
through the unpathed snows? I have my reward in unexpected
renovation of health, and in an enjoyment that I had forgotten, or
never have known, of the sublimity of these hills in their winter
desolateness."

The scene changes often to New York during this middle period
of Catharine Sedgwick's life, and the letters to young Kate touch on
a variety of things: an account of a fancy dress ball to which one
of the Sedgwick girls went "prettily dressed but not in fancy."
Her mother told her she sent her as an American lady, a character
Mrs. Trollope would think "most fanciful of all." Another account
deals with the charms of Fanny Kemble whom Catharine calls "that
enchantress." She is, Catharine says, "most effective in a true
woman's character, fearful, tender and true. . . . I owe her some
delightful hours when I have felt something approaching to the
enraptured feeling of youth. There is no sensation more delicious
than that you experience from the mastery of genius, that restores
for a moment the flexibility of youth, and fires and melts you at
will." And, not losing track of the philanthropic aspect of life, wishing quite simply to have in young Kate a human being alive to the

good being done in the world, she adds at the end of the letter on
Fanny Kemble a few lines about a certain Joseph Curtis, of whom
she was later to do a memoir, founder of a Junior Republic for
boys, one of the earliest efforts of its kind.

We had a person to pass the evening a few nights since—a mechanic,
a jeweler. . . . He has about thirty boys who all live with him. His object
is to have them well taught their trade and well educated in other respects and to have vigilant moral education going on. They have a
republican self-government. They select juries from their own body and
always submit to the verdict rendered. During the cholera he determined
it was best to keep up the establishment. One of the boys had a dramatic
turn—wrote a little play. Some of them were fond of music and others
had a taste for drawing and made up scenery. Among them they got up
private theatricals and when all the rest of the city were flying, or in
consternation, they were well and gay, did their day's work. . . . He is
one of the most interesting philanthropists I have ever met with. . . .

In the early summer of 1833, the Robert Sedgwicks and Catharine
set out on a journey to Virginia Springs. Niece Kitty is given a
detailed description by her aunt of the seemingly haphazard but
pleasurable tour. En route to Richmond she writes:

The boat from Norfolk was delightful . . . a little cabin on deck for
the ladies, a sort of boudoir furnished with three sofas, low chairs, a
Boston rocking chair and mirrors enough for a party of Circassian
beauties. [At Richmond] Mr. Randolph—"Randolph of Wilton"—
called to see us and invited us to take a drive six miles to his estate of
Wilton. His parents are dead and this young man . . . has succeeded to
the estate. We went in a carriage and he on a fine blood-horse, and his
cousin Harrison on the best horse he could get, attended us. The estate
comprises 2196 acres of land on the James River and about 150 slaves.
[The house], the spacious wainscoted rooms, the high ceilings, the broad
staircase and fine hall give you a very magnificent idea of the grandeur
of its former proprietors. . . . But such ruin! Broken-down fences, a
falling piazza, defaced paint, bannisters tied up with rope, etc. The walls
of one of the apartments were covered with ancestral paintings. . . . The
slaves fancy this room is haunted and it is a common punishment for

the young offenders to shut them in this spectral apartment. . . . The general aspect of the house is that of a forlorn ruin. The gallant young proprietor has, however, an ample fortune and is going to put it in complete order and, as it is, he gives déjeuners and balls.

Of the slaves, Catharine noticed a contrast between the well-dressed, civil, accomplished hotel servants and those on the street and in the country who seemed downcast and often surly. In Richmond slaves were not permitted to be out after nine at night.

There follows an account of a sixty-mile drive over the Virginia roads of that era, starting before three o'clock on a rainy morning, driving through sand and clay that in the North would have been considered impassable. In the midst of a downpour the thorough-brace of the carriage broke. With the help of half a dozen Negroes the coach was pried up and "a chain made for the wheel shoe" was substituted. On through beautiful mountain scenery to a summit called the "Notch." This "the grandest scene my eyes ever lit on, save Niagara. . . . We forgot all our fatigues, anxieties, joltings . . . but it was such a brief pleasure that I am going up the mountain again this afternoon to enjoy one more view of it." At Virginia Springs they ate a sumptuous breakfast of venison steak and found the greatest abundance of "prime luxuries" including cleanliness and quiet and the great baths of which "no warm bath can be more delicious." But Catharine's enjoyment was a good deal marred by the "horrid blight of slavery which seems to me far worse since I have seen it."

From Stockbridge and Lenox during the summer that followed, a series of generous tributes issued from Miss Sedgwick's pen. One concerned Fanny Kemble Butler's recent book: "It is like herself, and she is a complex being, made up of glorious faculties, delightful accomplishments, immeasurable sensibility and half a hundred little faults. Let those find them and mark them who have an appetite so to do. I have not. . . ."

Then, a eulogy of Harriet Martineau who had paid an eight-day visit to the Berkshire valley on her return from a tour of the nation.

This first impression was later somewhat modified when Miss Sedg-wick and Miss Martineau took opposing sides in the course of the Civil War and when the Englishwoman showed herself to possess more than a touch of egotism and self-righteousness. Now, however, in the face of her immense accomplishment, she seemed someone to admire without reserve. For had she not done much "to still the cry of hunger forever in the poor man's cottage"?

A fresh encomium of Channing appeared in one of Miss Sedg-wick's letters at about this time, written after he had presided at the funeral of a Boston friend:

Dr. Channing made the prayer. His filial sentiment to the Deity always impresses me; it is not merely the confidence of a child to the father, but the tenderness that is most commonly felt to the mother; he is like the child who throws himself on his mother's bosom, sure there is repose there, and love enough for all his wants. His voice is the most tranquilizing sound I ever heard. I think if my passions were in ever such a storm, it would calm me. . . .

While in Boston, Catharine was much gratified to hear from "Miss P." (probably Elizabeth Peabody) of the pleasure a certain intelligent factory girl had had from reading *Home,* while a gentle-man of Miss P.'s acquaintance had left her one day to return to his library that he might go on reading *The Linwoods.* "It takes me half an hour to read a page," he said. "I should as soon think of galloping through Paradise." Catharine admits now, at last, to the satisfaction that "these bonbons" bring her. Also in Boston under the guidance, possibly, of Miss Peabody, certainly at Channing's behest, she had gone to hear Father Taylor at the Seaman's Bethel and had been stirred by this preacher's glowing zeal. "He does not scourge his brains by midnight lamps but comes panting with good news from his Father's house."

December 17, 1835, brought the Great Fire to New York City and to Catharine's active experience. It started close to her brother Robert's office on an evening when the mercury stood at zero and the hoses froze so that the firemen were helpless. Flames spread through the packed warehouses of the lower city and buildings were blown up in an attempt to arrest the flames. The fire continued to rage when Catharine went to bed and next morning she beheld a scene of sweeping desolation that reached from the ashes of the Stock Exchange to the water's edge, while carts and coaches moved in all directions filled with "boxes, cans and every species of commodity." The sidewalks were crowded with police, the militia, firemen and beggars carrying away half-burned blankets and other articles retrieved from annihilation—"a striking manifestation of the instability of human possessions." Catharine spent two almost sleepless nights in her room high in Jane Sedgwick's house, an improvised watchtower from whence she held a vigil over the simmering coals below. On the third night a band of Philadelphia firemen who had volunteered their help came to keep watch and Catharine could sleep until daylight, which brought a sight of the city "beyond any desolation I ever witnessed," and a hazy, murky atmosphere "where you do not see the bounds but only the fragments of walls defined in the mist—a world in ruins."

This was not to be the city's only catastrophe of the period for, less than two years later, came the spectacular financial crash in May of 1837, "a general bursting of bubbles" bringing panic, confusion and dismay. Dry-goods shops were "almost deserted save Stewart's, and you will see the line of counters with clerks on one side like so many ghosts. . . . Nothing is talked of but 'who has failed today' and the buried carcasses of today are covered by the fresh ones of tomorrow."

Invitations to parties within the world of fashion continued, however, most of them declined by Miss Sedgwick unless a new idea or an interesting human being was the bait. She wrote Kate of going to the house of her friend Eliza Cabot, now Mrs. Follen, who gave an abolition party for the Grimke sisters and she spoke of seeing Ellen Tree, "a very charming actress free from affectation of any sort; after Fanny, incomparably the first actress we have had." There was also a gathering at Jane Sedgwick's composed of Count Confalonieri, Albinola and Foresti, Bryant, Dr. Follen and brother Theodore. Catharine was sorry that Washington Irving declined because he was going to the country.

A certain number of philanthropic acts of Catharine's punctuated the days that flowed by. A visit after Sunday morning church to "poor Francis Brown—his arm mangled in a paper factory—amputated immediately after. He says he neither felt the crush nor the amputation. . . . It was more than I could look upon." Then there was the call she made upon Polish political exiles, the wife being ill. A young daughter came to the door while "two gentlemen opened a window upstairs and beckoned to a hackman turning the corner." When Catharine was admitted into the interior, "Mrs. G. raised herself from her pillow in a paroxysm of grief . . . and poor G. was screwing up a little coffin." She had given birth the day previous to a stillborn infant. A friend who sat beside her kept assuring the poor woman that she would presently find that all was for the best but "this obvious truth fell as impotent as such consolations usually do. . . . I could not help crying with her, there was something so simple and true in her grief." The daughter, Angélique, aged ten, was her mother's nurse and had packed away everything in the place, as the unfortunate people were obliged to move the next day. "A German woman who looked like one of Scott's old women and was all the time haranguing Madame on the inutility of weeping finally came up to the bedside, the little coffin tucked under one arm, and gesturing with the other!"

Among organized philanthropies, "The Woman's Prison Association of New York" made deep inroads on Miss Sedgwick's time. She had thrown herself eagerly into the work and for long years served as its president, regularly visiting prisons and hospitals, The Tombs, Blackwell and Randall Islands. Genial, outgoing and readily moved to compassion, her extraordinary power for winning confidence made her a sure target for the confessions of the sick and dying.

Now and then, Catharine's normally strong constitution suffered a setback which usually slipped into the long-established pattern of a severe sick headache. In her youth the heroic style of treatment had been in vogue: bleeding, blistering, a course of calomel, so drastic indeed that only the hardiest could withstand this attempt at cure.

But, headaches or no, her basic stability was of a more protracted kind than that of her brothers. During the summer of 1835 it became necessary for her to accompany her brother Charles to Saratoga Springs on a pilgrimage in search of health, and two or three years later Robert Sedgwick had a stroke. With the arrival of spring in 1839, however, he was so much improved that it was thought wise to speed his recovery by means of the favorite mid-Victorian panacea, sending him to Europe "for a change." A family party was thus formed consisting of Robert, his wife and his eldest daughter, Catharine and her favorite Kitty and one other among the nieces: five ladies and one gentleman. They sailed away on a month-long crossing bound for England. While they were gone, Theodore Sedgwick, head of the family, died of apoplexy, thus leaving Catharine with but half the original number of her brothers.

They landed in June at Portsmouth and were at once drawn into the glamorous pleasures of English hospitality which was lavishly proffered these particular guests from overseas. For in England, as later in Italy, Miss Sedgwick and oftentimes the whole Sedgwick party, which she drew after her as the magnet draws its filings, were fêted in very special fashion, owing partly to her reputation as a novelist, partly to letters of introduction from Fanny Kemble and lastly to the favors she had herself bestowed on various natives of these two countries.

Their entertainment began with the landing in Portsmouth, dwelling place of Basil Hall, a travel writer, who in America a few years earlier had spent some time in Stockbridge, met Catharine there and thought it his duty as a member of the master race to draw her attention to errors in the writing of her novel *Hope Leslie*. She had taken his criticism with a light touch and with a certain humor so that no serious constraint had arisen between them. Now came her reward, as he and his wife responded at once to the cards sent by the Sedgwicks on arrival, putting themselves at the disposal of the travelers, arranging a visit, among others, to Nelson's flagship, *Victory,* where they beheld the brass plate in the quarter-deck with its inscription, "Here Nelson fell," and were led to the narrow cockpit stateroom and shown the beam that supported the hero's head when he lay dying. Robert Sedgwick was overcome with emotion here and Catharine, watching her brother now, thought of the day when, a small boy, he ran up the lane at home, tossing his cap in the air and shouting: "Nelson! Victory!"

Later the party was conveyed to the Isle of Wight on the Naval Commandant's yacht, "the prettiest thing that has floated since Cleopatra's barge," and they had a fine sense of holiday delight at their first contact with the English countryside, with the hedges and flowering shrubs, the thatched and mossy cottages, gardens of verbena, stock, roses, with the songs of nightingale, lark, cuckoo, blackbird and, enhancing the whole, a rainbow arching high above the Solent.

Back at Portsmouth they walked about the country lanes and here Catharine slipped into the habit formed at home of conversing with the inhabitants, as had George Borrow in Wales, even entering cottages by the wayside where, owing to a certain note of sympathy which softened her inquiries, she was well received. She was pleased with the general air of neatness but distressed at tales of grinding poverty, the struggle for bread, the look of sadness upon the face of one man who supported his family by gathering from cliffs, supposedly inaccessible, the eggs of sea fowl and selling them to "people in a decline." For the privilege of this difficult and dangerous work he paid two guineas a year to the lord of the manor, and of prospects for his four sons Catharine was told there were none. Walking beside a young woman who staggered beneath a load of dry furze, Catharine begged to carry the woman's baby not a month old. Commenting on the young mother's healthy appearance, she was told: "Ah, that's natural to me. My mother had red cheeks in her coffin."

At Winchester, conveyed there by the Halls on a section of railroad but two days open and lined with hurrahing people, Catharine was overwhelmed by the Cathedral tombs with their contents of bones belonging to the Saxon kings from Canute to William Rufus. Here they stayed at the local inn and sat down to soup, salmon and mutton chops "served as in a gentleman's house, with elegance and accuracy." This was a vivid contrast to the inns of provincial America, while the grounds of the places they visited were perfection: "Every tree, shrub and little flower in its right place and nothing present that should not be there. Our grounds are like our society where you meet every degree of civilization," she wrote.

During much of the subsequent journey to London, Catharine and the nieces sat on top of the coach, having discovered the pleasures of this democratic way of procedure that included a fine view of the countryside and illuminating conversations with the coachman. Approaching Miss Mitford's house in a small village near Reading, the man pointed to a figure in the garden below. "Now, you would not take that little body there for the great author, would you?" The Sedgwicks descended, having written earlier to announce their coming. Miss Mitford, "truly a 'little body,'" with hair as white as snow, lived with her old father in a house as small as the humblest in a Berkshire village but maintaining four or five servants and a pair of horses. "I must show you my geraniums while it is light," Miss Mitford said in a sweet low tone, "for I love them next to my father."

At London, they took lodgings in Halfmoon Street: drawing room, dining room and four bedrooms, paying eight guineas a week, a sum that included firing and attendance. Firing comprised cooking. They sat often in their windows looking out at the passing scene, listening to the ballad singers, and Catharine was outraged by the display of grandeur in the carriages of the great, the role played therein by milord's coachman and other servants.

Fancy a man driving, with a militia general's hat, feathers and all, with three footmen, one seated beside him and two behind, all with white coats, scarlet plush breeches, white silk stockings, rosettes on their shoes and gold-headed batons in their whitegloved hands. There must be something "rotten in the state" when God's creatures, "possible angels," as our friend Dr. Channing calls all humankind, look up to a station behind a lord's coach as a privileged place.

Listening to Italian opera at Covent Garden, Catharine was interested to see that the "little Queen" sat in her box behind a curtain, as carefully hidden as an oriental monarch, in order to have her enjoyment unobserved and in tranquillity, but Catharine's own enjoyment of the evening was somewhat marred by the aspect of the leading ballerina, a lovely young girl whose skirt, it seems, was far too short, "her positions often disgusting. When she raised her leg to a right angle with her body, I could have exclaimed as Carlyle did, 'Merciful Heaven! Where will it end?'" Going to Sunday service in St. George's chapel at Windsor, Catharine felt the service careless and prescribed, with the hurried singsong of the prayers, and she thought with nostalgia of the summer services at home in the long parlor at Stockbridge, "the door open into the garden, the children strewn around the door step, their young faces touched with an expression . . . such as glows in the faces of the cherubs in the old pictures . . . the blue sky and everlasting hills in harmony with the pure and simple doctrine our friend Dr. Follen taught us. . . . Here, it is the temple that is greatest—the monuments of past ages."

The parties and encounters with the great now came thick and fast: a breakfast in the small, twenty-five-foot house of the famous and preternaturally kind Samuel Rogers, a house that looked out on the Green Park and held, among other treasures, the document in which Milton signed over to his publisher for ten pounds the copyright of *Paradise Lost*. Here, Catharine met Macaulay: "His conversation resembles his writings; it is rich and delightful. . . . Some may think he talks too much, but none, except from their own impatient vanity, could wish it were less."

Next morning they met Carlyle at lunch with Joanna Baillie, "Scott's favorite friend—a pleasant figure, delicate, erect, graceful, wears her own gray hair and the prettiest of brown silk gowns—free of pedantry and all modes of affectation."

Cutting across the English caste system by means of their various introductory letters, they had access to human beings who would not be apt to meet one another: suburban gentry, London aristocrats, writers, scholars, scaling thus the ladder of evening entertainment that ranged from six o'clock family tea with the Carlyles to a magnificent concert at Lansdowne House. Catharine, soon after her arrival, had dined with the Marquess of Lansdowne and his wife. He was the great Whig leader and counselor of Queen Victoria and was noted for his antislavery views. She had driven alone and in trepidation to the splendid house, "received by a half dozen servants in white and crimson liveries and announced through magnificent apartments." She felt, she said, no more embarrassed than she would at home and found "nothing of the studied stiffness we have heard alleged of English society." The concert was a different matter. It was held in a "superb gallery of sculpture with carved and gilded ceiling . . . one of the choicest collections of antiques in the kingdom. . . . When Kate and I entered, the apartments were filled with some hundreds of people of the first station and fashion in the land, luxuriously dressed and sparkling with diamonds, a sea of faces as strange as their diamonds to me. It was an overpowering kind of solitude." Catharine slipped into a vacant place and had begun to be quite comfortable in her solitary role when young Kate "with something of the feeling of Columbus' men on seeing land" exclaimed that two friends were approaching. "These gentlemen made their way to us and dissipated our forlornness." Later the Americans found that they had previously met several others: Bulwer and Mrs. Norton who was one of the four brilliant Sheridan sisters. Catharine had but recently read "that miserable deathbed letter from their penniless grandfather," and she was struck with the shifting scenes of life.

Of Carlyle, Miss Sedgwick said: "His head would throw a phrenologist into ecstasies . . . his eyes have a preternatural brilliancy," and she was reminded on seeing him of what Lockhart had said apropos of the size of Webster's head, that "he had brains enough to fill half a dozen hats." Carlyle spoke of Webster, saying that

"Webster's eyes were like dull furnaces that only wanted blowing on to lighten them up." And it made her happy to hear the Carlyles say that Emerson had "seemed to them an angel," that they had never lost their first impression of "his celestial nature."

There was an evening spent at the house of Henry Hallam, the historian; Sidney Smith was present, the famous wit who "seemed to have enjoyed his own fun and to have fattened on it." He had an unqualified admiration for Dickens and told them that ten thousand copies of each issue of *Nicholas Nickleby* had been sold. A youthful member of the company, recipient of some recent literary prize, "ventured to throw himself into the arena against this old iron king." But Sidney Smith took the young man in charge and "crackled him up, flesh, bones and all."

Of other people in London during this 1839 summer Catharine tells us that meeting them "was like seeing the originals of familiar pictures: Jane Porter, Mrs. Opie, Mrs. Austen, Lockhart and Milman." Catharine, when young, had cried her eyes out over the tales of Mrs. Opie who had now adopted the Quaker faith and costume and who possessed "a fair and cheerful face." Another meeting was with Robert Owen of Lanark who, "pushing his theories with unabated zeal," wasted an hour trying to convince her he could make the world over and "set all to rights" if he could "substitute two or three truths for two or three prevailing errors."

Of a gentleman whom Catharine refers to as K—n, presumably the poet John Kenyon, she writes in glowing terms. The relationship had got off to a start from his having presented the Sedgwicks with a "ticket for six" to one of his breakfasts. Later Catharine dined with him, "the pleasantest dinner of all those in London." She had known of Kenyon before coming to England as the friend of many of their friends at home and as the author of "very charming published poetry." He is, she states in her journal, the "personification of the English gentleman of Addison's time. . . . I have heard more clever things from him than from anyone else in London . . . his manners those of a man who has all the world's conventionalities at his command and yet whose nature is too strong for them, so that the stream of humanity comes gushing fresh from its fountain without heeding the prescribed channels." Had the warm sensibilities of Catharine Sedgwick been touched, at fifty, her spinster heart moved by this altogether charming gentleman who turns up in her company again in Italy? How understandable this would seem to be and how urgently the good fairy in us propels us toward the wish for a romantic consummation.

In summary of her impressions after a month in London, Catharine was struck with the identity of English and New England character but shocked to find how very little interest in America there was and what immense ignorance of her country prevailed. Young Kate, for example, was asked if there were a theater there. And in spite of her generous and widespread entertainment, she saw nothing to change a long-held opinion "that there is something in the Anglo-Saxon race essentially averse to the spirit and grace of society. I have seen," she says, "more invention, spirit and ease in one soirée in a German family at New York than I have ever seen here. . . . An Englishman has an uncomfortable consciousness of the presence and observation of others; an immense love of approbation, with either a shyness or a defiance of opinion." She went on to note the striking number of single women who had an independent existence, separate pursuits, much influence. She observed their greater leisure and their opportunity for intellectual cultivation as opposed to many at home and she exclaimed over the dowagers, up to seventy or over, who left their arms and neck bare. "Such parchment necks bedizened with diamonds, Macbeth's witches."

Catharine noted also the entire absence of taste within the middle class, so different from the French. As for the caste system, it appalled her. As absolute as in the Orient. "For the progress of the human race it was worth coming to the New World to get rid of it, worth all that our portion of the human family sacrificed, encountered, and suffered. . . . Travelers laugh at our pretensions to equality but our inequalities are as changing as the surface of the ocean, and this makes all the difference." And she made a comparison between a great London tailor come to their lodgings to take her brother Robert's measurements, his obsequiousness, his repetitive boastings of customers among the peerage, with the fine, self-respecting personality of the little tailor at home in Stockbridge village whose education and that of his children made them excellent citizens of the best sort.

The Sedgwicks left London by way of the Tower stairs from whence they were rowed out in a poor little boat, the best they could obtain, to the steamer *Soho,* lying in the Thames waiting to take them to Antwerp. The small ship carried many more passengers than could be accommodated with berths, and the surplus was strewn over the saloon floor after loiterers had been driven at a late hour from the dining-room table. At Antwerp they were charmed with their hotel, occupying three sides of a paved court, and with the mistress in her full petticoat who came out to meet them.

From Brussels they were driven to the battlefield of Waterloo. Catharine sat, characteristically, on the box beside the coachman and came to be known as *"la dame qui s'assit a côté du cocher."* They drove through villages where men and women sitting on benches before house doors drank beer and ate cakes, and the babies were pink and contented, while Catharine listened to the coachman's detailed saga concerning two courtships, his father's and his own. At Waterloo it thrilled her to be shown the spot where Wellington gave his ringing order: "Up, Guards, and at them!" And here, where grew the thickest corn in all Belgium, it saddened her to think of the reason for this tremendous fertility induced by the blood of the dead and wounded who lay strewn far and wide after the battle with no one to tend them while the water in small pools standing here and there was red and clotted with blood. On the way to Aix la Chapelle, Catharine watched small girls of five making hay and smoking pipes and, arrived at that town on a feast day, she found a great crowd assembled before the cathedral. The people fell to their knees as a priest and his attendants, on a high balcony above, displayed cathedral relics, the Virgin's chemise, the swaddling clothes, said to have been presented to Charlemagne by a Persian king.

The trip continued by steamer up the Rhine from Cologne to Bonn and the Sedgwicks were delighted with the simple, kindly manners of their fellow travelers but were somewhat discountenanced by one lady on board who, although having the *air noble,* stared at them nonetheless through her lorgnon. At Bonn they presented letters of introduction to the celebrated Schlegel who invited them to visit him: an old gentleman past seventy wearing a becoming black velvet cap cut round and making a halo of white hair beneath. He showed them his bust done in Carrara marble and more than once referred to the decay of the original since the bust was made. Vanity was not peculiar to women, Catharine decided.

Another letter intended for Bonn turned out to be an introduction to the lady of the Rhine steamer, a Madame M. with "happy eyes." She owned a superb establishment filled with antique gems, pictures, sculpture and, as they warmed to each other, she took the Sedgwicks on a tour of sightseeing, guiding them to the Botanical Gardens where they were taken in hand by a celebrated botanist, one of a large family of brothers devoted to the same science. *"Une aristocracie botanique,"* said Mme. M. Among other plants they were shown a collection of American specimens and here Catharine found herself back in her Ice Glen at Stockbridge surrounded by familiar friends. "I felt very much as if I ought to speak to them as they did to me."

Out walking again with Mme. M. on a pure summer afternoon up a steep winding path planted with grapes, on the way to the ruins of Godesberg Castle, they had tea on the summit where German ladies sat in a group on the piazza, having come out on a fine day to knit and gossip and eat cold roast fowl, Westphalia ham, melon and Swiss cheese. On leaving Bonn to continue up the Rhine, they were seen off by their new friend, Mme. M., who, saying farewell just before the steamer sailed, impulsively sent her footman back for her cloak and went with them as far as Andernech, not far from Coblenz, the site of one of her many villas.

At Wiesbaden, there came a month's halt in the Sedgwick itinerary where the baths were presumed to be a tonic for Robert's health. Catharine and young Kate acted as purveyors for the party and, all good hotels being filled, inquired at a bookshop for rooms and were instantly led across the street where an "honest German" provided them with bedrooms and parlor, including breakfast and supper. Dinner at five o'clock they had at the table d'hôte of a large hotel and here the quantity of meats, vegetables and sweets was such as to require two hours of capable, industrious serving, while the questions asked Miss Sedgwick showed an amazing ignorance concerning the United States. "Is English spoken in America? Who is the sovereign of your country?"

While the older Sedgwicks remain behind, Catharine and the three nieces continue by boat up the Rhine. On board they blush for a fellow countryman who boasts of the prowess and speed of American steamships as compared to the European, but they are universally delighted with German manners which extend all the way from peasant to prince. "They always seem to be feeling a gentle pressure from the cord that interlaces them to their species." The servants, ever prompt, faithful, cheerful, are blessedly free from the cringing servility of servants in England.

Villages bordering the Rhine, "a mass of wretched dwellings stuck against moldering walls," arouse the pity in Catharine's heart. Men and women cultivating the vine along steep precipices, carry the manure in buckets on their shoulders, but, steeped to the very lips in poverty, they are a "smiling, kindly people." Ashore during an hour, Catharine converses with an old man who invites them into his garden, offering them plums served on grape leaves. There is a "gentleness and sensibility in his voice" as he tells her the story of his life and informs her of the sufferings of the poor who live on potatoes and *"some* black bread and one half pound of meat per family on Sundays." Alms boxes exist in every hotel, opened each month and the contents distributed by the proprietor. Again Catharine is overwhelmed by the cruel contrasts in the fortunes of the human race as, on the return journey to Wiesbaden, passengers are served in quantity with such varied foods as soup, boiled meat, croquettes, sausage, tongue, vegetables, macaroni, pudding with fruit sauce, followed by "a procession of joints, mutton, veal and venison, stewed fruit, calf's foot jelly and blanc mange. For dessert, apricots, cherries, mulberries, pears and a variety of confectionery." A glutton's dream.

When the end of the month at Wiesbaden arrived, Catharine, who at home had never been trusted to buy a go-cart, now selected and bought a traveling carriage for the Sedgwick journey into Switzerland and Italy. Their first stop was Frankfort. Presenting their letters, they were entertained there at dinner by a banker, in a "delicious atmosphere of fruit and flowers," and they went to the theater that began in daylight and ended at 9 p.m. where "ladies unattended wear their ordinary dress and the price of a box ticket is fifty cents," like an "assembly collecting for a lyceum lecture in a New England village." At Kronthal, while the Robert Sedgwicks paused to take the cure, Catharine and her train of young women climbed mountains, visited ruined castles and were invited into wayside cottages. They watched a gathering of peasants bidding for chestnuts at an auction sale, a most important item of local food, and they lunched with the miller at his mill on tender boiled beef, bread and butter smeared with honey, and white wine. Friends they made everywhere among servants and tradespeople, the man who delivered newly purchased trunks and a young seamstress, a "quiet, modest and respectful girl" who kissed them all at parting, including Robert.

"I leave this country with an interest, respect and attachment that I did not expect to feel for any country after leaving England," Catharine writes. "I feel richer for the delightful recollection I carry with me of the urbanity of the Germans. Never can I forget the *'Guten Tag,' 'Guten Abend,' 'Guten Nacht,'* murmured by the soft voices of the peasants from under their drooping loads as we passed them on their walks." And she admires as well the activity, boldness and freedom of the German mind, the fact, for example, that a wife and husband, by law, share their property equally. "This it is," a gentleman said to Catharine, "that makes our wives so intelligent in the management of their concerns, so industrious, so economical." Of the ruling classes, however, Catharine wonders whether they may be storing up trouble for the future. Not only are the young people moving toward lives of greater independence, objecting to parents' ever-recurring questioning—"Where were you yesterday? Where do you go tomorrow?"—but, more serious, she senses future rebellion in the lower orders, debarred as they are from political action. "They will hardly go on quietly wearing a master's uniform, doing his work, eating black bread and potatoes as if this were their fair share." German serenity is indeed pleasant to encounter "but is it not the serenity of the mighty ocean that wants but the moving of the wind to rise in resistless waves?"

The posting journey from Frankfurt to Basle was a matter of 225 miles, the horses, four of them, changed every six miles. The postilion, his trumpet suspended by a cord, two bright-colored worsted tassels bobbing down his back, sat on the near wheel horse and guided the leaders with rope reins. Their progress was slow but steady: Darmstadt, Heidelberg, Carlsruhe, Baden Baden, Frieburg with its beautiful cathedral. Catharine joined the vesper service there at twilight. "You do not ask or think by what name this religion is called. . . . You feel the wants of their natures are the wants of your own and your worship is spontaneous." Basle, Bienne, the lovely little island where Rousseau lived—the Alps. "I left them lunching at Arleberg and walked on alone. All my life I have been longing to come to Switzerland and now it seems as if, like a rainbow, it would fade away while I look at it."

Arrived in Berne, they stayed with a sister of Dr. Follen. Catharine brooded on what it must have cost Follen to leave the family, that scene. The house's terraced gardens fell to the Aar, the Alps were his daily companion. How sad was the lot of all refugees to our land of the free. "Is our welcome too often a cold and stinted one? Do we not often regard them with distrust . . . rather than supply to them, as far as may be, the lost charities of home?"

At Geneva they attended service in the cathedral where Calvin

preached and toward evening Catharine and Kate drove out to call
on the Sismondis at Chesne. The house was hidden behind a hedge,
a low cottage under fine old trees. In the foreground a Gothic
church, Mont Blanc for background. Catharine was happy to find
here the matching tranquillity and elevation of the owner's philo-
sophic mind. What pleasure to see face to face at last this friend of
long standing! She and Kate were received with warmth and were
told that in Geneva proper Confalonieri awaited them. "After an
hour we came away perfectly satisfied. Not a look, a word, or tone
of voice had reminded us we were meeting for the first time." They
returned with the whole party to dine. Madame Sismondi had said,
"It is but sitting a little closer." Sismondi was sixty-seven, short,
stout, with brilliant hazel eyes and "soul-lit" expression. Madame
said she wished he were twenty-one and she nineteen. Sismondi replied that he should not care to live his life over again, it had been
so happy, he should not dare trust the chances.

On a fair morning of October, Catharine and her inseparable
Kate walked out to breakfast with the Sismondis. He breakfasted
on curds and cream. A good-natured discussion ensued between
husband and wife as to who should be invited there that evening.
Strangers had arrived with letters. Madame objected to certain
among them, one very silly woman, another who would count on a
grand soirée. Sismondi was for including them all and he set out
after breakfast in his carriage "to make visits to these people, with
much the feeling that a bountiful man has in going among the poor
with a purse full of money." At the evening party, tea and cakes
were served around a circular table. Miss Sedgwick had a conversation with de Canolles, a celebrated botanist and admirer of Gray,
Nuttall and Elliott. Canolles, discussing Swiss peasants, said it was
easy to recognize the Protestant from the Catholic canton by the
extreme wretchedness of the people in the latter, even though they
were far more lighthearted than their richer neighbors. This was
because of their being able to throw off the burden of their sins at
confession and because they lived without the haunting desire to
improve their condition. Catharine wondered whether their condi-

tion was not that of "brutes grazing in the fields. Those who have a prospect, strain every nerve to press forward."

Madame Sismondi, British by birth, made a little dissertation, that delighted her hearers, on the character of Genevese women, "the most exemplary she has known." Their so-called "pedantic virtues" sprang from exactness, not pedantry. At fifteen, every girl entered on a course of religious instruction from the pastor, which excluded other studies and all amusements. This planted an ineffaceable impression in the youthful mind. Often astonished at the nice discrimination of her servants, Madame Sismondi asked: "Where did you learn this?" "Ah, Madame, we learn a great deal during our year of instruction," they replied. Another local institution, the *Société des Dimanches,* was composed of children whose mothers were friends. Joining the society at the age of five, the little girls met under the watchful eye of an older woman each Sunday afternoon. The girl who first married bestowed her name on the society and, as soon as this occurred, men also were admitted. These meetings continued through life and often took the place of her family for the solitary, and, if one of them was in financial straits, help was freely given. Sismondi listened with pleasure to his wife's animated account, drew his chair close, put an arm about her and said: *"Je te remercie, mon cœur."*

The Sedgwicks went out to visit Ferney, the village that had formed itself about Voltaire who lived there for twenty years. Here he built a church for others to worship in and, for himself, a château and grounds, at present badly mauled by sightseers who, among other depredations, had torn the bed curtain to shreds. Catharine, seeing the house, was made chiefly aware of Voltaire's vanity and ignobility of mind, a strange contrast to his love of justice and passion for mankind's freedom. In the château salon she beheld a painting of him being guided by Henri IV to the throne of Apollo, and in his bedroom, emblematical figures representing the four quarters of the globe approached to do him homage. On the grounds without, an old man, son of Voltaire's gardener who as a boy had accompanied the great writer on his walks, carrying his notebook for him, showed Catharine a book of seals removed by Voltaire himself from the letters arriving for him. This was a habit of long standing that had enabled him to familiarize himself with his correspondents, that he might avoid opening those communications he knew would be distasteful. He had scribbled comments across the envelopes such as: *"J. J. Rousseau—un bouillant."* The most common epithet was *"Fou."*

The moment came when the gentle pleasures of Switzerland had to be left behind. The Sedgwicks were sad in having to go from the lingering quiet, the little plodding steamer on Lake Geneva, the washerwomen who "scrub, beat and rinse" in the waters of the lake, one of whom told Catharine a nightdress of hers had been "drowned"; the guides, fine men, who led the party on muleback to the Mer de Glace. And they wished for a longer enjoyment of the well-ordered, healthy hospitality of Geneva and the friendships formed under the aegis of the Sismondis. "I rather think the heart grows by traveling," Catharine wrote Charles at home.

On the drive to Italy through the Haute Savoie they crossed the Alps at Mt. Cenis. Five mules, each with his muleteer, dragged the heavy traveling carriage while the coachman with his horses followed in the rear. Catharine walked most of the way, rising alone at dawn to see the sanctuary where lay the bones of St. François de Sales and la Mère Chantal, side by side. "I like to enter a Catholic church in the gray of the morning while the lights on the altar are struggling through the misty dawn, while the people that glide in and drop down before the images are as shadowy as the pictures themselves." The inn beyond the Savoy barrier promised a meal of lake trout, but going out into the kitchen they found the floor strewn with "eggshells, bones and vegetable refuse." This cured their appetites. Down then into the fair plains of Italy. The first stopping point was Turin. At ten in the morning Catharine sat in the hotel window looking over the piazza with its band of street musicians, its soldiers, priests, peasants, its juggler who drew a great crowd that scattered as the royal carriage drove through. The King rode past attended by servants in scarlet livery while mendicant barefooted friars with long beards collected alms.

The Sedgwicks sent off a note to Silvio Pellico, librarian to a marchesa and friend of the Spielberg refugees now in America. He came at once, "a sort of etching of a man with delicate features . . . a more shadowy Dr. Channing. His manners have a sweetness and gentleness that correspond with his spiritual appearance."

A half bushel of letters from home, after a month's fasting, awaited them at Milan, forty francs' worth from the post office. They spent the evening reading them, then sent off letters of their own to various friends of the Italian exiles. Most of these people were, at October's end, still at their villas outside Milan. But they came in to call nonetheless and received the Sedgwicks "with un-measured cordiality." Count Confalioneri, their familiar companion, took them about Milan to "lionize" them and they drove in his carriage to see the sights.

An evening at La Scala Opera brought pleasure mingled with a certain degree of displeasure to Catharine's New England sensibili-ties, as the Milanese gentlemen came close to the Sedgwick box to stare at the girls, while the corps de ballet again performed in a way to shock her. She noted in the lobby the presence of the Aus-trian police with their tall furred helmets and their swords, and she watched with interest the ladies who received callers in their boxes fitted out with carpets, tables, sofas. Presently they made a new friend in the cordial "Mme. T." who, from her villa at Desio, drove in to call upon them. She invited them to her town house decorated with "the perfection of Parisian taste, the masterly workmanship of England and the beautiful art of her own country—all subservient to wealth almost unlimited." Here were painted ceilings, mosaic floors, a stained glass window designed by Palladio whose erstwhile studio they were taken to see. At the country villa there were even greater wonders to exhibit, a veritable page from the Arabian Nights; conservatories filled with five or six thousand camellia plants; an ancient abbey restored by Palladio holding a theater and a museum for antiques, while from the bell tower one could see half the plains of Lombardy with Alps for background. They walked about the winding shore of a lake filled with water brought from Lake Como and embellished with an aerial bridge where, at one end, stood a monument to Tasso and nearby, a glorified fisherman's hut decorated with frescoes telling of the poet's life.

An evening, before quitting Milan, was spent with the author of *I Promessi Sposi* and his family. "Manzoni is a little past fifty with an intellectual and rather handsome face and a striking expression of goodness, his manner gentlemanly and modest." Catharine was able to tell him of the American translation of *I Promessi Sposi*. He had not heard of it and was both surprised and gratified. The Sedgwicks declined an invitation to pass a day at his country house, not wanting to invade his privacy, and they were always to regret it. They declined also an invitation to stay for a week at Mme. T.'s villa, deciding instead to drive on toward Venice. "So our bills are paid, our post horses ordered and we are going, feeling as if we had lived a little life here. . . . There is no such lengthener of human life as traveling."

At seven on a November morning with Venus low in the sky above them they set out for Verona and Lago di Garda. The post horses were small but more spirited than the heavy German horses and faster. Roses bloomed at the various stations and into the coach windows women thrust trays piled high with grapes, apples, pears. They drove through Vicenza where Palladio was born and on into Padua where Petrarch was a canon in the church and Galileo lectured at the University. Catharine was deeply moved by these reminders of noble achievement out of the long past and she was gladdened on the drive through the Lombardy plains to see them heavy with corn, olive, mulberry and the growing vine, all a source of power and vigor for the benefit of the free Italian cities. At Venice she arose before dawn to attend early Mass at St. Mark's, and in the midst of the cathedral's splendor her attention was held by a penitent, a young man with bronzed face and tangled hair who had "a wild, savage desolation about him" that she would long remember. "He strode through the kneeling congregation as if he were on the sea beach, not pausing till he reached the steps before the high altar when he threw himself prostrate upon them as if he would have buried his face in the marble. The people were passing up and down, jostling him, treading on him; he moved no more than if he had been struck dead there. It seemed to me that I could hear the cry from his soul, 'God be merciful to me, a sinner!' " She returned after Mass to the "superb suite of apartments" put at their disposal by Confalonieri. Here it was that his wife had lived when she sued for his pardon at the Austrian court.

Days of sightseeing follow, "five beautiful days mingled with luxurious floating in our gondola." They are rowed out one morning as far as San Lazzaro in the sea to the Armenian convent where Byron received his lessons "when his lordship took the whim to study Armenian and to swim across to us from the Lido." In Venice their one acquaintance is "a Venetian exquisite" unable to answer the questions put to him by the eager Catharine. The education of women? He shrugs and says, *"Ça commence."* Passing a madhouse, Miss Sedgwick inquires whether the patients are well cared for. In reply he strokes his mustache: *"Assez bien*—Luck is a lord." By contrast, Catharine is impressed with the fine seriousness of their gondolier, "the most sagacious of cicerones," who, when they leave for good, stands in his gondola at the foot of the stone staircase, hat in hand, in his close-fitted, scarlet-corded dress, his fine black hair waving off his bronzed forehead. "I told him how glad we should be to see him some bright day in New York."

The Sedgwicks in Italy continued to remain within the reconnaissant aura of their refugee friends' families. Ferrara, the next spot in which they lingered, "a clean fine old city with immense unoccupied houses and wide, grass-grown streets," had been the home town of Foresti who for sixteen years, persecuted and under sentence of death, was incarcerated in the Spielberg dungeon. Catharine's admiration for this man, "lover of justice and freedom," was immense, for she believed that if his youth, his high position and his country were restored to him under similar oppressive circumstances, he would again sacrifice himself as he had earlier. Before leaving Ferrara, the Sedgwicks went to pay their respects to Foresti's sister, a lady who had gone into a decline when her brother was imprisoned and who was now slowly dying. They found her shrunken, a tragic figure of fate, dressed in mourning, her situation so moving that all, including Robert, "wept together."

And now, at November's end, with the crops in and the vintage over, bad weather descended upon the travelers as, slowly, they drove toward Rome. Rain fell as they crossed the Apennines, drawn by three pairs of horses and a yoke of oxen, "a slow drag which we continued until six in the evening." Catharine particularly enjoyed the stops at out-of-the-way inns where the people were social and frank, "where you have the whole family to serve you with their amusing individualities, and all eager and indefatigable." They were given bread and delicious butter and fresh eggs with their tea, generous fires in the morning and a pair of chickens for the day's lunch, all for one dollar each. Setting forth in the mists of early morning, out of long-established habit, in spite of the warnings of the French courier, Catharine walked in advance of the carriage through wild and solitary country. She seems, embarked in this sort of enterprise, never to have known fear.

At Siena they were obliged to put up with a small, fireless apartment because the best ones were being saved for a *"milord Anglais."* All English travelers were "milords" to the Italians and, now and then, the Sedgwicks encountered these autocrats at the various posts where horses were changed. One carriage in particular impressed itself on the Sedgwick mind, its occupants a gentleman, his pretty young wife, courier, maid, and three lap dogs. The lady was engaged in feeding the dogs with raisins and biscuits, giving no heed to the clatter of several blind and maimed old beggars about the carriage door, finally closing the door upon them, a shocking experience for Catharine who said that "this turning aside from human necessities to pamper brutes seems to me one of those 'fantastic tricks at which the angels weep.'"

Finally, well before Christmas, Catharine, full of emotion, is able to write the words *"We are in Rome."* Here, the poet Kenyon was on hand for the winter and another old friend had seen to their lodgings near Monte Cavallo looking out on the Viminal, with a highly cultivated garden below and the sun shining on them from its rising to its setting. They felt, one and all, they were "suddenly come into possession of an independent fortune." They began their stay with a visit to St. Peter's on a feast day and Catharine's reaction was detached and impartial as always. She described the Pope as "an ugly old man with a big nose and a stupid expression," and, although she grants that the cardinals "as a class of men, are very noble in their appearance," she was far from approving their actions.

As we stood in the vestibule awaiting our carriage, cardinal after cardinal drove off; and as I saw each heavy coach with fat, black horses, gilded and tasseled harness and its complement of three footmen and embroidered liveries dash through an ignorant, wretched multitude, nearly running over the blind and the lame, those words of doom occurred to me: "Woe be to the shepherds of Israel that feed themselves. Should not the shepherds feed the flocks?"

And then, characteristically, tired of waiting, Catharine and Kate turned their backs on the throng and walked home. The walk, however, did not free the two women from their sense of the oppression and power of the mighty Church, for, in passing a cold dark den lighted only by the half-open door, they saw a group of children, under four years, in charge of a woman who knitted the morning away while teaching them their prayers in Latin accompanied by the proper genuflections. What a contrast to the "warm, well-lighted schools at home."

Impressions of delight continued, however, to mingle in Catharine's warm heart with pity for the poor of the land.

I cannot convey to you what I have enjoyed and am enjoying from painting, sculpture and architecture; and when I shudder at the idea of leaving all these magnificent and lovely forms, I doubt the wisdom of our New-World people coming here to acquire hankerings which cannot be appeased at home. I would advise no American to come to Italy who has not strong domestic ties or some absorbing pursuit at home.

Roses were in bloom on December 29 in the Borghese Gardens when Catharine went forth to spend several hours with an English friend, walking later the glades and avenues of the Villa Doria, ending the day with a glimpse of the lovely little circular temple designed by Bramante that stands on the Janiculum Hill hidden away in a court next San Pietro in Montorio. She visited many of the Roman palaces and, in one, found the rooms warmed by a fire and a table spread with books, drawings and the "delicate needlework" of a lady who had been driven away by their entrance.

"I walk these splendid edifices daily with the enthusiasm . . . of a pilgrim," Catharine writes her brother. But never out of mind is the chilled and destitute population seeking the warmth of the sun under the protection of some high Roman wall. Their plight is all the more inexcusable, she tells us, for, according to her friend Sismondi, if the Campagna were properly cultivated there would be food for all, that malaria-ridden Campagna then in the hands of eighty landowners who, squeezing from it the highest possible revenue, import labor out of the north and the south, five hundred families yearly, of whom many die each year, to work under overseers traversing the fields on horseback, and to sleep on the open ground or in the entrances to the catacombs.

But it is difficult to remember the dark and the tragic when flowers in stalls piled high send out their sweet and permeating odor, when the lovely sound of church bells rings the soul heavenward, when the broad Spanish steps edging the house where Keats so sadly died are massed with potted azaleas in colors of the moon, when on *festa* days their coachman arrives bringing small presents, "jonquils, violets or smoking chestnuts." Small wonder that Catharine writing home to announce their departure should say: "We have left Rome . . . after a sojourn of but two months, with the fond feeling of lovers."

Bidding farewell to a weeping landlord and his wife, they drive in February along the road to Naples through the "solemn solitude" of the Campagna, from Rome to the Alban Hills, passing the broken line of ancient aqueducts where there is "scarcely an indication of the presence of man, scarcely the note of a bird or the sound of an animal to break the silence." On through the Pontine marshes, down the Appian Way and a stop at noon on the turf beside the road while the carriage horses eat. Here, Robert takes his siesta, his wife brings out her needlework, young Kate reads aloud from a book presented her by an Italian officer, and another of the nieces decorates her bonnet with ivy and fresh flowers placed that morning by the waiter at her breakfast plate to signalize the coming of spring.

"Delightful lodgings" at 28 Santa Lucia awaited them at Naples, lodgings once again engaged for them by the faithful Kenyon. There were also in the background the American chargé, Mr. Throop, and the consul, Mr. Hammett, and for their further entertainment, they were possessed of introductory letters to several distinguished Neapolitans as well as to the general of the King's army. Throop procured for them invitations to a court ball where "women with stupid faces were covered with diamonds," where the royal family supped on fish and oysters and game, where each table supported a wild boar stuck with silver arrows and where "the ladies gathered hungrily about the tables and ate like good trencher women."

This was the court of King Ferdinand II, the notorious "Bomba" whose reign climaxed the Bourbon misrule of Naples and whose son was, twenty years later, to be deposed by Garibaldi and Cavour. Now, in 1840, the sensitive, sensible soul of Catharine Sedgwick was outraged by the flagrant discrepancies of existence between rich and poor, by the King's avarice, the people's suffering. "A man who can get work earns only, by the hardest kind of labor in summertime, sixteen cents a day and he pays a tax of three dollars for every bushel of salt he consumes." When Catharine spoke to Hammett of the extreme abjectness of the Neapolitan people, of shopkeepers' recurrent demands for more than the price agreed upon, his answer was: "Ah, they are so very poor." So poor and so utterly without any prospect of help, it seemed to her as she listened to the tales of horror that would not let her mind rest: the scourge of cholera when, of the sum raised to alleviate distress, no more than a tenth part had remained for the people, the bulk of it going into the King's coffers, the King's drive into the city from his place of refuge in the country as, speaking to the crowds that swarmed about his carriage, he ordered them into the churches that they might there do penance for the sins that had brought this plague upon them. And the visit to the courts of law where a bribe to the judge was as common as the customary fee to lawyers at home. And the story of the young writer, a brave, earnest youth who, publishing a diatribe on the abuses wrought upon the poor, was thrown into prison with the "furiously mad." And the sight of the fine equipages drawn up before house doors awaiting the morning exit of luxury-loving gentry while "men in the heyday of life, one pillowed on the body of another," slept their hunger off in the entrance vestibules.

Previous to the Sedgwicks' departure from Naples, they made an expedition with several of their friends to the Bay of Baia. Here, on the drive out, Catharine looked across to Pozzuoli, the ancient Puteoli, and thought with infinite pleasure of the moment when St. Paul, "the brave apostle," had first set foot on Roman ground there. They left their carriage presently and climbed through a defile to have a view of the Queen's oyster-eating lodge and they were met on their return by a "group of young, Moorish-looking girls who were selling bits of precious marbles from the ruins" of the Cumaean caves. The scene was full of beauty, the Bay of Naples and Vesuvius beyond, the Apennines snow-capped, and Capri in the blue distance. An old woman sat on the fragment of a marble column, "the living image of the Cumaean Sibyl," holding above her head a tambourine on which she played one of the wild airs to which they dance the tarantella, accompanying it with her cracked voice. Two "joyous girls" proceeded to dance around Kenyon, leaping and clapping their hands. "Apart stood four girls as grave and fixed as Caryatids, with immense piles of brush on their heads, which they had just brought down from the hills, and we cold pilgrims from the north were looking on." Kenyon, who had begun by regarding the girls as troublesome, gave himself up by degrees to the spirit of the scene. "The floodgates of poetry were opened, and over his soul-lit face there was an indescribable shade of melancholy, as if by magic he were beholding the elder and classic time which before had been imperfectly transmitted by poetry, painting, sculpture. He threw a shower of silver among the happy creatures as we drove off."

The month of April, 1840, was now well on its way to completion and the moment of departure for home almost at hand as the party turned northward en route for Genoa, the port of sailing. They lingered again in Rome during the mourning and rejoicing of Holy Week, then drove on across the Apennines. During the three-mile ascent, walking as usual most of the way to save the horses, Catharine was moved to sympathy for the driver of the ox team engaged to aid the pull when, a few miles from the summit, one of the beasts fell dead. His owner's distress, throwing himself on the ground, beating his breast, reminded her of "Lear's anguish over the dead body of Cordelia."

In Florence, Miss Sedgwick was shown about the city by an American friend, Richard Henry Wilde, an ex-Congressman, now spending agreeable hours of leisure in "ferreting out the life of Dante from Tuscan archives." Still clinging to the city, Catharine felt, was the aura of its days of early freedom, sprung from the strength of its governing guilds, those "twelve companies of arts and trades" formed in the thirteenth century by the working classes when "each man was master and lord in his own house," when workmen "in their poor and rustic lives did most virtuous deeds and contributed far more to the honor of their families and their country than those who lived more luxuriously." After seeing the two great collections in the galleries of the Pitti and the Palazzo Vecchio, Catharine wrote her brother at home: "I feel fully what was so well said by the old man who for seventy years had shown a famous picture in the Escurial: 'We are the shadows, they are the realities!'" And now, carrying with them the store of their year's journeying across the face of Europe, the travelers set their faces toward their "earthly heaven," their home in the New World.

There were yet rather more than twenty-five years ahead of Catharine Sedgwick, and much useful labor as well as many pleasant moments. But one feels, nevertheless, reading her letters, that the cream had been skimmed from the bowl of life, that slowly, inexorably, the mandates of decline, the eating of the bitter curds, began with the return from Europe and the death, a few months later, of her brother Robert.

In answer to Dr. Dewey's letter of condolence, Catharine sent a heartbroken reply: "God only knows how I have loved my brothers, the union I have had with them. No closer tie has ever weakened that which began with my being. . . . Our lives have flowed in one stream; and with Robert so long, that now I feel as if half my life were buried in his grave. . . . He is gone, gone when I did not expect to lose him. . . . Weakened as I am, the lights seem all going out. . . . I have had praise and flattery and I have not been insensible to them; but God knows they have never weighed for one moment against affection, and I would give all the world could offer to me of them for one tone of Robert's voice. . . ."

Her brother Charles was left, but she regards him "with a fear that he will vanish from me while I look at him." The year following brought the deaths of Catharine's sister Frances, of Dr. Channing and of Charles' son, a suicide in Europe. Also the removal from close proximity of her much loved niece Kate, who, at November's end, married William Minot, Junior, and went to live in Boston.

Writing again to Dr. Dewey, the Unitarian divine, who became more and more of a prop for Catharine as her life drew toward its close, she said:

You have heard of Channing's death, and perhaps that he passed the summer here at Lenox, and in a free and happy condition of mind and healthy state of body such as he often said he did not remember to have enjoyed from his childhood. . . . He seemed to have thrown off every shackle, to be rid of his precision, and he was so affectionate and playful with the young people that those who had not before known him wondered anyone should fear Dr. Channing. He liked our anti-conventionalism—our free ways of going on—and he went away with more than half a promise to return to us next summer. Before he reached Bennington he took the cold of which he there died. Died! What a word to apply to the passage of such a spirit into the immortal world!

In February of 1844, Catharine went to stay with Fanny Kemble in Philadelphia. She tells Kate that the "wit and instruction of London" has bestowed a fine polish upon the actress' talent and that her bitter marital experience has matured her character. They sat up, the two women, night after night, talking into the early morning hours, such, Catharine says, was the flow of Fanny's rich, fresh thoughts.

Later, during August, life at Lenox appeared to bring its usual rural joys, for Catharine describes a picnic on the lake given by her for the little children and their parents. "We mustered seventy-nine. It was very successful. Who ever failed when children and summer, freedom and green fields were the element of the festival?" But during the fall, clinging sadness again forced its way into her consciousness. To Kate, Catharine wrote of a sad and empty home-coming, the Lenox house unsouled, uncarpeted, stacked with chairs and tables in apparent mutiny. And at Stockbridge, where Catharine and her sister Eliza went to spend a few days in December, they tried, alone as they now were, to recapture a little of the house's youth, tried to tell each other, but with waning conviction, that "the dead are *not* dead."

There were two trips to the Hudson River with a few years intervening between them. First, a charming experience in Rhinebeck at the house of an old lady, Mrs. Garretson, sister of Chancellor Livingston, "one of the two last of the old race of Livingstons. . . . There were twelve of them who led strong, joyous lives, all having royal estates in the Manor, with iron physical and rich intellectual constitutions. They ate and drank after the old fashion, turtle soup, mince pies and Madeira wine for dinner, hot suppers at night . . . laughing together over their breakfast table. . . . *All* lived to slip far beyond the prescribed boundary of man's life, and here is Mrs. Garretson absolutely unimpaired at ninety-two." At tea, with the best cups set out for Catharine, "the old lady presided with a sort of lofty grace, and drank green tea and ate strawberries and cream." They sat on a piazza enclosed in roses looking out, beyond a lawn with noble old trees, over a magnificent stretch of the river studded with a little fleet of sloops. Catharine had made this call on Mrs. Garretson because one of her servants had composed "some pretty verses" to Miss Sedgwick by way of thanks for the writing of *Live and Let Live.*

The later trip to the Hudson was for the purpose of visiting Highland Gardens and its environs with the accomplished Charles Downing, landscape architect, and the Swedish Frederika Bremer who was shortly to journey down another river of very different aspect at the side of Dorothea Dix. With these two companions and others, Catharine went for a picnic up the mountain above Beacon where the view was glorious to see. They had capon and champagne and there were "all manner of merry things said and done." The two ladies took to each other only by degrees but with ultimate enthusiasm. Catharine described Miss Bremer as "a little lady with most lovely little hands" and a mouth like Longfellow's. She was rather taken aback, however, by Miss Bremer's clothes: a gray gown and a black watered-silk mantilla. "So she comes to breakfast, so to dinner, and so she appears in the evening." But she had modesty and a "most sweet gentleness, simple and sincere as a child," and she entertained the company by playing Swedish airs and teaching them Swedish jigs. Also, she found time to paint a watercolor of Miss Sedgwick. Catharine predicts there will be an affiliation between Miss Bremer and the Transcendentalists although "she is not like them, foggy, but has, *au fond,* a sound, rocky foundation and clear good sense." And "she has tones of voice so full of humanity and of experienced suffering that they almost bring tears." Frederika, on her side, felt her "soul a little slumbrous" while with Catharine during the first days, "her pleasant countenance without evidence of real genius, though indicating kindness and good will." Presently, however, there was such a degree of cordiality emanating from Catharine that Frederika's initial doubts were blown away and she came to believe she "could live with her as with a heavenly soul in which one has entire trust."

The death of one more long-time friend, the Swiss Sismondi, was announced to Catharine by his widow who quoted a passage from her husband's journal saying how greatly he had enjoyed her and how touched they both had been by one of her little books. *"Il est charmant, et de morale et d'art de contes. . . . On l'aime et on l'admire pour un si bel usage de ses talents."*

Another writer, the poet Bryant, was still very much alive, however, and we hear of a visit made him by Catharine in Maytime at Springbank, his place in Roslyn, Long Island. She was enchanted with the old-fashioned house facing Great Neck Bay, and with the lovely shaded walk and rural bridge leading to the cottage *orné* of her host's daughter.

In 1848, Catharine published *The Boy of Mount Rhigi,* the last of her purely didactic tales, written to impress the public with the pressures for good and evil brought about by environment in the education of the young—the story of two boys reared under drastically differing conditions, one of them blessed with good fortune, the other with bad. The good boy influences the bad in commendable fashion as the story unrolls and, with a substantial bit of luck thrown in by the author, it weaves its way to a happy ending. Catharine's clergymen friends, Dr. Dewey and Dr. Bellows, were warm in their praise of the book, assuring her that she will never realize the good she has done.

In November, 1849, Catharine describes a visit made to the dignified Mrs. Robert Sedgwick at the Stockbridge house by Lucy Stone, female apostle of Women's Rights. "She does not look older than four and twenty. She is thirty-one, we are told, and the possessor of rare gifts . . . one of the very sweetest voices I ever heard, a readiness of speech and grace that furnish the external qualifications of an orator (a lovely countenance, too), and the intensity, entire forgetfulness and divine calmness that fit her to speak in the great cause she has undertaken. She has some of the slang words and slang phrases of her clique, but if she could have your Aunt Susan to travel with her, and be as docile to her wise hints as she was here, the ministry would be quite perfect." Might not Henry James have taken this young lady for model in his drawing of the lovely Verena Tarrant, in *The Bostonians?* Miss Sedgwick did not live to read this book. But she would, no doubt, have been sympathetic to the methods of the writer in search of copy, and amused at his perspicacity.

Meanwhile, there arose a new cause to be defended, a cause that deeply stirred Catharine's heart. French, Greek, Italian patriots had each received, in successive years, the loyalty and sympathy of the Sedgwick family and had been able to count on the tradition of Stockbridge for support. Now, in 1851, came the Hungarians and their great hero, Kossuth. At first, it was a member of the advance guard whom they received, a young man, exile from his country, who was "like a boy coming to his home in a holiday. . . . We certainly have had great happiness from exiles," wrote Catharine. And her happiness was emphatic when she heard that a ship was to be sent to bring Kossuth to America. Later, at Sedgwick instigation, presumably, the town of Stockbridge organized a fair for the Hungarians, with the farmers' wives, "everyone joining in." Catharine could not rest until she had made sure that Kate in Boston had heard the hero speak. "No such orator has been, or in all probability will be, heard again. And, for his cause, it is the rock of eternal justice. . . . I never had so profound an impression from the presence of any human being. . . . An earnest soul creates souls."

In June, at New York during the following year, she was again hard at work planning a lecture for Kossuth, the proceeds to go to his impoverished family. Such a benefit could not, of course, be instigated by the lecturer himself and its inception, therefore, depended on Catharine and her friends. Whereas during the first winter of the Hungarian patriot's stay his popularity had been immense, the public, fickle as always, had now turned to newer affairs. And so, fearing a debacle on the evening of the lecture, "after discouragement and almost despair," they had, finally, complete success. "It was one of the *blissful* moments of life when we got to the Tabernacle that memorable night and found it full. . . . And what a lecture it was!" Continuing, Catharine says: "He seems to me to take rank with the noble army of martyrs. . . . He paid us one beautiful visit."

This visit may have been to Charles Sedgwick's house in Lenox, a house now transplanted from its original position in the village to a spot on the brow of a hill near the entrance to the town. A wing had been built for Catharine with piazza and a terrace that looked out over twenty miles of valley. Here she gave her much-coveted breakfast parties, up at six on summer mornings to gather flowers and strawberries from her garden, to bake muffins in her tiny kitchen. "Cooking is the only accomplishment of which I am vain," she tells her friends, one of whom assures us that "her vivacity, shrewdness and tact in conversation were never more charming than at these Arcadian repasts."

On the subject of the achievements and failures among current writers at this epoch, Catharine was articulate. Mrs. Charles Sedgwick had just read aloud to the family *The House of the Seven Gables*. Catharine comments that in spite of its "stamp of unquestionable genius . . . its elegance and finish that is like the work of a master sculptor . . . the book is an affliction. It has the unity and simple construction of a Greek tragedy, but without the relief of divine qualities or great events; and the man takes such savage delight in repeating and repeating the raw head and bloody bones of his imagination. . . . There is too much force for the subject. It is as if a railroad should be built and a locomotive started to transport skeletons, specimens, and one bird of paradise."

At Margaret Fuller's death, Catharine wrote Mrs. Channing: "From first to last she was a woman of noble aims, and, with all her egotism, unselfish in action. The longer I live, the more presumptuous and futile it seems to me to attempt judgment of character, and Miss Fuller's was exceptional. Her truth was exemplary

and all her conduct . . . her Italian life beautiful. The close had the
solemnity of a fulfilled prophecy and was it not merciful?"

Of Thackeray, whose first lecture she heard in New York, she
says:

It was an able one, written in classic English and given with a manly
dignity and simplicity. . . . If there were a detective police for the follies
and infirmities of human nature, he would be elected chiefly by accla-
mation. But I have no appetite for this sagacity. . . . I prefer those nice
analyses that find sustenance instead of detecting poison; the one work
is for our Channings, the other for Thackeray and the wise in their
generation. I apply all this, however, to the impression received from
Thackeray's novels; his lectures, I believe, will be free from this characteristic fault, much more humane and genial than his books.

Emily Brontë, Catharine does not like, does not understand. She
hopes that Kate has not wasted her time on " 'that little family in
Hell,' living and dying at *Wuthering Heights*. It is a most signal
waste of talent." But, in contrast, presently, because of George Eliot's power of conveying tragedy, Catharine is obliged to "resolutely
shut up *The Mill on the Floss,* not being able to meet the storm that
I hear rumbling in the distance and that I am sure is to pour down
on poor Maggie's devoted head. . . . This 'Mill' has delighted me.
It has turned out such an amount of good grist . . . it deals sturdily
with the real stuff that life is made of."

A winter in New York followed, for Catharine, which Charles
shared with her. He had been ill and it was considered wise to have
him near city doctors, while his wife, because of the school at home
that was hers to supervise, remained at Lenox. To Kate she writes:
"You ask me what I have been doing all winter. Little, my dear
child, but watch your father's face and do what I can to minister
to his comfort and shift one heavy burden for another. I have written some small matters, and tried my hand at a heavy one, but
heaviness is the prevailing element."

She was continually occupied in good works, nevertheless, whenever in New York City, and her letters carried the sound, often,
of that fatigue so familiar to conscientious women, "the crowding

and stuffing of every moment." There were the visits to a "colored, ragged school" in the dismal St. Giles district, there were her duties in connection with the Prison Society three days in the week, and the special befriending of Sing Sing's celebrated matron who "has nerves to explore alone the Seven Circles of Dante's Hell" and who plans to send one hundred thirty intelligent and virtuous women to San Francisco to infuse them into that chaotic mass, thus to leaven it. Apparently, some among Catharine's friends had urged her to take on less in connection with these various causes, following on an illness of her own. But she assured them that their anxiety was quite groundless, that she had been rather run down during the summer, owing partly to the heat, that sometimes she is a little wearied in town and often heartsick. "But I believe," she says, "the little charity I do is conservative in its tendency. It takes me out of doors and is solacing to the heart after the heavy disappointments and amidst the wearing, small trials of life. . . . I feel its value more than I ever did and take far more pains to nourish it than when I was younger and happier, and it seemed fairer."

From Lenox, true to form, Catharine's letters were in more cheerful vein. To Kate, in connection with the idea of immortality, she says that "the year seems to bear no record that will not pass with the leaves of the flowers that have dropped. But this is nonsense! If it is by continual dropping that the rock is worn, so it is by minute accretions that the gem is formed, and our meetings and partings—our smiles and tears—that have made up the years' life, have nourished those affections that constitute immortality. . . ." In reply to an invitation to visit the Minots at Woodbourne in Roxbury, Massachusetts, she declines because of other engagements and also for her inability to leave her garden wherein, after an absence, she finds her "flowers looking like children whose mother has been spending the day out." She was grateful, however. "Thanks, dear child and dear William, for your kindness to me. . . . I don't believe an own mother ever had truer happiness in visiting her child than I have in going to you."

Charles Sedgwick's health continued to fail, however, and he was sent off on a trip, by way of cure, with his sister to watch and tend him. They were invited to join an excursion party of several hundred to visit the Falls of St. Anthony and the cities of St. Paul and St. Louis. There were "people from all parts of the country, politicians, painters, writers, sculptors, Europeans, young ladies and old —all headed for the Mississippi—five steamers and bands of music chartered for the Falls." Charles, it seems, was in mounting spirits, "his mercury at the very top of the scale" and he was "the charm of the boat—young men hanging about him to hear his jokes." The excursion was "prosperous to the end. Not the slightest accident, not even a detention of more than fifteen minutes in a journey of 2740 miles." In St. Louis they saw William G. Eliot, "Saint of the West," the disciple of Channing who preached the "Boston Religion," and whose moral influence was said to be greater than that of any other man in the region. "He makes men of all sects tributary to him, and to co-operate with him." The day they were there, a Croesus, though of a different faith, gave Eliot property to the amount of 30,000 dollars to build an industrial school. An attractive man, like Channing in his spiritual quality, but, as a practical and out-of-doors man, he had greater freedom and frankness.

Back at Lenox with the trip behind them, Charles grew continually weaker. Catharine writes Kate of her father: "When I look at him, I feel as if he were on the verge of a translation." On August 3, 1856, he died. This, for Catharine, accelerated the unwinding of her own being. For a long time she could not bring herself to leave the house which had been his. "Here every object is associated with my brother, with sweet memories of loving words and looks and deeds. . . . His life was an angel visit from beginning to end . . . the gladness he put into my life; the sorrows he rooted out of it." And, thinking back on their youth, she remembered a letter he had written her when once she left home briefly: "Everything in the house and about it seems to be waiting for your presence. Your flowers will not bloom . . . and the clouds cast their shadow on the earth as if there were none here fit to shine on. When are you coming home?"

The funeral service was at Lenox and the burial was in the tree-shaded Sedgwick circle within the Stockbridge cemetery, both remarkable as a manifestation of community admiration and love. During a "tremendous searching storm" at four in the afternoon, the house and grounds were crowded with people from every quarter and of every kind. Twenty-four Irishmen begged leave to carry his body on their shoulders to Stockbridge six miles away. They said they would go on their knees if it would serve to show their love. Because of the storm's violence, they were permitted to carry the coffin for only half a mile at each end of the journey but they walked all the way, the water often up to their knees. A procession of great length followed the body to the grave where four of Charles' nephews gently shoveled the earth to cover it, and a great assemblage stood for an hour in the midst of the rain to see the last office performed. "It was unspeakably affecting; more so than anything I ever saw." Thus wrote a local reporter of the scene.

An obituary in a Boston journal soon after his death described the unusual qualities that made up Charles Sedgwick's character:

Living in a sequestered village, without fame in his profession, without wealth or distinction, no man, perhaps in the whole state, was more beloved, admired and cherished than he. He had a combination of qualities as rare as genius. He was as honest, as brave, as clear headed as any man, and he had the tenderness, the fine instincts and the subtle perceptions of a woman. . . . Every move for political freedom and for the removal of social evils had his attention, not as a matter of duty but as a matter of course. It was part of his life. The criminal in the neighboring gaol and the dog at the door, never looked in Mr. Sedgwick's face, nor heard his voice, without feeling he had a friend.

There was the story of one of the servants in the house who, overhearing his humorous addresses to his cow, while he patted and fed her, exclaimed: "Ah! I had rather be Mr. Sedgwick than anybody in the wide world, and next to that I had rather be Mr. Sedgwick's cow."

What was there now for Catharine Maria Sedgwick, aging spinster bereft of sisters and brothers, what but to write another book?

Without delay or apparent hesitation, she got out her quill pen and her sheets of foolscap and set to work. The result was that, six or seven months after Charles' death, she was informing Kate that her "book gets on very well," that she is doing from eighteen to twenty pages a day, that she is working up to the last ounce of her strength. The book bore the title, *Married or Single,* and Catharine told Dr. Dewey in July of 1857 that she was sending him a copy in the course of a week. Now that it was finished, her spirits were low and she feared her friends might be mortified either by the silence of the critics or their adverse comments. "But don't feel bad for me, my dear friend, and do not let your wife."

In the preface Catharine Sedgwick says she will be happy if the novel does anything to lessen the stigma placed on the term, "old maid." The main theme deals with the right of every woman to lead an independent life. It is confused as to plot but the final emergence of the heroine hand in hand with a hero of magnanimous character, betrothed to him after he has at last succeeded in overcoming her purpose of remaining single, makes agreeable reading. One asks oneself whether, unconsciously, the book was not written to bring Catharine a vicarious security without the bonds of matrimony, a state for which in life she had so greatly longed and which she had ever been denied. From the conscious plane, however, emerge many of her ideas on the issues of the day: a little satire on Transcendentalism, her ardent sympathy for the runaway slave, and so on. But if *Married or Single* failed to keep pace with the best of her novels, the critics did not cause her any appreciable amount of annoyance, while an English edition of the book did. She was much harassed by its "shabby style," the omission of the preface, the altered captions to chapters and bald variations within the text. And she planned to inquire of Ticknor and Fields what might be the best method of righting the indignity.

One more book, her last, she wrote the following year, a short *Memoir of Joseph Curtis,* jeweler, teacher, reformer, philanthropist, a kind of saint with a capacity for befriending and taming the young as St. Francis befriended the birds. Miss Sedgwick had known and admired Curtis before his death and with him had visited the "Corner House" where his apprentices lived in a kind of productive harmony. She had been so impressed with the man's quality and his quiet achievement that she remained haunted by the wish to let the world know of him and his impressive labors. This she does, telling his tale in moving fashion, quoting an encomium from Peter Cooper, one of Curtis' supporters, who stated: "I regard him as the best and truest pattern of a perfect man that it has ever fallen to my lot to know." A fine finale for the quill pen of Catharine Maria Sedgwick, this little paean of praise which her friend Bryant preferred to any of her other books.

And now, one by one, the wives and husbands of Catharine's brothers and sisters took their way out of the world, leaving, eventually, one whole generation to be represented by her alone. Three years after Charles' death, Jane Sedgwick, widow of Henry, died, a loss that Catharine felt keenly because of the close ties established at the start of their relationship. The year following, it was the news of Eliza Cabot Follen's death that saddened her, the more so as the last communication between them was Catharine's refusal to attend a meeting in Boston of the Anti-Slavery Society, because she could not, somehow, rise to Eliza's ardent point of view.

The Civil War, however, moved Catharine profoundly. At the secession of South Carolina, "that bullying state," she quotes a few family remarks with which she agreed: "Let the damned little thing go!" and "Plow them under, plow them under! It has been a little wasp from the beginning!" But as the conflict grew wider she became more and more an emotional part of it. "I have an intense desire," she writes a friend in 1861, "to live to see the conclusion of our present struggle; how order is to be brought out of the present confusion—how peace and good neighborhood are ever to follow upon this bitter hate. I am willing to see South Carolina humbled in the dust . . . but beyond South Carolina I have no ill will. The people are cursed and borne down by their slavery and maddened by their ambitious leaders. . . ." And she became truly a part of the general holocaust when young Major William Dwight Sedgwick, son of Charles and brother of Kate, was killed at Antietam.

Two final episodes in Stockbridge, the last that she tells us of, were both of them typical of her loyalty to this lifelong home. On a fearfully cold morning, seventeen degrees below zero, she arose from a bed in which she had lain "uneasy" all night, being "stiff with old age and growling rheumatism," and walked to the bridge and back before breakfast. She saw the sun rise in a golden flood of light and the "mountains that guard this sacred valley lighting up as the gates of Heaven opened. The smoke from the village rose in solid white columns, and not a footstep outside save G., and his lips were too stiff to answer my salutation." The other episode, occurring in the heat of summer, was the laying of the cornerstone of a Catholic church in a "beautiful spot under the shadow of Laurel Hill," a spot chosen by young Jane Minot Sedgwick, a convert to the faith, who presented the church to the town. Catharine thought back to the days when Mass was held forty years before at the hatter's little shop for half a dozen poor Irish, whereas today there was a "close procession of Irish Catholics from one end of the village to the other." It was, Catharine tells us, a great day for young Jane who had been indefatigable in her exertions, and half canonized by her friends and followers. "Oh, see Miss Jane's good, beautiful face!" said one.

Back at Lenox, in a quasi-empty house, there was now the failing health of two old ladies to consider, that of Mrs. Charles Sedgwick who died within the year, and of Catharine herself growing visibly weaker. It was presently decided by the Minots that "Aunt Kitty" should quit the Berkshires for good and go to live with them at Woodbourne. Obedient to her adopted child, Catharine left Lenox on April 1, 1863, and on the day after her arrival at West Roxbury had her first attack of what was then diagnosed as epilepsy. Whether true epilepsy or a malady due to some other cause, the attacks continued to come during these last four years of her life.

"Since my illness," she writes her niece, Susan Butler, "I have in some respects behaved with the humility that one would think should always attend us. . . . I don't lay out my future, nor count upon it. I receive gratefully my life from day to day. . . . Whatever Kate tells me I may do, I do, and none other. . . . I am treated like a duchess by such friends as few duchesses have." And a year later she tells Dr. Dewey: "I am better, though from the nature of my illness, always in dread. . . . I walk out in spite of the cold and I sit for hours on the lounge in the piazza looking at the green trees." She mentions her pleasure in reading the New York *Evening Post* which Bryant is at present editing, an old familiar friend, the paper, which she had known from its first establishment sixty-three years before. Because of a present decrease in her income, due to the war, she has decided to discontinue her subscription, to her deep regret. Bryant, however, hearing of this, continued it for her.

One final trip, to visit friends in Boston, Catharine describes with pleasure. "I have been here for the last three weeks and had much enjoyment from seeing old friends and have had the honor and pleasure of a call from Whittier. He has a face and manner fitting his high gifts. . . . I have walked daily and sat for two hours in the Public Garden. Am I not a brave old woman?"

Dr. Dewey tells us that the handwriting of this letter was very tremulous and the few that followed it were for the greater part dictated. Her mind, nonetheless, remained clear, the disease making only gradual inroads on her brain and taking the characteristic form of increased and less discriminating admiration for everything around her.

Several years earlier, before her last illness, Catharine had written Kate: "We cling to life; it is the law of our being; and it is my continual prayer to be delivered from fear and anxiety; to be thankful for the continuance of my powers and faculties to this time . . . and in God's mercy to meet the summons that must come soon. I *am* cowardly . . . I am glad now to have done with the subject. I quite agree with Emerson who, in his chapter on *Manners* says, 'If you have a cold, or have had a fever, or a sunstroke, or a thunder stroke, never speak of it.'" She had been able, almost entirely able, to live up to this precept. Her laments were few, her rejoicing was frequent. To Susan Butler she wrote now, on July 19, 1867: "I have a balcony out of Kate's window in the pine wood where I lie all day and where the mercies and love of God are continually pressing upon my senses. But 'tis hard work, Susy, to be sick and helpless and useless!"

Before this letter reached its destination, Catharine Sedgwick had forever done with fever and cold, with fear and with the outgoing love that is fear's enemy. She went then to lie in peace beneath a cross carved in a pattern of ivy that stands between the graves of two great friends: Mumbet, the slave, and her brother Charles.